The Old Testan
An Intro

Second Edition: Revised and Expanded

Other titles in the T&T Clark Approaches to
Biblical Studies series include:

The Old Testament in the New:
An Introduction

Second Edition: Revised and Expanded

Steve Moyise

Bloomsbury T&T Clark
An imprint of Bloomsbury Publishing Plc

B L O O M S B U R Y
LONDON • NEW DELHI • NEW YORK • SYDNEY

Bloomsbury T&T Clark

An imprint of Bloomsbury Publishing Plc

Imprint previously known as T&T Clark

50 Bedford Square	1385 Broadway
London	New York
WC1B 3DP	NY 10018
UK	USA

www.bloomsbury.com

BLOOMSBURY, T&T CLARK and the Diana logo are trademarks of Bloomsbury Publishing Plc

First edition published 2000, reprinted 2001, 2004. This second edition published 2015

British Library Cataloguing-in-Publication Data
A catalogue record for this book is available from the British Library.

ISBN: HB:	978-0-56765-634-6
PB:	978-0-56765-633-9
ePDF:	978-0-56765-635-3
ePub:	978-0-56765-636-0

Library of Congress Cataloging-in-Publication Data
A catalog record for this book is available from the Library of Congress.

Typeset by Fakenham Prepress Solutions, Fakenham, Norfolk NR21 8NN
Printed and bound in India

Contents

Preface to Second Edition

Much has happened in the study of the 'Old Testament in the New' since 2001. As well as significant monographs published on individual books, such as Holly Carey (2009) and Kelly O'Brian (2010) on Mark's Gospel, Kenneth Litwak (2005) and Peter Mallen (2008) on Luke-Acts and Susan Docherty (2009) and Gerd Steyn (2011) on Hebrews, a number of series have begun. Tom Hatina has edited *Biblical Interpretation in Early Christian Gospels*, with volumes on Mark (2006), Matthew (2008) and Luke (2010). Maarten Menken and I have edited the series, *The New Testament and the Scriptures of Israel*, with volumes on the use of Genesis (2012), Deuteronomy (2007), Psalms (2004), Isaiah (2005) and the Minor Prophets (2009). There is now a *Commentary on the New Testament Use of the Old Testament* (Beale and Carson, 2007) and a number of scholars have produced their *magnum opus*: Francis Watson, *Paul and the Hermeneutics of Faith* (2004), Greg Beale, *A New Testament Biblical Theology* (2011) and Tom Wright, *Paul and the Faithfulness of God* (2013). In order to do justice to this material, each chapter has been revised and expanded and two new chapters have been added. The first of these comes after the four Gospels and looks at Jesus' own use of the Old Testament (drawing on my *Jesus and Scripture*, 2010). The second comes after the study of 1 and 2 Peter and Jude and looks at James and the Epistles of John. It is my hope that this second edition will prompt a new generation of students, ministers and lay people to engage with what C. H. Dodd called, *The Substructure of New Testament Theology* (1952).

Introduction

> For I handed on to you as of first importance what I in turn had
> received: that Christ died for our sins in accordance with the scrip-
> tures, and that he was buried, and that he was raised on the third day
> in accordance with the scriptures. (1 Cor 15.3–4)

In this summary of the gospel, Paul is keen to demonstrate that the
gospel he preaches is the same as that preached by the early disciples.
He has not introduced novelty, as some are suggesting, nor does he
claim any great originality. He passed on what he himself received.
Having established this, he then moves on to the substance of the
gospel. It concerns a person, namely Jesus Christ, though it is not clear
whether *christos* is being used here as a name ('Jesus Christ died for
our sins') or as a title ('the Messiah died for our sins'). Either way, the
central thrust (judging by its repetition) is that his death and resurrection are both 'in accordance with the scriptures'. In other words,
Christianity did not spring out of a vacuum but is in direct continuity with the religion enshrined in what Christians now call the Old
Testament. Not only did Paul pass on what he himself received; the
gospel itself is in accord with those writings which for centuries had
been received and passed on by the Jews.

The emphasis here is on the death and resurrection of Jesus but
Matthew also sees the details of Jesus' birth as a fulfilment of scripture.
For example, in the infancy stories (Matt 1–2) we are told that scripture
predicted the nature of his birth (1.23), its location in Bethlehem (2.6),
the flight to Egypt and his departure when safe to do so (2.15), Herod's

slaughter of the innocents (2.18) and his final settling at Nazareth (2.23). The stories are rehearsed each Christmas and taken by many to prove the supernatural origins of Christianity. Both the beginning and end of Jesus' life is said to be 'in accordance with the scriptures'. This is taken one stage further when Paul and other New Testament writers see the emergence of the Church (Gal 4.21–31), its persecution by the Jews (Rev 3.9), the inclusion of Gentiles (Rom 9.25) and even specific issues like choosing a replacement for Judas (Acts 1.20) and the payment of Church workers (1 Cor 9.9), as prophesied in scripture. The Old Testament (some scholars prefer 'First Testament' or 'Hebrew Bible' since there was no 'New Testament' at this point) apparently contains a blueprint of events which would come to pass in the first century. And this is supported (then and now) by such verses as:

> Then he [Jesus] said to them, 'These are my words that I spoke to you while I was still with you – that everything written about me in the law of Moses, the prophets, and the psalms must be fulfilled.' Then he opened their minds to understand the scriptures, and he said to them, 'Thus it is written, that the Messiah is to suffer and to rise from the dead on the third day, and that repentance and forgiveness of sins is to be proclaimed in his name to all nations, beginning from Jerusalem.' (Luke 24.44–47)

> For whatever was written in former days was written for our instruction, so that by steadfastness and by the encouragement of the scriptures we might have hope. (Rom 15.4)

> First of all you must understand this, that no prophecy of scripture is a matter of one's own interpretation, because no prophecy ever came by human will, but men and women moved by the Holy Spirit spoke from God. (2 Pet 1.20–21)

However, Jewish scholars have always protested that many of the cited texts have been taken out of context. For example, the famous prophecy of the birth of a child in Isa 7.14, when read in its own context, is clearly talking about a contemporary of the prophet. The promise in vv 7–9, that the nations who are presently threatening

Jerusalem will be destroyed, is ratified by a sign: 'Therefore the Lord himself will give you a sign. Look, the young woman is with child and shall bear a son, and shall name him Immanuel.' (Isa 7.14). The Greek translation of the Hebrew scriptures (known as the Septuagint or LXX, from the tradition that it was produced by 70 scholars) rendered the Hebrew *almah* ('young woman') with *parthenos* ('virgin'). This allows Matthew to quote it as a proof-text for the virginal conception of Jesus. But the words that follow Isa 7.14 say: 'For before the child knows how to refuse the evil and choose the good, the land before whose two kings you are in dread will be deserted' (Isa 7.16). If this is a prediction of the birth of Jesus 700 years hence, then it makes utter nonsense of the story being narrated in Isaiah. Some early Christians even claimed that the original reading of Isa 7.14 was 'virgin' and that the Jews changed it to 'young woman' so as to deny the virgin birth.

Furthermore, Matthew's claim (2.23) that the holy family settled in a town called Nazareth in order to fulfil the prophecy, 'He will be called a Nazorean', stumbles on the fact that no such text exists. Indeed, the town Nazareth is never mentioned in the Old Testament. Modern scholars have suggested that Matthew might be thinking of the Nazarite vow in Num 6 or perhaps the Hebrew word for 'branch' (*neser*) in Isa 11.1. But the fact remains that nowhere in the Hebrew or Greek Old Testament is there a text that says, 'He will be called a Nazorean.'

Discussion of the Old Testament in the New is thus sometimes conducted along the lines of those who are prepared to believe the Bible and those who are not. If Matthew says that Isaiah predicted the virgin birth of Jesus, then that must be what Isaiah meant, however puzzling it seems to us. If Matthew says there is a text that predicts the holy family will settle at Nazareth, he must have known one, even if it is now lost to us. Sometimes this is simply asserted as a requirement of faith. To doubt either of these things is to doubt the truthfulness of the Bible and the truthfulness of the God that gave the Bible. Other times it is supported by such reasoning as, 'Matthew would not have tried to convince his readers with proof-texts that he knew did not exist or obviously meant something else. His opponents would merely have to look up the texts in order to refute him.'

On the other hand, the movement known as the Enlightenment has made people suspicious of accepting 'truth' simply because a powerful body demands it. If words mean anything, then Isaiah is expecting the birth of a child in his generation and not 700 years hence, as Matthew appears to suggest. Some are prepared to give this a sympathetic interpretation. For example, it has been argued that while the original text referred to Isaiah's time, Matthew sees an amazing parallel whereby the birth of a child is once again to be the sign of a great act of God. Such correspondences are known as 'typology' and have been important for understanding the use of the Old Testament in the New. Others, however, are less sympathetic and accuse Matthew of simply taking the text out of context and giving it a Christian meaning that it did not have in its original setting. Even Dick (Richard) France, who suggests that reading Matthew on his own terms will 'achieve a more respectful appreciation of his literary ability and skill', acknowledges that our 'cultural and religious traditions would not allow us to write like this' (1994, p. 134).

An interpreted text

In our day, copyright laws mean that authors need to quote accurately, attend to the original setting of the utterance and then draw conclusions. In the ancient world, texts were living traditions, regularly updated to apply to new situations. The task of the interpreter then was not to discern what the text meant in the past but what it means now in the present. As the author of Hebrews put it, 'Long ago God spoke to our ancestors in many and various ways by the prophets, but in these last days he has spoken to us by a Son' (Heb 1.1). This does not necessarily mean that the old is now void (though according to Heb 8.13, parts of it are) but it does mean that it is now viewed in the light of later revelation. Paul can even speak of the impossibility of understanding the scriptures prior to Christ:

But their minds were hardened. Indeed, to this very day, when they hear the reading of the old covenant, that same veil is still there, since only in Christ is it set aside … whenever Moses is read, a veil lies over their minds; but when one turns to the Lord, the veil is removed. (2 Cor 3.14–16)

As we will see in our next chapter, this has important implications for how texts were quoted in the first century. For example, because of the significance of Jesus' life, death and resurrection, Bethlehem was soon regarded as an important place. And so Matthew quotes Mic 5.2 in the form, 'And you, Bethlehem, in the land of Judah, are by no means least among the rulers of Judah' (Matt 2.6). But the actual text of Mic 5.2 says that Bethlehem *is* the least among the tribes of Judah. Matthew (or the sources on which he depends) has inserted the Greek word *oudamos* ('by no means') into the quotation in order to make his point. To us this seems fraudulent. We would have first quoted the text accurately (with due acknowledgements) and then made the point that though the place is small in size, it is in fact very significant because Jesus was born there. But first century interpretation was quite happy to make this point by telescoping all this into a *single modified quotation.*

Another practice was to form composite quotations by taking part of one verse and combining it with part of another. In Acts 1, the disciples have to decide what to do about the treachery of Judas. Peter concludes that they must elect another to take his place because it is written in the book of Psalms, 'Let his homestead become desolate, and let there be no one to live in it'; and 'Let another take his position of overseer' (1.20). However, this seems less impressive when it is noted that the first phrase comes from Psalm 69.25 and the second from Psalm 109.8, neither of which have any obvious connection with Judas. The point is that we are always dealing with an *interpreted* text. There is no obvious connection between these psalms and the decision to elect a replacement for Judas. Indeed, in the original, the relevant verse is in the plural ('May *their* camp be a desolation; let no one live in *their* tents.').

All this means that when we come to describe the use of the Old Testament in the New, we must be careful to distinguish between how it looks to us and how it may have looked to them. Scholars have sometimes used words like 'arbitrary' or 'ad hoc' to describe the use of the Old Testament in the New. And from our point of view, it sometimes appears that way. But it is fairly certain that it did not appear 'arbitrary' or 'ad hoc' to them. Thus in the example above, we can note that Psalm 69 contains the phrases 'for my thirst they gave me vinegar to drink' (69.21) and 'the insults of those who insult you have fallen on me' (69.9). It was therefore 'obvious' to the early Christians that this psalm was about Jesus. And given that belief, it was not an enormous step to deduce that what the psalm says about the fate of his enemies applies supremely to Judas. Thus we must be very cautious when we hear arguments like, 'Matthew would never have done such and such.' The New Testament authors lived in a very different world to ours.

Quotations, allusions and echoes

Studies on the Old Testament in the New have found it helpful to distinguish between quotations, allusions and echoes. The former are usually indicated by a citation formula such as 'it is written' (Mark 1.2) or 'this was to fulfil' (Matt 2.15), though some think this should not be rigidly applied. Paul Trudinger, for example, prefers a definition such as the presence of 'word combinations in a form in which one would not have used them had it not been for a knowledge of their occurrence in this particular form in another source' (1966, p. 84). This allows him to find a number of quotations in the book of Revelation, where no such formulae are used. Though it can only be a rough guide, the number of quotations listed in *The Greek New Testament* (United Bible Society) are:

Matthew	54	2 Corinthians	10
Mark	27	Galatians	10
Luke	25	Hebrews	37

John	14	James	4
Acts	40	1 Peter	12
Romans	60	2 Peter	1
1 Corinthians	17	Revelation	0

Allusions are less precise, picking up on a few key words and usually woven into the new composition. They are clearly more difficult to detect than quotations, though Greg Beale insists that there should be an 'incomparable or unique parallel in wording, syntax, concept, or cluster of motifs in the same order or structure' (2012, p. 31). However, there is debate as to whether an allusion must be the result of conscious intention. For example, many people today use expressions like 'no peace for the wicked' or 'the powers that be' without having any idea that they come from the Bible. But to someone who knows the Bible well, they are instantly recognizable as allusions to Isa 48.22 and Rom 13.1. Others, perhaps the majority, would have some inkling that they come from the Bible but would have no idea where to find them. Thus estimates of the number of Old Testament allusions in a given book vary enormously. For the book of Revelation, this has ranged from about 250 to well over a 1000. Not surprisingly, scholars have tried to refine the criteria used for detecting such allusions (see Paulien, 2001, pp. 113–29).

Finally, scholars often speak of 'echoes' when the allusion is so slight that conscious intention is unlikely. The biblical authors were so immersed in scripture that they naturally used many of its idioms and expressions as their own. But they were not intending to 'allude' to a text as part of an argument or as an important feature of their composition; it just came naturally. Thus George Caird says that the author of Revelation 'constantly echoes the Old Testament writings (without ever actually quoting them), partly because this was the language which came most naturally to him, partly because of the powerful emotive effect of familiar associations, and partly no doubt because his vision had actually taken its form, though not its content, from the permanent furniture of his well-stocked mind' (1980, p. 74). Some regard 'echoes' as too tenuous and would prefer the more neutral term, 'literary parallels'. Others, however, regard echoes as important. After all, music critics do not confine their comments to the loudest instruments of the orchestra. It is often the subtle sounds at the very brink of hearing that determine the quality of the performance. And echoes can be quite loud if you are standing between two mountains.

Conclusion

In order to understand how the Old Testament functions in the New, we must immerse ourselves in the writings of the time. In our next chapter, we will look at a number of texts that are either contemporary with the New Testament writings (Dead Sea Scrolls, Philo, Josephus) or written shortly after (the Rabbis). This will help us to see what texts were available in the first century, how they were viewed, and what techniques were being used to interpret them (exegesis). However, we will also use modern approaches to biblical interpretation to describe how it appears to us. For example, we might conclude that there is no logical connection between Psalm 69.25 and finding a replacement for Judas. To us, such exegesis looks 'arbitrary' or even 'gratuitous' and we would not approve of such techniques today. But we should not thereby conclude that it appeared 'arbitrary' or 'gratuitous' to them. Given their experiences and mind-set, the connection was probably obvious. In this study, we are interested both in how it might have looked to them and how it appears to us.

Further reading

Greg Beale has written a number of books on the use of the Old Testament in the New, including a 1000 page biblical theology (to be discussed later). However, a good introduction to the topic is his *Handbook on the New Testament Use of the Old Testament* (2012), with chapters on the challenges facing the interpreter, definitions of quotation, allusion and echo, the relevance of background material, a summary of the different ways the Old Testament is used in the New Testament and the presuppositions that govern such uses. Also useful is the trilogy of books that I have written: *Jesus and Scripture* (2010), *Paul and Scripture* (2010) and *The Later New Testament Writings and Scripture* (2012). Evangelical scholarship is naturally interested in how the New Testament uses the Old Testament since one of its main tenets is the unity of scripture. However, there is no single evangelical view of the matter and the views of Walter Kaiser, Darrell Bock and Peter Enns are debated in *Three Views on the New Testament Use of the Old Testament* (2007), edited by Stanley Gundry. Finally, although not an introductory book, the most useful reference work on the subject is the *Commentary on the New Testament Use of the Old Testament* (2007), edited by Greg Beale and Dan Carson. It offers commentary on all of the quotations and major allusions in the New Testament and we will refer to a number of its authors in the course of this book.

Questions

1. What is the difference between a quotation, an allusion and an echo?
2. Why is it important to understand the quotations in the New Testament in the light of other first century texts?
3. If Isa 7.14 is read in the light of its surrounding context, what does it appear to be referring to?

1

Texts and Interpretation in the First Century

For much of Church history, the only comparisons that could be made with the New Testament were the later rabbinical writings. But since the discovery of the Dead Sea Scrolls from 1947–1956, we now have a vast array of texts dating from about 200 BCE–50 CE. The origins of the community are disputed but their interest in scriptural interpretation, particularly the desire to see their own history and key personnel as its fulfilment, leads to important parallels with the New Testament. There has also been something of a revival in studies of Philo (a Jewish philosopher, c. 20 BCE–50 CE) and Josephus (a Jewish historian, c. 37–100 CE). In this chapter, we will consider a variety of passages from these three bodies of literature which provide an important context for understanding the texts that were available in the first century and how they were being interpreted. We will begin with five texts found at Qumran, chosen to illustrate the diversity of approaches to interpreting texts in the first century.

The Habakkuk scroll (1QpHab)

This commentary was one of the first discoveries at Qumran and was published in 1950. The scroll works through the first two chapters of Habakkuk, quoting one or two verses followed by commentary. The commentary section is introduced by the word *pesher*, which means 'interpreted'. The interpretation applies the text directly to events and people of the author's period. The texts here quoted are taken from the translation by Geza Vermes (1997), as it is easily available. For convenience, the biblical text is printed in italics. Words in parenthesis represent gaps in the scroll and are a reconstruction of what most probably was there (in the opinion of Vermes).

> *I will take my stand to watch and will station myself upon my fortress. I will watch to see what He will say to me and how [He will answer] my complaint. And the Lord answered [and said to me, 'Write down the vision and make it plain] upon the tablets, that [he who reads] may read it speedily ...* and God told Habakkuk to write down that which would happen to the final generation, but He did not make known to him when time would come to an end. And as for that which He said, *That he who reads may read it speedily*: interpreted this concerns the Teacher of Righteousness, to whom God made known all the mysteries of the words of His servants the Prophets. (1QpHab 6.12–7.5)

There are three things to note here. First, the actual form of the quoted text. Up until the discovery of the Dead Sea Scrolls, our earliest manuscripts of the Hebrew Bible were from the tenth century CE (the so-called Masoretic Text or MT). Here, we have someone quoting Habakkuk from around 50 BCE. What is the relationship between the two texts? In this case, they are virtually identical, thus testifying to the supreme accuracy of textual transmission across a millennium. However, as we shall see in our other examples, there are sometimes significant variations between the quoted text and the Masoretic text lying behind our printed Bibles. In the light of the accuracy of transmission, this is best understood as evidence for the existence of variant versions of the biblical text. This was already known to us from the LXX, where some of its stranger readings had already suggested that its translators were working from a different form of the Hebrew text to that which has come down to us.

Second, the text is applied directly to the 'Teacher of Righteousness', 'to whom God made known all the mysteries of the words of His servants the Prophets' (an allusion to Amos 3.7). According to Hartmut Stegemann (1998), this person was high priest in Jerusalem until ousted by Jonathan in 152 BCE. He then fled to Syria and called upon other exiled groups to join him in a more faithful obedience to the Torah. The result was the movement known as the Essenes. Josephus estimates that around the middle of the first century BCE, there were about 4000 Essenes and 6000 Pharisees (he also mentions Sadducees and Zealots, but these were numbered in hundreds). After the Teacher's death around 110 BCE, some of the Essenes moved to the desert (Qumran) and devoted themselves to Torah observance, scriptural interpretation and intensive scroll production. Stegemann suggests that prior to the Teacher of Righteousness, the words of the prophets were generally thought to apply to a distant future (Dan 12.9). But the Teacher and his followers 'were firmly convinced that they were living in the last phase of the history of the world, just before the last judgement of God and the dawn of the time of salvation' (1998, p. 122). This resulted in a particular attitude to the biblical prophets:

> A special insight on the part of the Teacher of Righteousness consisted in the concept that nothing that God had once had the biblical prophets commit to writing had ever referred to situations of those prophet's own time. From the outset, all of it had been God's solemn pronouncements for the last phase of history – precisely that time, then, in which the Teacher of Righteousness was living. (1998, p. 122)

The importance of this for an understanding of John the Baptist, Jesus and the early Church is clear. John comes on to the scene crying out, 'Repent, for the kingdom of heaven has come near' (Matt 3.2). Jesus reads from the scroll of Isaiah and says, 'Today this scripture has been fulfilled in your hearing' (Luke 4.21). Paul claims that the exodus story was 'written down to instruct us, on whom the ends of the ages have come' (1 Cor 10.11). Clearly they share the same eschatological orientation that the time of fulfilment is at hand. It remains to be seen whether they also share the same methods of interpreting the biblical text.

Third, adjustments are made to the meaning of the text in order to apply it to the Teacher of Righteousness. In particular, the thrust of the original passage is that God did grant Habakkuk's request for a vision and told him 'to make it plain on tablets'. However, the author of the commentary wants to claim that the words have remained a mystery until God revealed their meaning to the Teacher of Righteousness. As this would appear to contradict what Habakkuk says, the author draws a distinction between 'describing' the events of the end and 'knowing' when this would take place. It is interesting that the first of these (that Habakkuk was writing about the final generation) is simply assumed. It is only the claim that the Teacher of Righteousness knows when it will happen that requires assertion.

The Florilegium (4QFlor)

First published in 1968, this text is known as a florilegium ('collection') of messianic texts. It begins with God's promise to David to establish an everlasting dynasty (2 Sam 7.10–14), which is then linked to the promise of Amos 9.11, that God will raise up the fallen tent of David (both texts are quoted in the New Testament). The author envisages two messianic figures, the 'Branch of David' and the 'Interpreter of the Law'. These will meet opposition, since Psalm 2.1 says that the 'rulers take counsel together, against the Lord and his anointed' (also quoted in Acts 4.26), and this is then identified with the last days spoken about in Dan 12.10:

> *The Lord declares to you that he will build you a House. I will raise up your seed after you. I will establish the throne of his kingdom [for ever]. I [will be] his father and he shall be my son.* He is the Branch of David who shall arise with the Interpreter of the Law [to rule] in Zion [at the end] of time. As it is written, *I will raise up the tent of David that is fallen.* That is to say, the fallen tent of David is he who shall arise to save Israel … *[Why] do the nations rage … [and the] princes take counsel together against the Lord and against [His Messiah]?* Interpreted, this saying concerns [the kings of the nations] … This is the time of which it is written in the book of Daniel, the prophet: *But the wicked shall do wickedly and shall not understand, but the righteous shall purify themselves and make themselves white* (1.10–13, 18–19; 2.1–3)

In 1920, Rendell Harris put forward the idea that the early Christians probably made collections of key texts so as to facilitate teaching and debate. He pointed to the collection of texts found in Rom 3.10–18 and the way that New Testament quotations sometimes agree in wording against all known versions of the Old Testament (such as the 'stone' passages quoted in Rom 9.33 and 1 Pet 2.6). The implication was that the New Testament authors were not so much quoting the actual scriptures but quoting certain collections or *testimonia*. He thought this explains why texts are often quoted out of context.

This view was challenged by C. H. Dodd in an important work called *According to the Scriptures* (1952). Dodd argued that quotations were often the tip of the iceberg and are only understandable on the assumption that the readers would be aware of the larger context. Thus the reference to Judas's successor in Psalm 69.25 only makes sense if the reader is aware that the whole psalm is about Christ's suffering. In other words, it is hard to imagine anyone selecting Psalm 69.25 to go into such a collection without its surrounding context. It is much more likely, said Dodd, that Christians focused on particular parts of scripture, such as Isa 53, Dan 7 and Psalm 69. He also pointed out that there was no evidence for the existence of such collections.

Scholars have generally sided with Dodd on this matter but the discovery of such collections at Qumran has at least refuted the last point. Collections of texts *were* made and it is difficult to imagine Paul unrolling a 10-metre scroll every time he wanted to quote a particular verse from Genesis or Isaiah. He must surely have used notes of some kind. As we shall see in due course, scholars are divided as to whether it was important for the reader to know the actual context of the quoted text or whether it was enough to understand how the words were being interpreted in the present.

The Hymn scroll (1QH)

The Hymn scroll was first published in 1954 and appears to be modelled on the biblical psalms. Svend Holm-Nielsen (1960) counts

150 allusions to the psalms and about 120 to Isaiah. Some of the hymns appear to be referring to the experiences of the community but some sound more individual and were probably written by the Teacher himself. What is of interest is the way that the author identifies with the feelings and experiences of the Psalmist. No attempt is made to show that the Psalmist was 'really' talking about a future figure. The language is simply adopted as the most appropriate way of describing his own experiences.

This is sometimes called 'typology', where a 'biblical event, person, or institution' serves as an 'example or pattern for other events, persons, or institutions' (Baker 1994, p. 327). Michael Fishbane notes that typology is already deeply embedded in the Old Testament. For example, Isa 65.17–25 adopts the language of the creation stories in order to reflect the 'hope that the imminent end will be *like* the beginning, when once, before history, harmony reigned supreme' (1985, p. 354). Future salvation is modelled on the exodus story (Isa 43.16), Sinai images are transferred to Zion (Psalm 68.16–18) and the new temple will be modelled on the old (Ezek 40-48). Furthermore, Noah is presented as a new Adam (Gen 9.1–9) and Joshua as a new Moses (Josh 1–3). 1QH continues this trend by having the Teacher of Righteousness take on the persona of the Psalmist and other Old Testament figures.

> They caused [me] to be like a ship on the deeps of the [sea]
> and like a fortified city before [the aggressor],
> [and] like a woman in travail with her first-born child,
> upon whose belly pangs have come and grievous pains,
> filling with anguish her child-bearing crucible.
> For the children have come to the throes of Death,
> And she labours in her pains who bears a man.
> For amid the throes of Death she shall bring forth a man-child,
> and amid the pains of Hell
> there shall spring from her child-bearing crucible
> a Marvellous Mighty Counsellor;
> and a man shall be delivered from out of the throes. (1QH Hymn 4)

Beale would argue that a genuine typological correspondence must be more than just an analogy between a 'biblical event, person, or institution'; there must also be a 'forward-looking element or foreshadowing' in the Old Testament context and an 'escalation' or 'heightening' in the New (2012, p. 14). This is an important point and will figure in many of our discussions but it is worth noting that it is not something that can be objectively applied. Beale thinks that Jesus is the fulfilment of Israel's hopes in a way that the Qumran teacher is not and so any application of texts to Jesus will automatically contain an element of 'escalation' or 'heightening'. However, at least on a formal level, the New Testament and the Qumran writers are doing similar things.

The Melchizedek Scroll (11QMelch)

It has often puzzled scholars why the author of Hebrews, in order to make the point that Jesus is our high priest and lives to make intercession for us, launches into an obscure piece of exegesis concerning the figure of Melchizedek. In the Old Testament, he is briefly mentioned in Gen 14 and Psalm 110 has a line that says, 'You are a priest for ever according to the order of Melchizedek.' The author of Hebrews argues that scripture knows of two priesthoods. The levitical priesthood offers sacrifices day by day, which, by their very repetition, shows that they are unable to take away sins (Heb 10). Jesus, on the other hand, is a priest for ever, according to the order of Melchizedek. He offered himself once and for all, as a perfect sacrifice for sins.

The Qumran library has now brought to light a document known as 11QMelch (11Q means it was found in cave 11) which links the year of jubilee (Lev 25, Deut 15) with the proclamation of 'liberty to the captives' from Isa 61 (the synagogue reading in Luke 4). In 11QMelch, it would appear that Melchizedek is the one who will proclaim this liberty and forgive sins (it is not absolutely certain due to the fragmentary nature of the text). Psalm 82.1 is then quoted to show that Melchizedek has a place in the divine council and is even called *elohim*. Vermes explains that while *elohim* normally means 'God', it can sometimes mean 'judge', and that is probably the meaning here. He suggests that the discovery of this document not only sheds light on Hebrews 'but also on the development of the messianic concept in the New Testament and early Christianity' (1997, p. 500).

> [*To proclaim liberty to the captives.* Its interpretation is that He] will assign them to the Sons of Heaven and to the inheritance of Melchizedek f[or He will cast] their [lot] amid the po[rtions of Melchize]dek, who will return them there and will proclaim to them liberty, forgiving them [the wrong-doings] of all their iniquities ... For this is the moment of the Year of Grace for Melchizedek. [And h]e will, by his strength, judge the holy ones of God, executing judgement as it is written concerning him in the Songs of David, who said, ELOHIM *has taken his place in the divine council; in the midst of the gods he holds judgement.* (11Q Melch 4–10)

The Damascus Document (CD)

Two medieval manuscripts of this document were discovered in 1896 in a store room (*geniza*) of an old Cairo synagogue (CD is short for Cairo Damascus Document) and published in 1910. It is believed they were taken there by the Karaites in the tenth century CE. A manuscript from Cave 1 contains a version of the *Damascus Document*, along with the *Rule of the Community* (1QS 1–3), the *Manual of Discipline* (1QS 5–11), the *Rule of the Congregation* (1QSa) and the *Rule of Blessings* (1QSb). A further ten fragmentary copies have been found in caves 4, 5 and 6 and date from around 75–50 BCE. The original was probably composed about 100 BCE. In CD 7.14–21, the threat of Amos 5.25–26, that Israel will be exiled to Damascus, is changed into a promise and then allegorized so as to predict the origins of the community:

> Did you bring to me sacrifices and offerings the forty years in the wilderness, O house of Israel? You shall take up Sakkuth your king, and Kaiwan your star-god, your images that you made for yourselves; therefore I will take you into exile beyond Damascus, says the Lord, whose name is the God of hosts. (Amos 5.25–26)

I will exile the tabernacle of your king and the bases of your statues from my tent to Damascus. The Books of the Law are the *tabernacle* of the king; as God said, *I will raise up the tabernacle of David which is fallen.* The king is the congregation; and the *bases of the statues* are the books of the Prophets whose sayings Israel despised. The *star* is the Interpreter of the Law who shall come to Damascus; as it is written, *A star shall come forth out of Jacob and a sceptre shall rise out of Israel.* (CD 7.14–21)

It would appear that the author of the Damascus Document took 'Sakkuth' not as a proper name ('Saturn') but the Hebrew word *sukkuth*, which means 'tabernacle'. The ancient scrolls consisted only of consonants, the reader having to supply the vowels from oral tradition. It was only much later that vowel signs were actually included with the text. Thus either by accident or design, the author of the document read the consonants s-k-t as *sukkut(h)* and not the name 'Sakkut(h)'. He then linked this with the 'fallen tabernacle' spoken about in Amos 9.11. The negative reference to Israel following their star-god 'Kaiwan' is omitted and replaced with a positive mention of the star who shall come forth from Jacob (Num 24.17). Allegory and word-play are then used to make other associations. Thus by some complex and technical exegesis, the author has found in scripture a prophecy for the establishment in Damascus of a community devoted to biblical study, led by the Interpreter of the Law.

Amos 5.25–26 is also quoted in the New Testament. In Stephen's speech (Acts 7), he quotes the incident of the golden calf and then says that because of their idolatry, God handed them over to worship the host of heaven. This is then supported by a quotation from Amos 5.25–26. The text is not allegorized or given a contemporary application but the wording has been adjusted. 'Sakkuth' and 'Kaiwan' are replaced by 'Moloch' and 'Rephan' (a change already present in the LXX) and 'Damascus' (Israel's northern exile) is replaced by 'Babylon' (Judah's southern exile). As quoted in Acts 7.42–43, the text now reads: 'Did you offer to me slain victims and sacrifices for forty years in the wilderness, O house of Israel? No; you took along the tent of Moloch, and the star of your God Rephan, the images that you made to worship; so I will remove you beyond Babylon.'

Philo

Philo was a Jewish philosopher who interpreted the scriptures (mainly the law), in terms of Greek philosophy. Working with the LXX, which he believed to be inspired, he used a range of rhetorical practices (mainly allegory), to show that the scriptures were in harmony with Greek philosophy. For example, Gen 4.1 says: 'Now the man knew his wife Eve, and she conceived and bore Cain, saying, "I have produced a man with the help of the Lord"'. This 'double agency', as we might call it, is taken by Philo to refer to the Greek idea that human beings consist of an earthly body (which will die) and 'the virtues' (which are immortal). In a work called *De Cherubim* (a reference to Gen 3.24), he explains:

> A husband unites with his wife, and the male human being with the female human being in a union which tends to the generation of children, in strict accordance with and obedience to nature. But it is not lawful for virtues, which are the parents of many perfect things, to associate with a mortal husband. But they, without having received the power of generation from any other being, will never be able by themselves alone to conceive anything. Who, then, is it who sows good seed in them, except the Father of the universe, the uncreated God, he who is the parent of all things? (*Cher* 43–44)

Philo often argued from silence. Scripture does not say that Isaac 'knew' Rebecca (Gen 25.21) or that Moses 'knew' Zipporah (Exod 2.21) and so he concludes that Rebecca 'became pregnant by the agency of him who received the supplication' and Zipporah 'found that she conceived by no mortal man' (*Cher* 47). It is unlikely that Philo is speaking about an actual 'virgin birth' because his focus is on 'the virtues' but some scholars, such as Roger Aus (2004, pp. 61–63), think that this is the contextual background for understanding why it was thought that Jesus had to be born of a virgin.

Josephus

Josephus was a Jewish historian who wrote a history of the Jewish people up to and including the war with the Romans in 70 CE. In much of his *Antiquities of the Jews*, he summarizes the biblical material but there are also some interesting embellishments. For example, the reason that Pharaoh vowed to kill the Hebrew children at the beginning of the book of Exodus was because a scribe had foretold the birth of a liberator, and this was communicated to Moses's father, Amram, in a dream:

> One of those sacred scribes, who are very sagacious in foretelling future events, truly told the king, that about this time there would be born a child to the Israelites, who, if he were reared, would bring the Egyptian dominion low, and would raise the Israelites; that he would excel all men in virtue, and obtain a glory that would be remembered through all ages. A man whose name was Amram … betook himself to prayer to God, and entreated him to have compassion … Accordingly God had mercy on him, and was moved by his supplication. He stood by him in his sleep, and exhorted him … this child of yours … shall deliver the Hebrew nation from the distress they are under from the Egyptians. (*Ant.* 2.205, 210–16 abbreviated).

Now it is commonly thought that Matthew's story of Herod's slaughter of the children of Bethlehem (Matt 2.16) was intended to evoke the similar story of Pharaoh's killing of the Hebrew children (Exod 1.22). However, if Josephus's account was well known at the time Matthew wrote his Gospel (thought to be about 75–85 CE), then he might also have intended other parallels. For example, Joseph is told in a dream that Mary's child 'will save his people from their sins' (Matt 1.21) and Herod's plan to kill the children of Bethlehem is sparked by the news that prophecies have been made about Jesus:

> In the time of King Herod, after Jesus was born in Bethlehem of Judea, wise men from the East came to Jerusalem, asking, 'Where is the child who has been born king of the Jews? For we observed his star at its rising, and have come to pay him homage.' *When King Herod heard this*, he was frightened, and all Jerusalem with him; and

calling together all the chief priests and scribes of the people, he inquired of them where the Messiah was to be born. They told him, 'In Bethlehem of Judea; *for so it has been written by the prophet:* "And you, Bethlehem, in the land of Judah, are by no means least among the rulers of Judah; for from you shall come a ruler who is to shepherd my people Israel."' (Matt 2.1–6)

First-century texts

Allowing for the fact that sometimes the ancient authors (New Testament and Qumran) changed the wording of their texts, the evidence still points to the fact that the biblical text was available in a number of versions in the first century. This is true both for the Hebrew text and its Greek translation. Too often, scholars have spoken of 'agreeing with the LXX' or 'going against the Hebrew', when what is actually meant is that the quoted text differs from our Masoretic Text and Rahlfs' reconstruction of the Greek text (1935), based on the great fourth and fifth century manuscripts known as Alexandrinus (A), Vaticanus (B) and Sinaiticus (X). Indeed, there is debate as to whether there ever was a single LXX text, from which all other versions derive. Certainly the various books of the Hebrew Bible were translated at different times and by different authors. This is clear from the very different styles of translation. Some are literal and wooden (Pentateuch), others are much freer (Proverbs). Some are much longer than the Hebrew books now in our possession (Job, Daniel) and the Greek version of Jeremiah has the chapters in a different order. Accordingly, a reference to Jer 38.15 (LXX) will not correspond with Jer 38.15 in an English Bible (which is based on the Masoretic Hebrew text) but will normally be included in parenthesis (in this case, it is Jer 31.15).

It would also appear that some of the Greek translations of the Hebrew underwent revision in order to bring them closer to a particular Hebrew text. New Testament quotations from the book of Daniel, for example, tend to agree with a version known as Theodotion rather than the Septuagint. In modern editions of the LXX, both texts are usually printed (see Further reading for details of English translations).

We must also reckon with the Aramaic paraphrases known as the Targums (or *Targumim* to give them their Hebrew plural). Though the origins of the synagogue are debated, it would appear that a reading of scripture (Hebrew) was followed by an explanation in Aramaic, and this is the form in which most people would have learnt scripture. Unfortunately, these are only found in late manuscripts (the Cairo Geniza yielded seven manuscripts from around the seventh-ninth centuries) and so their significance for New Testament interpretation is debated. But their early existence is not in doubt, since two were found at Qumran (Leviticus and Job), which Stegemann dates to the second century BCE.

Anthony Hanson makes considerable use of the Targums in order to explain peculiar or difficult readings. He argues that though the readings might only be known to us from a ninth century manuscript, the copyist hardly obtained such readings from the New Testament. It is more likely that both the ninth century manuscript and our New Testament manuscripts are dependent on an earlier form of the tradition. Other scholars, however, are more cautious, observing that a lot can happen in nine centuries! As an example of the sort of expansions included in the Targums, Gen 2.7 ('then the Lord God formed man from the dust of the ground, and breathed into his nostrils the breath of life; and the man became a living being') has become in Targum Pseudo-Jonathan:

> And the Lord God created man in two formations; and took dust from the place of the house of the sanctuary, and from the four winds of the world, and mixed from all the waters of the world, and created him red, black and white; and breathed into his nostrils the inspiration of life, and there was in the body of Adam the inspiration of a speaking spirit, unto the illumination of the eyes and the hearing of the ears. (quoted in Hanson 1983, p. 24)

Lastly, as we have already noted, it may be that the early Christians made their own collections/translations of important texts and that at least some of the New Testament quotations were taken from them rather than directly from an ancient scroll. Indeed, given the physical difficulty of finding a particular passage in a long scroll, it is unlikely that any of the authors quoted texts in the modern sense of physically locating the actual passage and copying it. Thus when we come to analyse the New Testament quotations, we will have to bear in mind that they might be quoting from one or more of the following:

1. A Hebrew text similar to the Masoretic Text of the tenth century CE
2. A different type of Hebrew text
3. A Greek text similar to that found in Alexandrinus, Vaticanus and Sinaiticus
4. A different or revised form of Greek text
5. An Aramaic translation/paraphrase of a Hebrew text
6. A Christian collection or translation

Rabbinic exegesis

Though the discovery of the Dead Sea Scrolls has put rabbinic parallels in the shade, valuable work was done by Joseph Bonsirven (1939) and William Davies (1948) on the importance of rabbinic Judaism for understanding Jesus and Paul. Rabbi Hillel (*c.* 100 CE) was responsible for drawing up seven exegetical 'rules' (*middoth*) for biblical inter-pretation. It is unclear if such 'rules' were intended to *govern* exegesis or are a later *rationalization* of what was actually taking place. They are often cited by their Hebrew names, which gives the impression of precision and technicality but they are actually quite general and can be paralleled in Hellenistic writings. Taken together, it can be seen that a vast array of possibilities opens up for how a text can legitimately be interpreted. Hanson (1983, p. 21) summarizes them like this:

1. One may argue from the greater to the smaller and vice versa.
2. Analogous or equivalent expressions may be applied interchangeably.
3. One may argue from the particular to the general.
4. Vice versa

5. An inference may be made by putting several passages together.
6. A difficulty in one text may be resolved by comparing it with another text which has points of resemblance.
7. The meaning of a passage may be established by its context.

As an example, consider Paul's argument in Rom 4. He begins by quoting Gen 15.6, 'Abraham believed God, and it was reckoned to him as righteousness.' The crucial point for Paul is the meaning of the word 'reckoned' and so he cites another text (rule 2) where this word occurs: 'Blessed are those whose iniquities are forgiven, and whose sins are covered; blessed is the one against whom the Lord will not *reckon* sin' (Psalm 32.1–2). By assuming a connection between these two texts, Paul is able to link the idea of 'God reckoning righteousness' with that of 'God not reckoning sin'. It also works in reverse. Gen 15.6 does not mention 'blessing' but the link with Psalm 32.1–2 allows Paul to ask, 'Is this blessedness, then, pronounced only on the circumcised, or also on the uncircumcised?' (Rom 4.9). Whether Paul was consciously following a 'rule' cannot easily be decided but his exegesis does provide a good example of it.

Conclusion

The discovery of the Dead Sea Scrolls has revolutionized the study of the Old Testament in the New. We now have a multitude of texts coming from a community of about the same period as the early Church, who also thought that scripture was being fulfilled in them. We have seen such techniques as typology, allegory, catch-word links, quoting from variant texts, altering the quoted text and reading the text in an unorthodox or surprising manner. We have also noted the attempt by Philo to link the Old Testament with Greek philosophy, and the way that Josephus embellishes the stories he tells. We have yet to discover whether the New Testament authors do likewise but this is the environment in which they must be set, either following such approaches or setting their mind against them. In the chapters that follow, we will first look at how the Gospels (and Acts) use the Old Testament to bring out the significance of Jesus, followed by a chapter on how Jesus himself used it. This is not as straightforward as it sounds, for Jesus' sayings in Aramaic have already undergone translation into Greek and perhaps also various embellishments. Following this, we will examine the use of the Old Testament in Paul, in Hebrews, in Peter and Jude, in James and the Letters of John, and in the book of Revelation. We will then conclude by outlining the main scholarly positions on the Old Testament in the New.

Further reading

Since the New Testament authors are writing in Greek for a Greek-speaking audience, their quotations are generally from the LXX (or a version of it). There have previously only been two translations of the LXX into English, that of the American scholar Charles Thomson (1808) and the English cleric, Sir Lancelot Brenton (1844). But in 2007, a group of scholars used the latest manuscript evidence to produce *A New English Translation of the Septuagint* (NETS), edited by Albert Pietersma and Benjamin Wright. This is an extremely useful resource for two reasons. First, each book or section of the LXX is introduced by a short essay on the characteristics of the particular LXX translator. Second, it has adopted the strategy of conforming the translation to the NRSV whenever the Greek and Hebrew are similar and departing from it when they are not. Thus the English reader can compare the NRSV with NETS and get some impression of the similarities and differences between the Greek and Hebrew versions, and the effect of these on the meaning of the text. For a good introduction to the LXX, see Jennifer Dines, *The Septuagint* (2004) and for more detailed study, see Timothy Michael Law, *When God Spoke Greek: The Septuagint and the Making of the Christian Bible* (2013). For an introduction to the Dead Sea Scrolls, see *The Oxford Handbook of the Dead Sea Scrolls* (2010), edited by Timothy

Lim and John Collins. This handbook of nearly 800 pages represents excellent value for money (paperback) and offers a comprehensive guide to the DSS and biblical interpretation. It is divided into eight sections (1) Archaeology and the discovery of the scrolls (2) Origins and history of the community (3) Relationship to other Jewish groups (4) Texts and interpretation (5) Religious themes (6) Relationship to Christianity (7) Relationship to later Judaism (8) New approaches. For a discussion of the likelihood of the early Christians making collections of quotations and scripture passages, see Martin Albl, *'And Scripture Cannot be Broken': The Form and Function of the Early Christian* Testimonia *Collections* (1999).

Questions

1. How have the Dead Sea Scrolls helped us to understand some of the quotations in the New Testament?
2. What are some of the differences between first century interpretation and how we would go about it today?
3. What are some of the difficulties in determining whether the New Testament authors have quoted their texts accurately?

The Old Testament in Mark

Though it is not always easy to decide what constitutes a quotation and what constitutes an allusion, even a tentative list of quotations in Mark reveals that it is only in the prologue (1.2–3) that he explicitly quotes scripture as editorial comment. All his other quotations are on the lips of characters in the story (mainly Jesus). This is in contrast to the other Gospels which provide a set of quotations as a sort of running commentary on the narrative. This does not mean that Mark provides no scriptural commentary on the events that he is narrating. There is in fact a rather extensive set of allusions and echoes that fill out Mark's narrative and engage the reader in a variety of ways. But it is only in his opening words that these constitute an explicit quotation and it is for this reason that scholars such as Joel Marcus (1992), Rikki Watts (1997) and Larry Perkins (2006) see this text as the key to understanding Mark's use of scripture.

Quotations in Mark's Gospel

Mark's opening quotation in 1.2–3

Mark opens his Gospel with what seems to be a title ('The beginning of the good news of Jesus Christ, the Son of God'), which is linked ('As it is written in the prophet Isaiah') with a composite quotation of Mal 3.1, Exod 23.20 and Isa 40.3 ('See, I am sending my messenger ahead of you, who will prepare your way, the voice of one crying out in the wilderness: "Prepare the way of the Lord, make his paths straight."') The ascription of this composite quotation to Isaiah has caused problems, both for ancient copyists and modern interpreters. Ancient copyists dealt with the discrepancy by omitting the word 'Isaiah' and turning 'prophet' into a plural. Thus most of our surviving manuscripts read, 'As it is written in the prophets' (hence KJV).

However, textual critics are virtually certain that the reference to Isaiah is original and so some explanation is required. One view is that Mark is using a testimony source where the texts had already been combined. Mark ascribes it to Isaiah either because he was unaware of its composite nature or because 'Isaiah' stands for 'prophets' in the same way that 'Psalms' (perhaps) can stand for 'writings' (see Luke 24.44). Later Jewish texts also offer such a combination (*Exod Rabba* 32.9; *Deut Rabba* 11.9) and if Jacob Mann's (1940) reconstruction of the ancient Jewish lectionary is correct, Mal 3 was the prophetic reading (*haphtarah*) that accompanied Exod 23.20.

On the other hand, Marcus thinks the ascription to Isaiah was deliberate because Mark wants to tell his readers that 'the beginning of the good news' is 'written in the prophet Isaiah'. Isa 40.3, he says, is not cited as a proof-text for the location of John's ministry (wilderness), or to clarify his relationship with Jesus (forerunner). It is quoted because the restoration promised in Isaiah is being fulfilled. Isaiah looked forward to a time when the heavens would be rent (64.1), the Spirit poured out (61.1), good news would be proclaimed (40.9-10) and God would come in power (40.10). Mark's introduction correspondingly speaks of the heavens torn open (1.10), the Spirit descending on Jesus (1.10), the good news proclaimed in Galilee (1.14) and the dawn of the kingdom of God (1.15). This new exodus framework is reinforced by quotations from Isaiah in Mark 4.12, 7.6–7 and 11.17 (see below) and one of the key expressions for discipleship in Mark's Gospel is following Jesus 'on the way' (8.28; 9.33; 10.32; 10.52). Thus the mystery of Mark's Gospel is that Jesus' path through suffering and death is in fact the 'fulfilment of that end so eagerly yearned for since Old Testament times: the triumphant march of the holy warrior, Yahweh, leading his people through the wilderness to their true homeland in a mighty demonstration of saving power'. (1992, p. 29)

Rikki Watts agrees but also wishes to do justice to the fact that the quotation is composite and contains a reference to Mal 3.1 (which itself is a reference to Exod 23.20). Thus Mark's aim is not only to signal the salvation background of Isaiah but also the judgement theme of Malachi:

> Mark's opening composite citation is intended to evoke two different but closely related schemata. First, the appeal to Isaiah 40 evinces Israel's great hope of Yahweh's coming to initiate her restorational NE [New Exodus]. Second, the allusion to Malachi not only recalls the delay of this NE but also sounds an ominous note of warning in that the nation must be prepared or else face purging judgement … These twin themes of the fulfilment of the delayed INE [Isaian New Exodus] promise and possible judgement due to lack of preparedness are fused in Mark's opening citation and together seem to establish the basic thematic contours for his presentation of Jesus. (1997, p. 370)

For Larry Perkins, it is the inclusion of Exod 23.20 in the composite quotation that is significant, for the book of Exodus is much more prominent in Mark's Gospel than the book of Malachi. There are direct quotations in Mark 7.10 (honour parents – Exod 20.12/21.17), Mark 10.19 (second half of the Ten Commandments – Exod 20.12–16) and Mark 12.26 (burning bush and God's self-revelation – Exod 3.6,15). There are specific allusions in Mark 2.27 (purpose of the Sabbath – Exod 20.8-10), Mark 14.12–13 (meaning of the Passover – Exod 12.6,14–20) and Mark 14.24 (establishing a covenant in blood – Exod 24.8) and there are also a number of common themes: journey, wilderness, temptation, plagues/miracles, self-revelation of God, Tabernacle/temple and hardness of heart. In the light of these parallels, Perkins says of Mark:

> It seems that he desires his readers to set the mission of Jesus within the larger story of Israel's formation as told in the Exodus narrative, but also to show that Jesus' mission is a separate, though connected,

stage in God's plans for Israel. Jesus will affirm God's word as revealed to Moses. He will offer a revised interpretation and understanding of God's covenantal intent for Israel. The deliberate conflation of the Exodus text with the Isaiah quotation probably indicates that the author wanted his readers to see the new exodus of Isaiah as a revised exodus paradigm. (2006, p. 104)

Parable purpose in 4.12

If Marcus is correct, then the quotation of Isa 6.9–10 in Mark 4.12 explains why this new exodus programme is meeting resistance, for Isaiah himself was told that Israel would reject his message. Indeed, his proclamation would serve to harden Israel so that they cannot escape the coming judgement:

> Go and say to this people: 'Keep listening, but do not comprehend; keep looking, but do not understand.' Make the mind of this people dull, and stop their ears, and shut their eyes, so that they may not look with their eyes, and listen with their ears, and comprehend with their minds, and turn and be healed. (Isa 6.9–10)

According to Mark, Jesus' proclamation has resulted in great success (1.22, 28, 33, 45) but also opposition (2.7, 16, 18, 24). In Mark 4, Jesus tells a parable (the sower) about the varied responses to the word of God (4.14–20) and explains to his disciples that there are insiders who understand and outsiders who do not. But what has perplexed commentators is that he goes on to explain that the reason Jesus teaches in parables is not to aid communication, as is commonly assumed, but to keep outsiders from understanding. He supports this by directly applying Isa 6.9–10 to his contemporaries:

> And he said to them, 'To you has been given the secret of the kingdom of God, but for those outside, everything comes in parables; in order that "they may indeed look, but not perceive, and may indeed listen, but not understand; so that they may not turn again and be forgiven".' (Mark 4.11–12)

Joachim Jeremias (1972, pp. 15–17) famously argued that this difficulty arose through mistranslation. The Greek word *parabole* translates the Hebrew *mashal*, which can mean riddle, puzzle, dark saying or oracle. Thus the original saying probably meant something like, 'for those outside, it all sounds like riddles'. But when this was translated into Greek, it became 'for those outside, everything comes in parables' and Mark added to the confusion by placing it in the middle of his parables chapter. C. E. B. Cranfield (1977, p. 155) pointed out that Mark's use of the passive ('and be forgiven') points to the Aramaic Targum rather than the LXX and is evidence that the saying goes back to Jesus. Thus the difficulty is probably to be explained by the difference between Semitic and Greek ways of thinking. William Telford, on the other hand, thinks it is quite deliberate.

> For Mark and his community, the very function of the parables has been reinterpreted. The parable is now seen, not as a vehicle for instruction or warning concerning the coming Kingdom of God, but as a vehicle for mystification. The parables reveal Jesus' message and status only to the initiated, in this case the Markan readership ... the parables were *meant* to harden Jewish hearts, *meant* to make them misunderstand, *meant* to conceal ... for history is governed by God's purposes which cannot be thwarted. (1999, p. 66)

Hypocrisy of the Pharisees in 7.6–7

Mark 7 has Jesus in dispute with the Pharisees over matters of the law (see below). Before that, the question ('Why do your disciples not live according to the tradition of the elders, but eat with defiled hands?') is met by the accusation 'Isaiah prophesied rightly about you hypocrites,' followed by a quotation of Isa 29.13 in the form: 'This people honours me with their lips, but their hearts are far from me; in vain do they worship me, teaching human precepts as doctrines.' Since the quotation follows the LXX and differs significantly from the Hebrew (which makes no mention of teaching human doctrines), many scholars think this saying reflects later Christian attitudes to

Judaism rather than something Jesus actually said. We will discuss this in chapter 6 but for now, we simply note that Mark uses Isaiah to accuse the Pharisees both of blindness (4.12) and hypocrisy (7.6–7).

Interpretation of the law in 7.10; 10.6–8; 10.19; 12.18–34

Though Mark does not reproduce much of Jesus' teaching, he does present Jesus as a powerful teacher ('They were astounded at his teaching, for he taught them as one having authority, and not as the scribes.') This is particularly evident in his ability to offer authoritative interpretations of the law. In 7.10, he accuses the Pharisees of using their tradition of Corban (devoting possessions to God) to avoid the plain meaning of the commandment to honour father and mother. In 10.6–8, Jesus is asked to enter the contemporary debate concerning grounds for divorce. Instead, he states that the Genesis texts are primary ('God made them male and female' and 'the two shall become one flesh'), while the certificate of divorce commanded in Deuteronomy was a concession to human weakness.

In 10.17–19, the rich young ruler's question ('what must I do to inherit eternal life?') is initially answered by a summary of the commandments ('You shall not murder; You shall not commit adultery; You shall not steal; You shall not bear false witness; You shall not defraud; Honour your father and mother'). It has perplexed commentators why Jesus only quotes the second half of the decalogue (in an order otherwise unattested) and not those concerned with God. When the man confidently replies, 'I have kept all these since my youth', Jesus invites him to give up his wealth and follow him, perhaps showing him the deeper meaning of these commandments.

In 12.18–27, a story is concocted about a succession of brothers who all had to marry the same woman because the previous brother dies. The aim of the story is to ridicule belief in the resurrection by demanding to know 'whose wife will she be?' Jesus replies by quoting a central affirmation of Jewish belief that God is the 'God of Abraham, the God of Isaac, and the God of Jacob', adding the interpretative comment: 'He is God not of the dead, but of the living.' One might have thought that Jesus would have quoted one of the texts that actually speak about resurrection, such as Dan 12.2 ('Many of those who sleep in the dust of the earth shall awake'). But perhaps it was more necessary to defend the point using texts from the Torah.

In 12.28–34, Jesus is asked to state the greatest commandment. He answers with the words of Deut 6.4–5 ('love the Lord your God with all your heart') but adds that there is a second ('You shall love your neighbour as yourself,') taken from Lev 19.18. Such a combination is not unique (*Testament of Dan* 5.3 says, 'Throughout all your life love the Lord, and one another with a true heart') but Jesus' comment that there is 'no other commandment (singular) greater than these' proved immensely significant for later Christian reflection (e.g. Rom 13.8–10; 1 John 4.7–21).

It may come as a surprise that Jesus' view of the law in these passages is entirely positive. He accuses the Pharisees of hypocrisy for putting their traditions *above* the law. In answer to the question about eternal life, the rich young ruler is not asked to have faith in Jesus but is directed to the commandments. Belief in resurrection is supported by reference to the 'book of Moses' (12.26) and the central message of Jesus is a combination of Deut 6.4–5 (love God) and Lev 19.18 (love neighbour). One could argue that forbidding divorce goes against Deut 24, which allows it providing the proper formalities are observed (the woman must be issued with a bill of divorce), but even here, Jesus' answer is based on quoting another part of the law. We could also add that when he heals a man suffering from leprosy in 1.40–44, he instructs him to go and offer the sacrifices commanded by Moses. Why then do most Christians assume that Jesus was against the law?

There are three main reasons that are usually cited. First, Mark includes a number of stories where Jesus is accused of breaking the Sabbath. Thus in Mark 2.23–28, Jesus allows his disciples to pick grain whilst walking through the fields, and in 3.1–6, he heals a man in a synagogue with a withered hand. But is Mark telling these stories to show that Jesus broke the Sabbath or that he truly understood its divine purpose? Second, at the conclusion of the debate about hand washing, Jesus makes the point that it is not what enters a person that makes them unclean but what is in their heart. Mark then adds the comment, 'Thus he declared all foods clean' (7.19). Many have deduced from this that Jesus was against the food laws but two things can be said about this: (1) It is not Jesus who is speaking but Mark; (2) There is no indication in the Gospels that Jesus or the disciples ever ate anything that the law prescribes as unclean (see Peter's comment in Acts 10.14). Most scholars think that Mark is drawing out an implication of Jesus' aphorism for his Gentile readers. Third, after Jesus says that the greatest commandment is to love God and neighbour, Mark has the scribe reply that this is 'much more important than all whole burnt offerings and sacrifices' (12.33). But such sentiments are common in the prophets (Hos 6.6; Mic 6.6) and does not mean that Jesus wished to abolish sacrifices, any more than the prophets did; it is a question of priorities. We will discuss this further in Chapter 6.

Messiah's entry into Jerusalem in 11.9–10

According to Mark, Jesus' entry into Jerusalem on a donkey was greeted with this acclamation:

Hosanna! (Psalm 118.25)
Blessed is the one who comes in the name of the Lord! (Psalm 118.26)
Blessed is the coming kingdom of our ancestor David! (Comment)
Hosanna in the highest heaven! (Psalm 148.1)

Psalm 118 is a festive Psalm, used at the feast of Tabernacles and the Passover. The line 'Blessed is the one who comes' originally applied to the pilgrims but the focus here is clearly on the *one* who comes, that is, Jesus. The third line does not appear to be a quotation, but a comment or response. Vincent Taylor (1952, p. 456) suggested that it might have been part of the liturgy and chanted antiphonally. But what was its meaning for Mark? Just prior to this episode, blind Bartimaeus acclaims Jesus 'Son of David', which the disciples attempt to silence (10.47–48) but Jesus apparently accepts ('your faith has made you well'). And in one further passage, Jesus himself asks how the Messiah could be David's son when David himself calls him Lord (see below). It would appear that behind Mark's Gospel lies a debate as to the adequacy or otherwise of seeing Jesus in terms of the common expectation of a Davidic deliverer (Isa 9.6-7; Jer 23.5; Ezek 34.23–24; Hos 3.5; Amos 9.11).

Purpose of the temple in 11.17

On the following day, Jesus 'entered the temple and began to drive out those who were selling ... and he overturned the tables of the money-changers' (11.15). He is then reported as quoting Isa 56.7, in combination with Jer 7.11 ('My house shall be called a house of prayer for all the nations? But you have made it a den of robbers.') To simplify somewhat, opinions as to the meaning of this episode depend on whether the key word in the composite quotation is thought to be 'prayer', 'nations' or 'robbers'. If it is 'prayer', then Jesus can be seen like one of the prophets of old who contrasts heart religion with hypocritical ritual. If it is 'nations,' then Jesus is forecasting the entry of the Gentiles into the people of God, including their full access to the temple (the episode probably took place in the court of the Gentiles). If it is 'robbers', then the note of judgement is uppermost, either as 'reformation' or 'destruction'. In the light of the cursing of the fig tree, which directly follows this episode, the latter is perhaps the more likely.

Rejection of the stone in 12.10–11

The parable of the vineyard (drawing on Isa 5) tells the story of a man sending various servants to collect his share of the produce. But the tenants abuse the servants and send them away empty-handed. So the man sends his only son, reasoning (oddly) that they will respect the heir and comply. But they kill the son and so the man has no choice but to 'destroy the tenants and give the vineyard to others'. The parable ends with a quotation from Psalm 118.22–23: 'The stone that the builders rejected has become the chief cornerstone. This is the Lord's doing; it is marvellous in our eyes'.

The quotation is somewhat surprising in that the parable appears to be a tragedy, whereas the psalm speaks of something 'marvellous'. The effect is to change the emphasis of the parable from the tragic means (the death of the son) to the positive outcome (the vineyard is given to others). Most scholars think this reflects later Christian doctrine (redemption through the death of Jesus and the consequent incorporation of the Gentiles) rather than the actual words of Jesus. It is one of three explicit quotations in Mark's Gospel that offer some sort of explanation for why Jesus died.

Puzzle of David's Lord in 12.36

While most of the disputes in the Gospel begin with a challenge to Jesus, Mark 12.35–37 has Jesus on the offensive. While teaching in the temple, Jesus asks, 'How can the scribes say that the Messiah is the son of David?' He then quotes Psalm 110.1 as a riddle, for if David calls him Lord, how can he be his son?

> The Lord said to my Lord,
> Sit at my right hand,
> until I put your enemies under your feet.

Many scholars have argued that Mark rejects a military Messiah in favour of a suffering servant but as Marcus notes, the issue is more subtle than that:

> Paradoxically … the Davidic image turns out to be both too triumphalistic and not triumphant enough … It is not triumphant enough because Jesus is victor not only over his earthly enemies but also, as his entire earthly ministry reveals, over their supernatural masters … That image, on the other hand, is too triumphant because the manner in which Jesus wins his definitive victory over his enemies is through his suffering and death. (1992, pp. 149–50)

It is unclear, however, whether Mark intends such a paradox or whether it appears paradoxical to us in the light of what we now know. It should also be noted that the final words of the quotation ('under your feet') are not from Psalm 110.1 but Psalm 8.6. The ending of Psalm 110.1 is 'until I make your enemies your footstool'.

Apocalyptic sayings in 13.24–26; 14.62

There has been much debate about the meaning of apocalyptic language. Certainly the majority opinion has been that Jesus predicted the end of the world and his own return to earth when quoting (or alluding) to Isa 13.10; 34.4; Dan 7.13 in Mark 13.

> But in those days, after that suffering, the sun will be darkened, and the moon will not give its light, and the stars will be falling from heaven, and the powers in the heavens will be shaken. Then they will see 'the Son of Man coming in clouds' with great power and glory. Then he will send out the angels, and gather his elect from the four winds, from the ends of the earth to the ends of heaven. (Mark 13.24–26)

However, Tom Wright (1996, pp. 612–53) strongly rejects this interpretation, arguing that the Israelite prophets used this language to describe an 'apocalyptic' event *in history*, not as a literal description of the *end of history*. Though it is in the nature of apocalyptic language to have multiple references, Wright believes this text is primarily speaking about the destruction of Jerusalem in 70 CE. That of course fits well with the statement that all these things will happen within a generation (13.30).

There are also difficulties in understanding the reference to Daniel's 'Son of Man'. In the Similitudes of Enoch, the 'Son of Man' is a heavenly deliverer and some think Jesus is identifying with such a figure. On the other hand, there are no texts which use 'Son of Man' in this way which can definitely be dated before the first century. Morna Hooker (1967) suggests that the references are not so much to a particular figure but the whole scenario of rejection and vindication. Thus when Jesus replies to the High Priest, 'you will see the Son of Man seated at the right hand', he is making the claim that he will be vindicated and their roles reversed (and the High Priest will come 'to see' this).

Striking the shepherd in 14.26

After the last supper, Jesus leads the disciples to the Mount of Olives and predicts their desertion, quoting the words of Zech 13.7 ('I will strike the shepherd and the sheep will be scattered.') The note of divine action is heightened by changing the imperative of the original ('Strike the shepherd') into the first person ('I will strike the shepherd'). However, the words that follow the quotation ('But after I am raised up, I will go before you to Galilee') change the emphasis to his subsequent resurrection. Marcus thinks that Mark is responsible for this since Peter's reply ('Even though all become deserters, I will not') and Jesus' response ('Truly I tell you, this day, this very night … you will deny me three times') simply ignore it. He concludes that Mark has introduced the reference to resurrection and reunion, producing a paradox (good coming from evil), as in the vineyard parable. This is the second of the three explicit quotations concerning Jesus' death, both of which contain an element of paradox.

Words from the cross in 15.34

It has been a puzzle and sometimes a theological embarrassment that God's Messiah ends his life with the cry, 'My God, my God, why have you forsaken me?' It is of course a quotation from Psalm 22.1 and one suggestion is that Jesus was seeking to invoke the whole of the psalm, especially its more positive ending: 'For he did not despise or abhor the affliction of the afflicted; he did not hide his face from me, but heard when I cried to him … Posterity will serve him; future generations will be told about the Lord, and proclaim his deliverance to a people yet unborn, saying that he has done it' (Psalm 22.24, 30-1).

However, most scholars find this unconvincing and look for a solution in various understandings of the atonement. Thus an ancient view of the incarnation was that 'only what is assumed can be saved'. If Jesus did not share the fears and anxieties of human existence, then he was not fully human and cannot therefore save humanity. On this view, he was indeed identifying with the Psalmist but in his forsakenness rather than his plea for help (Psalm 22.19-21) and what he will do if it is granted ('I will tell of your name …'). On a different view, Jesus died for our sins (1 Cor 15.3) and the anxiety in Gethsemane and the agony on the cross give us a glimpse of what that cost him. The forsakenness was not the product of fear but was his actual experience; at the moment of death, he was bearing the sins of the world and experiencing separation from God. Lastly, on the penal view of the atonement, Jesus became the object of God's wrath. Those that hold this view argue from the ransom saying (Mark 10.45) that Jesus not only died *for* us but also *instead* of us.

Looking back over the quotations, it is difficult to find an overall pattern and Tom Hatina (2002) has been particularly critical of those who claim to have found one. Clearly Isaiah is important to Mark but can quotations from Isa 6.9–10 (blindness), 13.10/34.4 (future devastation), 29.13 (hypocrisy) and 56.7 (purpose of the temple) really be used to support Marcus's view that the whole of Jesus' ministry is to be understood as the 'triumphant march of the holy warrior, Yahweh, leading his people though the wilderness to their true homeland in a mighty demonstration of saving power'? Marcus admits that Isaiah's 'triumphant march' has been subject to a 'radical, cross-centred adaptation' (1992, p. 36) and perhaps he is correct. But Hatina's point is that what this amounts to is the acknowledgement that what we have in Mark is very different to what we find in Isaiah and thus considerably weakens his case. In response, Marcus, Watts and Perkins would say that this only takes into account the explicit quotations; the parallels are greatly increased if we also consider Mark's allusions, to which we now turn.

Allusions in Mark's Gospel

The Suffering Servant

Though Isa 53 is never explicitly quoted in Mark's Gospel, many scholars believe that it has deeply influenced his thought and surfaces in the passion predictions of 9.31 and 10.33 ('the Son of Man will be *handed over*'), the ransom saying of 10.45 ('For the Son of man came not to be served but *to serve*, and to give his life a *ransom for many*') and the words at the last supper in 14.24 ('This is my blood of the covenant, which is *poured out for many*.'). Does Isa 53.10–12 lie behind these sayings?

> Yet it was the will of the Lord to crush him with pain. When you make his life an offering for sin, he shall see his offspring, and shall prolong his days; through him the will of the Lord shall prosper. Out of his anguish he shall see light; he shall find satisfaction through his knowledge. The righteous one, my *servant, shall make many righteous,* and he shall bear their iniquities. Therefore I will allot him a portion with the great, and he shall divide the spoil with the strong; because he *poured out* himself to death, and was numbered with the transgressors; yet he bore the sin of *many*, and made intercession for the transgressors.

This was the view of Cranfield, Taylor and Jeremias but Hooker (1959) sought to refute it by pointing out that:

1. The linguistic parallels are extremely weak. If we compare Mark's text with the LXX, we find that he uses a different word for service/servant, a different word for ransom and a different word for 'poured out';
2. Though Isa 53 is quoted elsewhere in the New Testament (Matt 8.17; Luke 22.37; Acts 8.32; 1 Pet 2.22), it is never from this so-called vicarious part;
3. There is no evidence prior to the first century that anyone was expecting a 'suffering servant';

4. Isa 49.3 explicitly identifies the servant with Israel (or perhaps a remnant of Israel) and this is the traditional Jewish interpretation.

On the other hand, most Christian readers are still struck by the almost uncanny resemblance to Jesus that Isa 53 affords. As France says,

> We find it hard to believe that allusions to so strikingly appropriate a figure in the Old Testament were merely by chance, or that the appropriateness of the figure escaped Jesus. To the Christian church the relevance of the Servant of Yahweh to the mission of Jesus has always been obvious; why should it be less obvious to him? (1982, p. 113)

The important thing for both sides in this debate is whether 'intention to allude' can be demonstrated. If it can, then although Mark does not draw attention to Isa 53 by explicit quotation, it could still be seen as the subtext that unlocks his understanding of Jesus. Indeed, it is possible to argue that allusions imply texts that are well known (or the allusion would be missed), whereas explicit quotations show the need to highlight them. It is clear that Isaiah is very important to Mark and this could be used as supporting evidence for the importance of Isa 53. On the other hand, if the lack of linguistic evidence and the lack of a precedent in contemporary Judaism makes 'intention to allude' a hazardous assumption, then it could be argued that the rejected stone of Psalm 118, the shepherd of Zech 13 or the righteous sufferer of Psalm 22 are all more important to Mark than Isa 53. Moo thinks all of these backgrounds are important for Mark but notes that 'Isaiah 53, like no other OT text, portrays vicarious, redemptive suffering, and portrays it as the very will of God' (1983, p. 171).

Zechariah 9–14

As well as the explicit quotation of Zech 13.7 in Mark 14.27, a good case can be made for the influence of Zech 13-14 on the whole of the passion narrative. For example, the scattering of the sheep in Zech

13.7 is followed in 13.9 by a refining ('as one refines silver') and a reinstatement ('They will call on my name, and I will answer them') which might explain the promise of reunion in Mark 14.28 (as Marcus argues). The action in Zechariah is to take place on the Mount of Olives. Admittedly, the war-like scene of Zech 14 is rather different to Mark's account of Gethsemane but this could be Mark's way of indicating the nature of Jesus' victory. It will be a time of strife, where 'each will seize the hand of a neighbour, and the hand of one will be raised against the other' (see Mark 13.12). And the final verse of Zechariah says that 'there shall no longer be traders in the house of the Lord' (Zech 14.21), a possible source for Jesus' cleansing of the temple.

The Righteous Sufferer

As well as the explicit quotation of Psalm 22.1 from the cross, the passion narrative contains other references to Psalm 22. For example, the dividing of Jesus' garments alludes to Psalm 22.18 ('they divide my clothes among themselves, and for my clothing they cast lots') and the mockery and wagging of heads alludes (or perhaps echoes) Psalm 22.7 ('All who see me mock at me; they make mouths at me, they shake their heads.') Other 'righteous sufferer' Psalms are also alluded to, most obviously the drink of vinegar in Mark 15.36 (Psalm 69.21). Marcus (1992, pp. 174–5) offers this table of parallels:

Mark		Psalm
14.1	by cunning, to kill	10.7–8
14.18	the one eating with me	41.9
14.34	very sad	42.5,11; 43.5
14.41	delivered into the hands of sinners	140.8
14.55	they sought to put him to death	37.32
14.57	false witnesses rising up	27.12; 35.11
14.61	silence before accusers	35.13–15
15.24	division of garments	22.18
15.29	mockery, head shaking	22.7

15.30-31	Save yourself!	22.8
15.32	reviling	22.6
15.34	cry of dereliction	22.1
15.36	gave him vinegar to drink	69.21
15.40	companions looked on from a distance	38.11

This does indeed show that Mark's description of Jesus owes much to the Psalms but as Stephen Ahearne-Kroll has pointed out, we must beware of constructing an abstract 'righteous sufferer' that does not in fact exist. In some of these Psalms, David is far from innocent and the theme is not so much 'vindication' as the 'willingness to challenge the suffering by demanding God's intervention and presence' (2007, p. 213). Thus if we genuinely seek to understand Mark's view of Jesus by taking into account the scriptural context of these Psalms, the result will be more complex than Jesus' willingness to die and God's willingness to vindicate. This 'righteous sufferer' is a modern construct in order to find an Old Testament pattern (or 'type') for Jesus, and so perhaps is Isaiah's new exodus. There is no doubting that Mark has drawn from these two bodies of literature in order to explain the significance of Jesus but it is questionable that either of them should be used as a 'framework' or 'template' for understanding the whole Gospel.

Conclusion

We noted at the beginning of this chapter that unlike Matthew and Luke, Mark does not provide a set of quotations to explain the various aspects of Jesus' life. However, it could be argued that his allusions play a similar role. Mark has told the story of Jesus' passion in such a way that it evokes the righteous sufferer of the psalms and probably also the suffering servant of Isaiah and the smitten shepherd of Zechariah. He does not try to *prove* that Jesus is any of these figures. He simply uses them as his 'palette' as he constructs his portrait of Jesus. In this, we can see similarities with the Teacher of Righteousness in the

Qumran writings, where the language of the Psalms and Isaiah are so prominent. It is of note that the three texts specifically quoted in connection with Jesus' death (Psalm 118.22–23; Zech 13.7; Psalm 22.1) are all subject to reinterpretation by being juxtaposed with Christian tradition: the workers of the vineyard are killed *but* the vineyard will be given to others; the shepherd is smitten *but* there will be a reunion; Jesus is forsaken *but* the disciples will see him again. Marcus uses the graphic image that it is as though the Old Testament traditions had been exposed to a 'Christological neutron bombardment' (1992, p. 41). If this is correct, the challenge for modern scholars is whether it is possible to reconstruct Mark's purposes from the 'irradiated remains' that are now part of Mark's Gospel.

Further reading

As well as the books cited in this chapter, it should be noted that France (2002) and Marcus (2000, 2009) have now produced significant commentaries where their most recent views can be found. Steve Moyise and Maarten Menken have edited a series of books that look at the use of particular Old Testament books in the New Testament (e.g. *Isaiah in the New Testament*; *Deuteronomy in the New Testament*). The chapters on Mark were written by Ahearne-Kroll (Genesis, 2012); Moyise (Deuteronomy, 2008); Watts (Psalms, 2004); Hooker (Isaiah, 2005) and Breytenbach (Minor Prophets, 2009). Another important series is that edited by Tom Hatina, which focuses on *Biblical Interpretation in Early Christian Gospels*. The volume on Mark (2006) includes studies on particular passages (1.1–15; 6.1–44; 15.1–39), the use made of particular books (Exodus, Zechariah) or passages (Hos 6.2) and particular themes (Son of Man; Servant of the Lord, Food laws). In 2009, Holly Carey offered a significant defence that Jesus' cry from the cross is intended to evoke the whole of the Psalm and that this in no way diminishes the emphasis on suffering.

She notes that vindication/resurrection has been as much a part of the passion narrative as death. Finally, Kelly O'Brian (2010) applies strict criteria for validating the presence of allusions and finds fourteen in Mark 14–15, mainly from the Psalms (2.7; 22.2, 8–9; 37.32; 42.6,12; 43.5; 69.22; 110.1), with a couple from Isaiah (36.21; 50.6) and Exodus (24.8; 20.16), along with Hos 6.2; Zech 13.7 and Amos 8.9-10. She notes that Mark shows no interest in establishing Jesus' innocence (as Luke does) and that Jesus is the 'representative head, who in dying for others, brings salvation near and enables the saints to inherit the Reign of God' (2010, p. 200).

Questions

1. Which Old Testament books are most quoted in Mark's Gospel? Is there a case for saying that one or more of them offers a template for understanding Jesus?
2. Which is more important for determining the meaning of Jesus' death – the quotations of Psalm 118.22-23, Zech 13.7 and Psalm 22.1 or the allusions to Isa 53?
3. Does the Old Testament context of Isa 13.10; 34.4; Dan 7.13 suggest that Jesus was speaking metaphorically in Mark 13?

3

The Old Testament in Matthew

Depending on how composite quotations are counted, there are about 54 quotations in Matthew's Gospel. They fall into three categories:

1. Matthew's own editorial comments. These are concentrated in the infancy narratives (1.23; 2.6, 15, 18, 23) and then spread through the Gospel (4.15; 8.17; 13.35; 21.5; 27.9). With the exception of 2.6, they are all introduced with a formula such as 'this happened so as to fulfil (*pleroun*) what was said by such and such a prophet'.
2. Quotations on the lips of Jesus. Matthew includes all of Mark's quotations but interestingly, they all occur in the latter half of the Gospel (beginning at 13.34). In the first half of the Gospel, Jesus quotes scripture in the temptation narrative (4.1–11), the Sermon on the Mount (Chs. 5–7), while dining with tax collectors (9.13), as part of the mission discourse (10.35), in the reply to John the Baptist (11.10) and four times in Chapter 12.
3. Quotations on the lips of others. This is a small group consisting of words by the devil (4.6), the Pharisees (19.7), the crowd (21.9), and the Sadducees (22.24).

We will divide our discussion into two sections. First, we will look at those quotations that are also in Mark but are treated differently by Matthew. Most scholars believe these to be Matthew's changes to Mark though the theory of Markan priority is not without its difficulties. Second, we will consider Matthew's formula quotations. As there is a much greater number of quotations to discuss, we will not in this chapter have a separate discussion of allusions.

Quotations in Mark but treated differently by Matthew

John the Baptist in 3.3

Instead of Mark's composite quotation of Mal 3.1/Exod 23.20/Isa 40.3, Matthew heralds the forerunner only with Isa 40.3, saving the Mal 3.1/ Exod 23.20 material for another occasion. This makes for a smoother introduction, as words from Isaiah now directly follow the ascription to 'Isaiah the prophet'. This could be seen as Matthew 'correcting' Mark but the fact that Luke also transfers the Mal 3.1/Exod 23.20 material to this same location suggests a more significant motive. In Matt 11, disciples of John the Baptist come to Jesus and ask, 'Are you the one who is to come, or are we to wait for another?' Jesus replies by citing Mal 3.1/Exod 23.20 and then says, 'and if you are willing to accept it, he is Elijah who is to come' (11.14). Thus the identification of John as Elijah is now a revelation of Jesus and quite explicit. There is therefore no need to have the composite quotation at the beginning. The fact that Luke does likewise suggests either that Luke followed Matthew's lead (Michael Goulder, 1989) or that they both followed a source other than Mark (generally known as Q from the German word for 'source', *Quelle*).

Parable purpose in 13.13–15

Matthew agrees with Mark in linking the purpose of the parables with the blindness saying of Isa 6.9–10 but there are a number of differences: (1) Before the quotation there is an additional saying, 'For to those who have, more will be given … but from those who have nothing, even what they have will be taken away;' (2) The quotation is first paraphrased ('seeing they do not perceive, and hearing they do not listen, nor do they understand') and then quoted in full; (3) The quotation is introduced by the Greek word *hoti* rather than *hina*. This suggests that the blindness is the *result* of the parables but not necessarily their *purpose*; (4) A fulfilment formula is used ('With them indeed is fulfilled the prophecy of Isaiah that says'); (5) The quotation follows the LXX and so ends on the more positive 'and I would heal them'. It cannot be said that Matthew has eliminated the predestination theme completely for he includes the saying, 'To you it has been given to know the secrets of the kingdom of heaven, but to them it has not been given' (13.11). But the stress does seem to have moved in the direction of the people's culpability rather than God's intention to keep them from the truth.

Interpretation of the law in 19.1–22 and 22.15–40

In the dispute about marriage and divorce (Mark 10.1–12, Matt 19.1–12), Matthew has three additional sayings. The first has the Pharisees replying, 'Why then did Moses command us to give a certificate?', to which Jesus replies, 'It was because you were so hard-hearted that Moses allowed you to divorce your wives, but from the beginning it was not so.' Second, the so called exemption clause is added to the prohibition of divorce ('except for unchastity'). Since this also occurs in the Sermon on the Mount ('But I say to you that anyone who divorces his wife, *except on the ground of unchastity*, causes her to commit adultery; and whoever marries a divorced woman commits adultery' – 5:32), many scholars regard this as Matthew's attempt to apply Jesus' words to his community (as does Paul in 1 Cor 7.10–16). Third, his disciples then ask whether it is better not to marry, to which Jesus replies with some rather obscure sayings about becoming 'eunuchs for the kingdom' (19.12).

It is somewhat surprising that none of the New Testament summaries of the commandments agree with any of the Old Testament lists (Exod 20, 34; Deut 5). Mark begins with murder, ends with honouring parents and adds a command about fraud (perhaps thought to be the result of coveting). Matthew agrees with Mark except that he adds the commandment to love one's neighbour (Lev 19.18) and omits the command about fraud. Luke and Paul both begin with adultery but Paul also includes commands about coveting and loving one's neighbour.

The variation might simply reflect the different ways the commandments were being recited in their respective churches, though Robert Gundry thinks that Matthew and Luke are deliberately omitting Mark's extraneous command about fraud.

Exod 20.12–17	Mark 10.19	Matt 19.18	Luke 18.19	Rom 13.9
honour parents	murder	murder	adultery	adultery
murder	adultery	adultery	murder	murder
adultery	stealing	stealing	stealing	stealing
stealing	false witness	false witness	false witness	coveting
false witness	defraud	honour parents	honour parents	
coveting	honour parents	love neighbour		love neighbour

The discussion about resurrection (Matt 22.23–33) is similar to that in Mark but in the discussion about the greatest commandment (22.34–40), Matthew omits the *Shema* ('Hear, O Israel: the Lord our God, the Lord is One') and the subsequent exchange where the Scribe takes Jesus to mean that loving God and neighbour are 'much more important than all whole burnt offerings and sacrifices'. It is easy to see why the latter was omitted because of its criticism of the law, which commands such sacrifices and burnt offerings, but omission of the former is surprising. Gundry (1994, p. 449) suggests that as a Jew writing to Jewish Christians, Matthew could assume monotheism in a way that Mark could not, and is therefore more interested in moving towards trinitarianism (28.19) than affirming monotheism. It should be noted that contrary to the view of many Christians, Matthew presents Jesus as upholding the law. He is sometimes in dispute about its meaning but that is what scribal tradition is all about.

> Do not think that I have come to abolish the law or the prophets; I have come not to abolish but to fulfil. For truly I tell you, until heaven and earth pass away, not one letter, not one stroke of a letter, will pass from the law until all is accomplished. Therefore, whoever breaks one of the least of these commandments, and teaches others to do the same, will be called least in the kingdom of heaven; but whoever does them and teaches them will be called great in the kingdom of heaven. (Matt 5.17–19)

Entry into Jerusalem in 21.5

Matthew links the entry into Jerusalem on a donkey with an explicit quotation of Zech 9.9, prefaced by words from Isa 62.11 ('Tell the daughter of Zion'). What is of interest in this quotation is that (1) It is introduced by a fulfilment formula and (2) The Hebrew parallelism 'mounted on a donkey, and on a colt, the foal of a donkey' has affected the way that Matthew has narrated the story:

Mark 11.2	Matt 21.2
Go into the village ahead of you,	Go into the village ahead of you,
and immediately as you enter it,	and immediately you will find
you will find tied there a colt that	a donkey tied, *and a colt with*
has never been ridden; untie it	*her*; untie *them* and bring *them*
and bring it.	to me.

It has sometimes been suggested that Matthew has misunderstood the Hebrew parallelism and has therefore invented another animal, leading to the rather odd picture of Jesus sitting on both animals or perhaps between them on a quasi-throne. However, Matthew is quite at home with Hebrew parallelism (4.16; 8.17) and it is more likely that he is emphasising the theological point that the passion is according to scripture. He is not asking the reader to picture Jesus sitting astride two animals but to understand the whole event as 'prophetic symbolism' (Nolland, p. 837). Gundry (1994, p. 408) thinks of the scene as a young foal tagging along after its mother but there is nothing to suggest that this is what Matthew is intending. Notice how John does a similar thing with the quotation about casting lots for Jesus' clothes in John 19.24.

Purpose of the temple in 21.13

Matthew includes the composite quotation of Isa 56.7 and Jer 7.11 but omits the words 'for all the nations'. Since Matthew's Gospel ends with the command to 'make disciples of all nations', this is surprising. However, on two occasions he has Jesus stating that his earthly ministry is confined to the house of Israel (10.6; 15.24), and so he might be making the point that the Jewish temple was never intended for Gentiles but the Christian Church now welcomes them. Alternatively, Matthew might have thought the reference to 'nations' implies that Jesus was simply protesting against exclusivism. By omitting it, Matthew focuses on Jesus' objection to Jewish unfaithfulness ('My house shall be called a house of prayer; but *you* are making it a den or robbers.')

Rejection of the stone in 21.42

Matthew follows the 'stone' saying with the interpretative comment, 'Therefore, I tell you, the kingdom of God will be taken away from you and given to a people that produces the fruits of the kingdom.' In the NRSV, there then follows another 'stone' saying (21.44) but it is absent from some manuscripts and is not printed in the NIV. It may have come from the Lukan parallel (20.18) and we will discuss it there.

Words from the cross in 27.46

Matthew's use of Psalm 22.1 is similar to Mark's, except he has Jesus saying 'Eli, Eli' rather than 'Eloi, Eloi', reflecting the Hebrew of the psalm rather than spoken Aramaic. Gundry thinks it also makes the confusion with Elijah more plausible. Otherwise, the major difference is in what follows, for as well as the rent curtain, we now have an earthquake and the saints of old coming out of their tombs. This appears to be an allusion to Ezek 37.13 ('And you shall know that I am the Lord, when I open your graves') and is now explicitly the reason for the Centurion's confession ('Truly this man was God's Son!' – 27.54). Since this incident only occurs in Matthew, it raises the important question of whether historical details have been invented to fit scriptural prophecy. Dodd denied this, arguing that the task of the early Church was to show that the events that had happened were a fulfilment of the ancient prophecies (Acts 2.22). It would substantially weaken their case if they were to invent incidents that could easily be shown to be false. This sounds plausible but it assumes that Matthew intended the story to be taken literally. Gundry thinks that Matthew is deliberately alluding to Ezek 37.13 (and Dan 12.2) as a way of claiming that Jesus' death marks the beginning of the general resurrection. We moderns might prefer it if he had first narrated the facts and then drawn his conclusions, but he was not a post-Enlightenment thinker. At any rate, if such an astounding occurrence had taken place, one would have expected it to be recorded somewhere ('look mum, Grandad's back').

Matthew's fulfilment quotations

In Mark, the opening quotation is the only one that functions as editorial comment. In Matthew, there are eleven such quotations which are all introduced (except 2.6) with the verb *pleroun* ('to fulfil'). Given that four of them appear to be Matthew's changes to Mark (Matt 8.17; 12.18; 13.35; 21.5), it would appear that Matthew is responsible for this important exegetical development.

Subject	Reference
Jesus' name and virginal conception (1.23)	Isa 7.14
Jesus' birth place in Bethlehem (2.6)	Mic 5.2
Jesus' departure from Egypt (2.15)	Hos 11.1
Wailing in Ramah for Bethlehem's children (2.18)	Jer 31.15
Jesus' home in Nazareth (2.23)	???
Jesus' dwelling in Capernaum (4.15)	Isa 9.1
Jesus' healing ministry (8.17)	Isa 53.4
Jesus' healing ministry (12.18)	Isa 42.1–4
Jesus' parabolic ministry (13.35)	Psalm 78.2
Jesus' triumphal entry (21.5)	Zech 9.9
Jesus' betrayal (27.9)	Zech 11.12

Our first observation is that they seem rather pedestrian. One might have expected (hoped?) that this additional exegetical activity might have clarified which scriptures were being used to explain Jesus death and resurrection or the nature of his messiahship. Instead, nearly half of them appear to focus on geography (Bethlehem, Egypt, Ramah, Nazareth, Capernaum). There is an increased usage of 'servant' texts (8.17; 12.18) but these are not used to elucidate the death of Jesus (Hooker's point). Rather, they show that Jesus' healing ministry was predicted by scripture (12.18), as was his parabolic ministry (13.35). The triumphal entry and betrayal are now explicitly linked to Zechariah by quotations, though one might have hoped for something more significant than the price of his betrayal ('thirty pieces of silver'). There is not space to look at all of these in detail but we will examine the five quotations in the infancy stories to see what they reveal about Matthew's use of scripture.

Jesus' name and the virginal conception in 1.23

The text that does stand out for its theological significance is Isa 7.14, which is used to support both the virginal conception of Jesus and his title as Emmanuel. In Mark's Gospel, the action begins with Jesus' baptism where the heavens are torn and the Spirit descends on him. Matthew is to record this (though the heavens are 'opened' rather than 'torn' and the whole episode is a vision granted to Jesus) but Matthew's story begins much earlier. Mary, while betrothed to Joseph, is found to be pregnant *ek pneumatos hagiou* ('from' or 'of' the Holy Spirit). Joseph, being a righteous man, wishes to avoid a scandal and determines to send her away. But his plans are changed by a visit from an angel, who reiterates that the conception is from/of the Holy Spirit. Joseph is then instructed to call the child (which will be a son), 'Jesus, for he will save his people from their sins' (1.21). Then comes the formula and citation of Isa 7.14: 'All this took place to fulfil what had been spoken by the Lord through the prophet: "Look, the virgin shall conceive and bear a son, and they shall name him Emmanuel," which means, "God is with us."'

Rather strangely, there appears to be a contradiction concerning the name of the child. Is he called Jesus or Emmanuel? We are told at the end of v. 25 that he was in fact called Jesus. So how is Isa 7.14 fulfilled with respect to the name? The answer, according to most commentators, lies in a change of the quoted text. In the original (Hebrew and Greek), the naming is in the second person ('you will name') but Matthew changes this to the third person ('they shall name'). Gundry says: 'This revision turns the quotation into a prediction of the church's confession. Just as "you [Joseph son of David] shall call his name Jesus, for he will save his people from their sins," so also "they [the people of Jesus] will call his name Immanuel"' (1994, p. 304).

The other major issue is whether Isa 7.14 actually speaks about a virginal conception. Two points are important. First, the Hebrew text uses the word *alma* ('young woman') rather than the specific word for virgin (*betula*). However, the LXX unusually rendered *alma* with *parthenos* (Gen 24.43 is the only other occasion) and Matthew quotes the text in this form. Second, regardless of the actual word used, the 'LXX probably means only that she who is now a virgin will later conceive and give birth: no miracle is involved' (Davies and Allison, 1988, p. 214). At any rate, the promise is not for a child 700 years hence for 'before the child knows how to refuse the evil and choose the good [i.e. weaned], the land before whose two kings you are in dread will be deserted' (Isa 7.16). However suggestive the text might be (a great act of God signalled by the birth of a child), it is clear that its original reference is to the political situation of the eighth century BCE. Whether it can be legitimately applied to a later period depends on one's understanding of meaning and reference. We will discuss this further in our final chapter.

Jesus' birth place in Bethlehem in 2.6

Were the Jews expecting the Messiah to come from Bethlehem, the city of David? There is little evidence to support it and in John 7.27 we read, 'Can it be that the authorities really know that this is the Messiah? Yet we know where this man is from; but when the Messiah comes, no one will know where he is from.' Matthew, on the other hand, has the scribes and chief priests answering Herod with the words: 'In Bethlehem of Judea; for so it has been written by the prophet: "And you, Bethlehem, in the land of Judah, are by no means least among the rulers of Judah; for from you shall come a ruler who is to shepherd my people Israel."' As with Isa 7.14, it all sounds very plausible the way Matthew has quoted it. But three things should be noted. First, Matthew (or his source) has introduced the word *oudamos* ('by no means') into the quotation of Mic 5.2. The original text (both Greek and Hebrew) states that Bethlehem is the least. Second, Matthew says least among the 'rulers' of Judah, but the Hebrew (*alpe*) means 'clans' not 'rulers'. The LXX is of no help for it rendered *alpe* with *chiliasin* ('thousands'). The explanation appears to be that either Matthew or someone before him took the Hebrew consonants to be the word *allupe*, which means 'princes' (and hence 'rulers'). Third, the final phrase is not found in Micah at all but appears to come from 2 Sam 5.2. Davies and Allison suggest that Matthew crosses over to this text in order to signal the importance of a Davidic Christology (1988, p. 243). They also think that Matthew is responsible for the changes made to the text of Mic 5.2.

Was Jesus in fact born in Bethlehem? If Matthew is correct that Mic 5.2 predicts the birth of the Messiah in Bethlehem, it may be that Matthew simply assumed that this was the case, without actually having any evidence for it. In other words, it could be another example of 'prophetic symbolism', like the saints coming alive in 27.52 or Jesus riding on two donkeys in 21.7. On the other hand, Mic 5.2 is never quoted in the Dead Sea Scrolls and we do not find any Jewish group on high alert for something significant happening in Bethlehem. Thus many scholars still agree with Dodd's judgement that

[F]ar from the nativity stories in Matthew and Luke having been composed for apologetic purposes, in order to meet a generally held belief that the Messiah must be born in Bethlehem, it was the fact that Jesus was actually born there that revived in Christian circles interest in a prophecy which played little part in contemporary Jewish thought. (1953, p. 91)

Jesus' departure from Egypt in 2.15

After the visit of the magi, Joseph is told to flee to Egypt for, 'Herod is about to search for the child, to destroy him.' He remains in Egypt until Herod dies. Then comes the fulfilment formula, 'This was to fulfil what had been spoken by the Lord through the prophet', followed by a quotation from Hos 11.1, 'Out of Egypt I have called my Son.' The text of Hosea is of course referring to Israel and the exodus, as the surrounding verses make clear:

> When Israel was a child, I loved him,
> and *out of Egypt I called my son.*
> The more I called them,
> the more they went from me;
> they kept sacrificing to the Baals,
> and offering incense to idols. (Hos 11.1–2).

Is Matthew trying to say that Jesus is to lead a new exodus? Certainly there are parallels between Jesus and Moses. They are both threatened as infants, find sojourn in a foreign land, stay there until the ruling power dies (Exod 4.19) and later (under God's command) leave Egypt for Palestine. But it is probably more complicated than that for (1) Moses flees *from* Egypt whereas Jesus flees *to* Egypt; (2) As God's son, the parallel is between Israel and Jesus not Moses and Jesus; (3) Matthew's quotation would have to look forward to 2.21, whereas all the other formula quotations refer back to what has just been narrated. Gundry concludes that, 'Matthew is not highlighting Jesus' later departure from Egypt as a new Exodus, but God's preservation of Jesus in Egypt as a sign of divine sonship' (1994, p. 34). But most scholars think that Matthew is drawing a parallel with the exodus. France (2007, p. 81) says that Matthew's quotation

> expresses in the most economical form a wide-ranging theology of
> the new exodus and of Jesus as the true Israel which plays a significant
> role throughout Matthew's Gospel. As usual, Matthew's christological
> interpretation consists not of exegesis of what the text quoted meant in

its original context, but of a far-reaching theological argument which takes the OT text and locates it within an over-arching scheme of fulfillment which finds in Jesus the end point of numerous prophetic trajectories. When Jesus "came out of Egypt," that was to be the signal for a new exodus in which Jesus would fill the role not only of the God-sent deliverer but also of God's "son" Israel himself.

Not all scholars would agree with the statement that Matthew was not interested in what Hosea originally meant. John Sailhamer (2001), for example, argues that Hosea would have understood Num 24.8 ('God who brings *him* out of Egypt') as a reference to the messiah and so his own words ('out of Egypt I called my son') are most probably a messianic prediction. Few have found this convincing but scholars such as Beale have sought to show that Matthew's exegesis is not arbitrary. He notes that Hosea looked forward to a day when the tribes would be reunited under 'one head' (1.11), most probably a Davidic figure (3.5), and that the future deliverance is thought of as a new exodus ('They shall come trembling like birds from Egypt' – 11.11). Hosea was not specifically thinking of Jesus' departure from Egypt but Matthew's application can be regarded as an 'organic expansion or development of meaning', like that of 'acorn to an oak tree, a bud to a flower, or a seed to an apple' (2012, p. 27).

Wailing in Ramah in 2.18

When Herod realizes he has been tricked, he orders the killing of all children aged two and under in and around Bethlehem (cf. Exod 1.22). According to Josephus (*Ant.* 15), Herod's reign was marked by such slaughters, though there is no direct evidence that this was true of Bethlehem. Be that as it may, our difficulty is to explain how Matthew thought this slaughter was a fulfilment of Jer 31.15 ('A voice was heard in Ramah, wailing and loud lamentation, Rachel weeping for her children; she refused to be consoled, because they are no more.') Had Matthew said that the pain of the slaughter was like the pain of the exile, one could suggest a number of reasons for the parallel: (1)

Tradition associated Rachel's burial place as either in Bethlehem (Gen 35.19) or near it (1 Sam 10.2); (2) In the light of Isa 10.29, Jer 31.15 and Hos 5.8, 'Ramah might be regarded as a city of sadness par excellence' (Davies and Allison, p. 269); (3) Jeremiah can be seen as the prophet of doom par excellence; (4) Jer 31 is a significant chapter for the early Church (e.g. Rom 11.27; 1 Cor 11.25; Heb 8.8–12), which may have led Matthew to 31.15. David Turner (2008, p. 95) concludes:

> In Jeremiah's view of the future, Rachel's mourning for her children would be consoled by Israel's return to the land and the making of a new covenant. The similar mourning of the mothers of Bethlehem also occurs in the context of hope, but the hope here is now about to be actualized through the sacrificial death and resurrection of the Messiah (Matt 26:27–28).

On this view, the typological comparison is not the 'suffering' of the two sets of mothers but the 'deliverance' that follows, resulting in the establishment of a new covenant. On the other hand, modern readers will find it difficult to celebrate a story where God miraculously rescues Jesus, while leaving the children of Bethlehem to be slaughtered. Later Christian tradition solved this by regarding the children as sharing in the sufferings of Christ and hence dying as martyrs, but it is by no means obvious that this was Matthew's view. Richard Erickson's solution is that the typology is not simply 'suffering' nor 'deliverance' but draws on the point that having fled from his enemy, Moses *returned* 'to stand before Pharaoh, fully identified with the people of Israel, in complete solidarity with them, becoming the channel of their deliverance and restoration' (1996, p. 21). Erickson's point is that this is precisely what Jesus does, standing side by side with his people even to the point of death.

Jesus' home in Nazareth in 2.23

The last formula quotation in the infancy stories concerns Jesus settling in Nazareth, which is said to be a fulfilment of the text, 'He will be called a Nazorean.' This is a difficulty since there is no such text in the Old Testament. It could of course be that Matthew is quoting a form of text that is now lost to us but against this is the fact that the town of Nazareth is never mentioned in the Old Testament. Most scholars think that he is probably using a word-play, either with *nazir* ('nazirite', as in Num 6; Judges 13), *neser* ('branch/root', as in Isa 11.1), *nazir* ('prince', as in Gen 49.26) or *noserim* ('watchmen', as in Jer 31.6). However, the problem with these suggestions is that they then make the link with Nazareth gratuitous. What is it that is being fulfilled by Jesus settling at Nazareth? Surely more than the fact that the letters can be rearranged to correspond to a known messianic title? This example is a stark reminder that the New Testament authors belonged to a very different world from our own. No doubt Matthew thought that it was both providential and exegetically significant that Jesus should settle in a town which sounds like one of the great 'deliverer' figures of old. Who are we to say that it is invalid or of little consequence? Aus (2004, p. 84) calls it a 'typically Jewish Christian haggadic embellishment', which is not based on historical facts but imaginative parallels. He denies that any form of deception is involved; it was the most natural way for a Jewish Christian like Matthew to express the profound truth that Jesus is Israel's final redeemer.

Conclusion

Matthew is much more concerned than Mark to link incidents in Jesus' life with explicit Old Testament texts. Some of Mark's allusions (Isa 53; Zech 9, 11) are now explicit quotations and the narrative is punctuated by a series of explanatory proof-texts. One might have expected this heightened exegetical activity to focus on such things as Jesus' relationship to God or the purpose of his death but they appear to be quite mundane. Of course, we must be careful not to impose a modern value judgement on the material (i.e. what we would consider mundane). Presumably Matthew thought these things were important. Indeed, Dale Allison suggests that Matthew's form of scriptural imitation 'was not an act of inferior repetition but an inspired act of fresh interpretation' (1993, p. 272). Many of the Qumran exegetical techniques are in evidence, including typology (Moses/Israel-Jesus), quoting variant texts ('virgin' instead of 'young woman'), altering texts (adding 'by no means'; changing 'you will call' to 'they will call') and reading texts in an unorthodox manner ('donkey and colt'). In one of the earliest studies to make use of the Dead Sea Scrolls, Krister Stendahl (1954) described Matthew's exegesis as *midrash pesher*, because it was similar to that found in the Habakkuk commentary (*pesher*).

We will note in Chapter 6 that Matthew goes out of his way to clarify that Jesus was a law-abiding Jew. Not only do we have specific statements like 'not one letter, not one stroke of a letter, will pass from the law until all is accomplished' (5.18), he also exhorts his disciples to keep the laws, for 'whoever does them and teaches them will be called great in the kingdom of heaven (5.19). It is also of note that in the dispute about hand washing, Mark adds his own inference: 'Thus he declared all foods clean' (Mark 7.19), but Matthew omits this. Certainly Jesus is against those who would use the law to avoid showing compassion (9.13; 12.7) and Matt 23 is a tirade against the hypocrisy of the Pharisees. But there is no indication that he wished to substitute a religion of love and grace for one of law and ritual.

Further reading

As well as co-authoring one of the best commentaries on Matthew (Davies and Allison, 1988/91/97), Allison has also written a fine study on *The New Moses: A Matthean Typology* (1993). The numerous parallels are not intended to denigrate Moses, he says, for 'the more one exalted Moses, the more one exalted Jesus … It was Moses' very greatness that allowed honor to pass from him to his superior look-alike' (pp. 275–76). There have been major studies on Matthew's use of Jeremiah (Knowles, 1993), Isaiah (Beaton, 2002) and Zechariah (Ham,

2005). The volume in the Hatina series (2008) contains chapters on particular texts (Matt 1.1; 1.23; 2.1–23; 8.17; 22.34–40) and the use of particular themes (Elijah, shepherd, healer-messiah). The chapter in the Beale and Carson Commentary (2007, pp. 1–109) was written by Craig Blomberg, who advocates a theory of double fulfilment. Thus there was a partial fulfilment of Isa 7.14 when Israel's enemies were destroyed but an even greater fulfilment in Jesus. The chapters on Matthew in the Moyise and Menken series were written by Brown (Genesis), Menken (Deuteronomy), Menken (Psalms), Beaton (Isaiah) and Ham (Isaiah). Maarten Menken (2004) has also written a monograph on the language of Matthew's quotations. Most scholars have concluded that Matthew deliberately modified his quotations to make his point but Menken argues that many of the changes had already been made in a revised version of the LXX. The last few years has also seen a fine set of detailed commentaries by scholars such as John Nolland (2005), Richard France (2007), David Turner (2008) and Craig Evans (2012). For the birth narratives, see my *Was the Birth of Jesus According to Scripture?* (2013).

Questions

1. What are the main differences between Matthew's and Mark's use of scripture?
2. In what ways does Matthew's use of scripture resemble that of the Dead Sea Scrolls?
3. In what sense can Jesus' birth be regarded as a fulfilment of scripture?

4

The Old Testament in Luke-Acts

Luke's Gospel contains about 25 quotations, half the number of Matthew and about the same as Mark. Bearing in mind that Luke is nearly twice as long as Mark, we can say that quotations in Luke are about half as frequent as in Matthew and Mark. Luke has all but four of Mark's quotations. For three of these, this is because he omits that section of Mark to which they belong (all of Mark 7 and Mark 10.1–12). The fourth is the reference to 'striking the shepherd' from Zech 13.7. This was probably not because of the quotation itself but because the episode ends with Jesus' promise, 'I will go before you to Galilee'. Since Luke only has appearances in and around Jerusalem, it is understandable that he drops the reference to Galilee (though it should be noted that Mark does not narrate any appearances in Galilee either). Most scholars regard Luke's Gospel as the first part of a two-volume work (compare Luke 1.1–4 and Acts 1.1–2) and we shall see how the contents of each affects our understanding of the other. However, it is also useful to compare Luke's Gospel with the other Gospels, especially as most scholars think that like Matthew, he has consciously changed some of the emphases of Mark. We will therefore begin by looking at the quotations that Luke shares with Mark (and Matthew), followed by those that are unique to him, first in the Gospel and then in Acts. As some of these additional quotations are from Isaiah, the case for a new exodus/servant of God framework for Luke is stronger than it was for Mark and some scholars now regard this as certain (Pao, 2000). However, a case can also be made for the importance of the Psalms and in particular, the figure of David, who is also called a servant of God (Acts 4.25).

Quotations shared with Mark (and Matthew)

John the Baptist in 3.4–6/7.27

Like Matthew, Luke uses the Exodus/Malachi material for Jesus' reply to
the disciples of John (Luke 7.18–35), leaving only words from Isaiah to
follow the ascription to Isaiah. However, unlike Matthew, he compen-
sates (as it were) by extending the quotation to include Isa 40.4–5.
Most scholars think this is because he liked the universal outlook of
Isa 40.6 ('and all flesh shall see the salvation of God'), a characteristic
found elsewhere in Luke. For example, his version of the genealogy
(3.23–38) goes back to Adam rather than just Abraham (Matt 1.1–17).
Acts 1.8 is seen as pivotal for understanding Luke's two-volume work:
'But you will receive power when the Holy Spirit has come upon you;
and you will be my witnesses in Jerusalem, in all Judea and Samaria,
and to the ends of the earth.' This is fulfilled at the end of Acts when
Paul proclaims the gospel in Rome. It is also of note that quoting Isa
40.5 ('Every valley shall be filled, and every mountain and hill shall be
made low') shows that we are talking about an eschatological event and
not simply the ministry of John the Baptist.

Parable purpose in 8.10

Like Mark, Luke introduces the quotation of Isa 6.9–10 with *hina* ('in
order that') but omits the final line ('so that they may not turn again
and be forgiven'), which considerably softens the statement. However,
Luke does have Paul quoting Isa 6.9–10 in full at the very end of the
book of Acts and it may be that he intends a progression, the hardening
having begun in Jesus' ministry, reaches a climax at the end of Acts.

Interpretation of the law in 10.25–28; 18.20; 20.27–40

Luke omits those sections of Mark which contain the disputes over corban
and divorce (Mark 7.6–10; 10.6–8). The citing of the commandments to the

rich young ruler (Mark 10.19) and the Sadducees' question about divorce (Mark 12.18–27) are much the same as in Mark. However, the citing of the twin commandments to love God and neighbour (Mark 12.28–34) comes earlier in Luke's Gospel, is cited by the lawyer rather than Jesus, and is followed by the parable of the Good Samaritan. Some scholars think these are Luke's redactional changes to Mark because the connection with the parable seems artificial. Charles Kimball (1994) denies this and argues that they are two quite separate incidents. He notes that the connection between the story and the parable can be adequately explained by reference to a rabbinic form of debate known as *yelammeddenu*, and he uses this to argue that it most likely goes back to Jesus. The parallels are:

1. It begins with a question ('What must I do to inherit eternal life?').
2. Relevant texts are introduced to elucidate the question (Deut 6.5 and Lev 19.18, linked by the word 'love').
3. A third text is introduced to arbitrate between the two texts (Lev 18.5: 'do this and you shall live').
4. A story or parable is told to illustrate key terms (the meaning of 'neighbour' and 'doing').
5. It concludes with an allusion back to the key text ('Go and do likewise', an allusion to Lev 19.18).

Messiah's entry into Jerusalem in 19.38

Luke inserts the word 'king' into the quotation of Psalm 118.26 ('Blessed is the *king* who comes'), suggested perhaps by Mark's phrase, 'Blessed is the coming kingdom', which he omits. Mark Strauss (1995, p. 349) thinks this is part of a deliberate strategy by Luke to show that God's promise to place one of David's descendants upon his throne has been fulfilled in Jesus. In the final phrase, where Mark and Matthew have, 'Hosanna in the highest heaven', Luke has, 'Peace in heaven, and glory in the highest heaven', echoing the angelic praise at the birth of Jesus (2.14). Like Matthew, Luke has earlier used Psalm 118.26 to conclude the lament over Jerusalem (13.35).

Purpose of the temple in 19.46

Luke omits the phrase 'for all the nations' from the quotation of Isa 56.7. Given Luke's interest in Gentiles, this is surprising and it might be evidence that this was absent from his version of Mark (since Matthew also omits it). Christopher Evans (1990, p. 688) suggests that Luke has dropped it because he does not believe that the nations will flock to the temple; rather, the gospel will go out to them, as in Acts 1.8.

Rejection of the stone in 20.17–18

Luke only quotes Psalm 118.22 ('The stone the builders rejected has become the cornerstone'), omitting the following verse that it was 'marvellous in our eyes'. Instead, he introduces words which allude to the stone of stumbling (Isa 8.14), which is frequently quoted in the New Testament (Acts 4.11; Rom 9.32–33; Eph 2.20; 1 Pet 2.4–8), and perhaps also to the stone of Daniel's vision which 'struck the statue on its feet of iron and clay and broke them in pieces' (Dan 2.34–35). The result is that the emphasis is much more on 'rejection' rather than 'transfer of ownership' (as in Mark and Matthew). Kimball says: 'Jesus employed the OT in a typological and prophetic manner in this exposition. He made a *pesher*-like claim to be the OT's rejected and judging stone, and he pictured himself as a type of rejected servant of God who, due to his sonship, is in a different class than the previous servants' (1994, p. 163). Whether the various endings of the parable of the vineyard actually go back to Jesus or are later additions will be discussed in Chapter 6.

Puzzle of David's Lord in 20.43

Luke quotes Psalm 110.1 without the gloss from Psalm 8 ('footstool' instead of 'under your feet'). Given his interest in the Spirit, it is surprising that he omits reference to David speaking in the Holy Spirit and writes, 'For David himself says in the book of Psalms'. Darrell

Bock (1989) sees this incident as the turning point in Luke's Gospel, where he begins to steer his readers away from a Davidic-Servant Christology towards the 'more than Messiah' Lordship Christology that is proclaimed in Acts. However, this appears to be an overstatement. At the climax of the Pentecost speech, Peter says, 'Therefore let the entire house of Israel know with certainty that God has made him *both Lord and Messiah*, this Jesus whom you crucified' (Acts 2.36). Both terms retain their importance for Luke.

Apocalyptic sayings in 21.25–27 and 22.69

Luke abbreviates Isa 34.4 to 'There will be signs in the sun, the moon, and the stars', apparently preferring his own description 'and on the earth distress among nations confused by the roaring of the sea and waves'. This is not a quotation but its phraseology is similar to Psalm 65.7, 46.3 and Wis 5.22 (a book found in the LXX but not the Hebrew Bible). During the trial before the high priest, Jesus alludes to Dan 7.13 in the words, 'From now on the Son of Man will be seated at the right hand of God' (22.69), which is more immediate than Matthew and Mark's 'you *will* see the Son of Man seated at the right hand'. Hans Conzelmann (1960) believed this was part of Luke's strategy to play down Mark's emphasis on an imminent end (see Luke 19.11 and Acts 1.6–8), though others have pointed out that if this were true, he would surely have omitted Mark's saying that 'this generation will not pass away until all these things have taken place' (Mark 13.30 = Luke 21.32).

Words from the cross in 23.46

Instead of the opening words of Psalm 22 (Matthew and Mark), Luke has Jesus say, 'Father, into your hands I commend my spirit', a quotation from Psalm 31.5. Evans (1990, p. 877) suggests that Mark's use of *exepneusen* ('breathed his last') might have suggested to Luke 'gave up his spirit' since *pneuma* in Greek means both 'breath' and 'spirit'. And as Luke has just had Jesus exhorting the penitent thief to 'trust in God', the cry of dereliction ('why have you forsaken me?') was 'hardly possible as a final utterance of the innocent martyr'. It should also be noted that Peter will argue in his Pentecost sermon (Acts 2.25–31) that Psalm 16.10 does not refer to David because he was 'abandoned to Hades' (the Greek word is 'forsaken') and must, therefore, apply to Christ, who was *not* abandoned/forsaken. This would not sit easily with a final cry from the cross, 'My God, my God, why have you forsaken me?'

Peter Doble (1996) agrees but he does not think that Luke is emphasizing Jesus' innocence. The Greek word *dikaios* in the Centurion's exclamation (23.47) is better translated 'righteous'. Luke's aim is to show that Jesus suffered as 'the righteous one' in accordance with scripture, notably the book of Wisdom. Doble uses this to counter the accusation that because Luke does not use sacrificial terminology like 'ransom', he has no theology of the cross. Luke believes that Jesus, the righteous one, was killed by God's enemies but God vindicated him by raising him from the dead. This is a theology of the cross; it is just different to that offered by Matthew and Mark.

Quotations not in Mark

Presentation of Jesus in the temple in 2.23–24

There are a considerable number of allusions in the infancy narratives but the two explicit quotations from scripture are both to do with Jesus' presentation in the temple. Lev 12.8 is quoted as explanation for the offering ('a pair of turtledoves or two young pigeons'), perhaps indicating the poverty of Mary and Joseph. Exod 13.3 ('Every firstborn male shall be designated as holy to the Lord') is of course applicable to all firstborn males but no doubt it was thought to be especially applicable to Jesus (see Luke 1.35). David Pao and Eckhard Schnabel (2007, p. 271) suggest that in 'fulfilling the requirements of the law, Jesus fulfills the past by bringing it to its climax'. However, Kenneth Litwak thinks this misses the point for the focus is not on Jesus but the pious lives of his parents and this will be repeated in the stories of Simeon and Anna that follow. Thus 'one of Luke's concerns is piety among his audience and he uses the Scriptures of Israel as a reinforcement. Piety includes obeying God, praying and fasting'. (2010, p. 131).

Temptation narrative in 4.4–12

Like Matthew, Luke expands Mark's brief statement of the temptation with three specific temptations and three replies from the book of Deuteronomy. In contrast to Israel's experience in the wilderness, Jesus trusts God for sustenance ('One does not live by bread alone' – Deut 8.4), refuses to fall into idolatry ('Worship the Lord your God, and serve him only'– Deut 6.16) and refuses to put God to the test ('Do not put the Lord your God to the test' – Deut 6.13). He thus proves faithful where Israel was unfaithful. There are parallels in rabbinic literature where the angel of death quotes from the Psalms and Moses gives three responses from Deut 32.1, 3, 4 (*Deut. Rabbah* 11.5). Interestingly, Matthew gives the three temptations ('tests' is a better word) in the order 'bread, testing God, worship'. In so doing, he ends with the sequence 'Away with you, Satan! … Then the devil left him' (4.10–11), which stresses Jesus' victory. Luke, on the other hand, ends with the sequence, '"Do not put the Lord your God to the test" … When the devil had finished every test, he departed from him until an opportune time' (4.12–13), which implies this is merely the first round of the battle.

Nazareth sermon in 4.18–19

Many scholars see this as Luke's masterstroke. Both Matthew and Mark record Jesus' rejection at Nazareth (Mark 6/Matt 13) but Luke brings it forward and gives it a specific setting. Jesus is asked to read in the synagogue and is given the scroll of the prophet Isaiah. It is unclear whether he chose the reading or Isa 61 was the reading set for the day.

Either way, what follows is not a reading from any known text of Isa 61 but a conflation of Isa 61.1–2 with a phrase from Isa 58.6:

> *The spirit of the Lord God is upon me, because the Lord has anointed me; he has sent me to bring good news to the oppressed,* to bind up the broken-hearted, *to proclaim liberty to the captives, and release to the prisoners* [LXX: *opening for the blind*]; *to proclaim the year of the Lord's favour,* and the day of vengeance of our God; to comfort all who mourn. (Isa 61.1–2)

> Is not this the fast that I choose: to loose the bonds of injustice, to undo the thongs of the yoke, *to let the oppressed go free,* and to break every yoke? (Isa 58.6)

> The Spirit of the Lord is upon me, because he has anointed me to bring good news to the poor. He has sent me to proclaim release to the captives and recovery of sight to the blind [Lit: opening for the blind], to let the oppressed go free, to proclaim the year of the Lord's favour. (Luke 4.18–19)

Two phrases are omitted from Isa 61.1–2 ('bind up the broken-hearted' and 'day of vengeance') and a phrase from Isa 58.6 ('let the oppressed go free') is inserted. Luke's text has four agreements with the LXX against the Hebrew MT, including the phrase 'opening for the blind' (the Hebrew has the obscure 'opening for the prisoners'). Furthermore, the link between Isa 61.1 and 58.6 appears to be the Greek word *aphesis* ('release'), whereas the Hebrew MT uses two different words. It seems unlikely, therefore, that this could represent an actual text from which Jesus could have read. Evans thinks it is Luke's own theological reflection on the significance of Jesus but Kimball wishes to defend its historicity, suggesting that it is most likely a summary of what Jesus said in his sermon (which is not recorded). He adds:

> In the linking of these texts, Jesus defined his ministry in terms of OT prophecy and fulfillment: he cited Isa. 61.1–2 to claim that he was the herald who proclaimed the messianic release and inserted Isa. 58.6d

to emphasize that he was also the agent of this spiritual liberation. (1994, p. 110)

Michael Prior (1995) makes a different point. He believes the reference to Isa 58 intensifies the social dimension of the prophetic message and provides a striking corrective to any religious practice which neglects the plight of the needy. Prior uses this as a basis for constructing a Lukan liberation theology. It should also be noted that the Qumran community saw Isa 61 as predicting the long awaited jubilee and in 11QMelch, this is linked to the coming of Melchizedek. The key difference, of course, is that Jesus went on to claim that, 'Today this scripture has been fulfilled in your hearing' (4.21). Some scholars have suggested that it might actually have been a jubilee year though there is no evidence that it was still being celebrated in Jesus' time. On the other hand, if it was a jubilee year but was being ignored, it would certainly add an extra dimension to the meaning of this event.

Isaiah 53.12 in 22.37

After the words of institution at the last supper, Luke has Jesus ask the disciples, 'When I sent you out without a purse, bag, or sandals, did you lack anything?' They reply, 'No, not a thing.' Jesus then adds the enigmatic saying that 'the one who has no sword must sell his cloak and buy one', followed by a quotation from Isa 53.12 ('And he was counted among the lawless'). Does this mean that Luke recognized Mark's allusions to Isa 53 and decided to be more explicit by including a specific quotation? Perhaps, although Hooker's point remains, that we are still not directed towards the vicarious part of the poem. Indeed, the linking of the quotation with the advice to buy a sword results in an extremely puzzling episode – hardly a clarification of the meaning of Jesus' death. Pao and Schabel seek to refute Hooker's point that Isa 53 was not a point of discussion in first century Judaism by citing two Qumran texts (4Q541, 4Q491) where a priestly figure appears to share some of the features of Isaiah's servant (mocked, abused, offers atonement for 'his generation'), though like the Isaiah Targum, there is no vicarious suffering. They conclude that Luke's explicit quotation of Isa 53.12 should be understood 'soteriologically, analogous to the main thrust of Isa. 53 ... Luke explains Jesus' suffering as the innocent righteous one, condemned as a transgressor, with reference to God's will' (2007, p. 389).

Hosea 10.8 in 23.30

On the way to the cross, Jesus addresses the 'daughters of Jerusalem' and warns them of dark times ahead. This is illustrated with words from Hos 10.8, that some will say to the mountains, 'Fall on us', so great will be their distress.

Before we consider the quotations in Acts, it is worth summarizing the case that Luke intends to present Jesus as enacting the Isaian new exodus. First, he extends the quotation of Isa 40.3 to include the eschatological 'every valley and hill shall be made low' and the universal 'all flesh shall see the salvation of God'. Second, he has Jesus specifically claiming to be the anointed prophet/servant of Isa 61 in the synagogue in Nazareth. Third, he has Jesus specifically quoting from Isa 53 concerning his death 'among the lawless'. Advocates of the new exodus theory then point out that this continues at strategic points in Acts, with the allusion to the servant's mission in 1.8 ('to the ends of the earth' – Isa 49.6), the quotation of Isa 53.7 ('Like a sheep he was led to the slaughter') in 8.32–33, Paul's application of the servant's mission ('I have set you to be a light for the Gentiles, so that you may bring salvation to the ends of the earth') to himself and his fellow mission-aries in 13.47, and the concluding quotation of Isa 6.9–10 in Acts 28.26–27. The puzzle, however, is that the sermons of Peter in Acts 2, 3, 4 and 5 are dominated by the Psalms rather than Isaiah and some texts seem to point in other directions.

Quotations in Acts

Judas' successor in 1.20

The betrayal of Judas presented a theological as well as an emotional problem for the disciples for as Peter says, 'he was numbered among us and was allotted his share in this ministry' (1.17). How was it that one of the twelve could become a traitor? And what should be done about it? According to Luke, Peter finds the answer 'written in the book of Psalms': '"Let his homestead become desolate, and let there be no one to live in it"; and "Let another take his position of overseer"' (1.20). At first glance, this seems a fortuitous text to find in the Psalms. However, as we saw in Chapter 1, it is in fact a composite quotation of two quite separate texts. The first comes from Psalm 69.25, a psalm already associated with Jesus' death in the early Church (Rom 11.9–10; 15.3). The particular verse quoted here is made to refer to the field that Judas is said to have purchased 'with the reward for his wickedness' (this is at odds with Matt 27.1–10). Because of Judas' death, this field/homestead is to remain desolate. In contrast, Psalm 109.8 ('May his days be few; may another seize his position') is quoted to show that a replacement must be found, though interestingly, this is not applied later when James is put to death (Acts 12.2). Luke was perhaps drawn to the psalm, which is not quoted elsewhere in the New Testament, by its use of *episkope* (position/ oversight). In the LXX, this is a general word but in 1 Tim 3.1, it is used for the work of an *episkopos* (bishop/ overseer). By using this term, Luke may be conferring on the apostles a title that was only to emerge much later.

Peter's Pentecost sermon in 2.17–35

Peter's sermon begins with a scriptural interpretation of the phenomenon of Pentecost. The strange behaviour is not to be explained by drunkenness ('for it is only nine o'clock in the morning') but by the words of the prophet Joel. Joel predicted that in the last days, God will pour out his Spirit upon all flesh and men and women will see visions, dream dreams and prophesy. This becomes the springboard for a proclamation of the death, resurrection and ascension of Jesus, which is supported by quotations from Psalms 16, 110 and 132. Peter's argument is that when David (the assumed author) wrote things like 'you will not abandon my soul to Hades, or let your Holy One experience corruption' and 'Sit at my right hand, until I make your enemies your footstool,' he was not talking about himself because he died 'and his tomb is with us today' (2.29). Therefore, he spoke as a prophet and his words look forward to the resurrection and ascension of God's true holy one, that is Jesus.

There are several interesting features about this use of scripture. First, it is facilitated by the use of the LXX. The Hebrew of Psalm 16.10 ('For you do not give me up to Sheol, or let your faithful one see the Pit') suggests protection from death (on this occasion) rather than death followed by resurrection. The LXX rendered the last phrase 'see corruption', which facilitates Luke's application to the resurrection. Second, from a historical point of view, it seems clear that David was speaking about himself ('You are my Lord; I have no good apart from you' – 16.2). If Peter is claiming (via Luke) that David was not speaking about himself, then either the words must be regarded as having multiple references or their meaning comes from God and has little to do with what David thought he was saying. We will discuss this further in our final chapter.

Peter's sermon in 3.13–25

This also begins by explaining an event that has just happened, in this case, a healing (3.1–10). Peter argues that it is not by his power or piety that the man has been healed but by the power of God, who raised Jesus to life, having been shamefully put to death by those present. But this was all according to God's plan 'so that times of refreshing may come from the presence of the Lord' (3.20). This is supported by an abbreviated quotation from Deut 18.15–19 (God will raise up a prophet like Moses), which is combined with the threat that disobedience leads to being cut off from the people (Lev 23.9). This is then followed by the promise to Abraham, 'Through your offspring all peoples on earth will be blessed' (Gen 22.18). The sermon ends with the statement, 'When God raised up his servant, he sent him first to you to bless you by turning each of you from your wicked ways' (3.26). It is not clear whether 'raised up his servant' is a reference to the resurrection or simply to the coming of Jesus. Perhaps the ambiguity is intentional. This collection of cross-linked texts has many parallels in the way scripture was used at Qumran.

Peter's reply to the rulers in 4.11

Peter and John are imprisoned for their preaching and in their defence, they quote Psalm 118.22 ('the stone that was rejected by you builders') claiming that 'Salvation is found in no-one else, for there is no other name under heaven given to people by which we must be saved' (4.12). It is surprising that Luke uses a different verb for 'rejected' (*exouthenein* – 'set at nought') from his earlier use of the same text in the Gospel (Luke 20.1). This could be seen as evidence for Luke's use of sources in the composition of Acts, for why else would he change the form of the quotation?

Rulers conspire against Jesus in 4.25–26

As the believers respond to threats by holding a prayer meeting, they quote the words of Psalm 2.1–2 that the nations, the kings of the earth and the rulers 'take counsel together against the Lord and his anointed'. This has been fulfilled when Herod (only mentioned in Luke's account of the trial), Pilate and the Gentiles 'gathered together against your holy servant Jesus, whom you anointed' (4.27). As we saw in chapter 2, the author of the Florilegium (4QFlor) quotes this same text to explain the persecution of the 'elect of Israel' (i.e. the Qumran community). Peter adds the point that this planned wickedness against Jesus was nevertheless foreseen by God and hence part of the divine plan ('whatever your hand and your plan had predestined to take place'). The moral question that this raises is discussed (though not really answered) in Paul's letter to the Romans (see Chapter 7).

Before looking at Stephen's speech, which is very different from Peter's evangelistic sermons, it will be useful to review Peter Doble's (2004, pp. 83–117) argument that it is the Psalms, rather than Isaiah, that is controlling Luke's narrative. First, when Luke wants to show how Peter proclaimed the suffering, death, resurrection and ascension of Jesus, he turns to Psalms 2, 16, 110, 118 and 132. As we will see below, Paul's speech in Acts 13 also draws on Psalms 2 and 16. Second, he notes how these Psalms also occur in Luke's Gospel. For example, Psalm 2.7 ('You are my son') occurs at Jesus' baptism, Psalm 110.1 is introduced by Jesus in dispute with the scribes (Luke 20.41–44), and Psalm 118.22 follows the parable of the vineyard. Third, David is mentioned by name 24 times in Luke–Acts and specifically as the one who speaks through the Psalms on 6 occasions (Luke 20.42; Acts 1.16; 2.25, 31, 34; 4.25). In contrast, Isaiah is only mentioned 5 times (Luke 3.4; 4.17; Acts 8.28, 30; 28.25) and although one must treat such statistics with caution, it is surely significant that the reader is constantly hearing the name 'David'. Fourth, scholars have searched in vain to find a text that predicts a suffering Messiah and have had to settle for a suffering servant. However, the Psalms are full of statements about King David's suffering and Jesus' last words in Luke are from just such a Davidic Psalm ('Father, into your hands I commend my spirit' – Psalm 31.5).

Stephen's speech in 7.3–50

Stephen's speech is different from the previous speeches in that it does not quote texts to support the death, resurrection or ascension of Christ. Instead, it offers a summary of Israelite history, focusing on how God's plan has frequently been opposed by those who should have known better. Joseph's brothers opposed him because they were jealous

(7.9). Moses thought that his people would understand that he was trying to liberate them but they said, 'Who made you ruler and judge over us?' (7.27). Nevertheless, he did lead them out of Egypt into the promised land but 'our ancestors refused to obey him' and told Aaron to make the golden calf. Moses ordered the building of the tabernacle but they rejected it (7.45). And you are just like them, says Stephen, for you have betrayed and killed the righteous one. At this they drag him out of the city and stone him.

Most of the quotations are simply part of retelling Israel's history but Amos 5.25–27 and Isa 66.1–2 have a more specific role. The first declares that Israel's worship in the wilderness was not to God but 'the host of heaven'. Luke's Greek follows the LXX in reading 'the tent of Moloch' (probably from a misreading of the Hebrew *melek*, which means 'king') and 'Rephan' instead of 'Kaiwan'. The change from Damascus (the northern exile) to Babylon (the southern exile) appears to be a conscious updating of the prophecy, either by Luke or someone before him.

Isa 66.1–2 is used to support the view that although God commanded the building of the tabernacle and allowed Solomon to build a temple, the 'Most High does not live in houses made by human hands' (7.48). This might account for the accusation against Stephen that he never stops speaking against this holy place' (6.13), though perhaps we are to understand this charge as a fabrication. It would appear that the early Church saw no contradiction between having its own meetings and attendance at the temple. It may be that Stephen represented a more radical form of the faith that wanted nothing to do with the temple and some scholars have suggested Samaritan influence (see John 4.21).

An Ethiopian ponders Isa 53 in 8.32–33

This is an interesting incident (if it is historically accurate) in that it shows that some worshippers had access to their own copies of biblical scrolls. The Ethiopian is puzzled as to whether the sheep led to the slaughter in Isa 53.7 is the prophet himself or another. This theme has been with us through most of the previous sermons. We are not told on this occasion what reasoning Philip used, only that 'starting with this scripture, he proclaimed to him the good news about Jesus' (8.35). This could mean that he showed him how the rest of Isa 53 speaks about Jesus or perhaps Isa 40–55. On the other hand, the previous sermons have focused on the Psalms and so 'starting with this scripture' could mean that he then moved to the familiar proof-texts of Psalms 2, 16, 110, 118, 132. In support of this, one could refer to the closing words of Jesus in Luke's Gospel, where he teaches his disciples that 'everything written about me in the law of Moses, the prophets, and the psalms must be fulfilled' (24.44). We are left with a question: Is the explicit quotation of Isa 53.7 further evidence for the Isaian new exodus theory or do the words 'starting with this scripture' suggest that we should think of broader influences?

Jewish tradition regarded Isaiah as a martyr (see Heb 11.37) and Bart Koet asks whether 'Isaiah and his death were one of the models for Luke's depiction of Jesus' life?' (2005, p. 97). If this is the case, then we have a parallel to what Doble argues for the Psalms: The mission of Jesus is modelled on the themes of the book of Isaiah *and* Isaiah himself.

Paul's speeches in 13.16–52

As in Stephen's speech, Paul offers a summary of Israelite history, though he jumps from David to Jesus, perhaps to strengthen the correspondence (typology) between them. He also uses the same proof text for the resurrection (Psalm 16) as we found in Peter's Pentecost sermon and makes the connection more explicit by declaring that David 'died, was laid beside his ancestors, *and experienced corruption*' (13.36). Two further quotations are linked to this. Psalm 2.7 has God declaring to Israel's king: 'You are my Son; today I have begotten you.' These words appear in the baptism and transfiguration narratives, though it is not clear whether they refer to Jesus' birth, resurrection or something about his nature. Those familiar with the Nicene creed will probably connect 'begotten' with 'eternal generation' and take 'today' to be timeless. But this seems unlikely for a first century Jew, though the text of the psalm is certainly suggestive. The second quotation is from Isa 55.3 ('I will give you the holy promises made to David.') The link is probably an example of Hillel's second rule (*gezerah shawa*), with the 'Holy one' (*hosion*) of Psalm 16 suggesting the 'holy promises' (*hosia* – lit. 'holy things') of Isa 55. It is of note that the choice of Isa 55.3 is because of its reference to David and connection with the Psalm 16, not to reinforce an Isaian pattern.

There are two further quotations in the sermon. Hab 1.5 is quoted as a warning ('Beware, therefore, that what the prophets said does not happen to you.') But the narrative then suggests that this is precisely what does happen, for on the following Sabbath, Paul quotes Isa 49.6 ('I have set you to be a light for the Gentiles') as divine warrant for turning to the Gentiles. Thus of the five quotations in this sermon, the first three are seen as already fulfilled, the fourth isn't when spoken but is by the following Sabbath, resulting in the fifth quotation about to be fulfilled. One might contrast this with Qumran where much of what scripture says is still to take place.

Peter Mallen regards Paul's application of the servant's mission (Isa 49.6) to himself and fellow evangelists as extremely significant. Hooker's objection to seeing Isa 53 as the key to understanding Jesus' death is that there are not many explicit quotations in the New Testament and even when they do occur, as in Luke 22.37 and Acts 8.32–33, they do not refer to the vicarious section of the chapter. For Mallen, the answer to this is that Luke's interest in the servant passages is not simply to explain Jesus' death but to provide a 'job description or outline for Jesus' mission and that of his followers' (2008, p. 207). He further notes that this puts a question mark against seeing the Isaian new exodus as *governing* Luke's narrative, for Isaiah's themes have also undergone transformation:

> The New Exodus hope for the restoration of Israel, clearly sounded
> at the beginning of the narrative and partially fulfilled in the opening
> chapters of Acts, threatens to unravel completely by the end of the

narrative. Gentiles have apparently become the predominant part of God's restored people and Luke's readers would probably be aware that Jerusalem now lies in ruins. One must therefore seriously question the claim that the New Exodus provides the hermeneutical key to understand the entire narrative. (2008, p. 189)

James' speech in 15.13–21

During the so-called Jerusalem council, James quotes Amos 9.11–12 to support the view that God's purposes have always been to include Gentiles among the people of God. However, if Amos 9.11–12 is read in an English translation (which follows the Hebrew), one might question the relevance of a text which says that God will raise up the fallen booth of David 'in order that they may possess the remnant of Edom and all the nations who are called by my name'. The explanation appears to be that James is quoting from a Greek text that read 'Adam' for 'Edom' (the consonants are the same) to form the phrase, 'in order that the rest of *humanity* might seek the Lord'. But is James, the brother of Jesus, likely to have quoted from a Greek mistranslation in the middle of Jerusalem? Probably not but the reference is clearly significant for Luke, for the quotation of Amos 5.25–27 in Stephen's speech is the only other quotation from Amos in the New Testament. As Huub van de Sandt (2009, pp. 57–77) points out, Amos 9.12 is the only text in the Old Testament where the divine name is called over the Gentiles and Luke clearly sees a connection between the two texts. The first is introduced with the words, 'But God turned away from them' (7.42) and the second begins, 'After this I will return' (15.16). In fact, Amos 9.11 begins with the words, 'On that day' (Greek and Hebrew) but Luke has changed the wording to make the link with Amos 5 clearer.

Paul's defence before the high priest in 23.5

In a curious incident where Paul does not recognize the high priest, he acknowledges that Exod 22.27 says, 'You shall not speak evil of a leader of your people.' Howard Marshall (1980) suggests irony ('I did not think that such a man who could give such an order could be the high priest') but Gert Steyn (1995) says the important thing is not so much the content of the quotation but the fact of it. Paul is presented as a loyal Jew who knows the law and respects it.

The final quotation of Isa 6 in 28.26–27

The hardening and blindness spoken about in Isa 6.9–10 is abbreviated and paraphrased in Mark 4.12 (the purpose of the parables), John 12.40 (Jewish rejection of Jesus) and Rom 11.8 (Israel's rejection of the gospel). Interestingly, a much fuller quotation appears in the Matthaean parallel to Mark 4.12 and this is identical to what we now find at the very end of Acts (Luke 8.10 is even more abbreviated than Mark 4.12). Did Luke wish to save the full force of the quotation to the end of his two-volume work? Steyn (1995) notes that the LXX differs from the Hebrew by putting more emphasis on the people's culpability for their blindness rather than predestination, leaving open the possibility of repentance. Some have suggested that the aim of Luke–Acts is to show how the Gentiles have accepted the gospel and the Jews rejected it. On this understanding, the quotation of Isa 6 at the end of Acts is final. But others think that the message of Luke-Acts is that while some Jews have rejected the gospel, a new community of Jews and Gentiles has been formed.

Allusions in Luke–Acts

There are a huge number of allusions listed in the back of the Nestle-Aland edition of the Greek New Testament and is beyond the scope of this short introductory book. However, it is worth giving a few examples to give something of the flavour of Luke's allusive style.

Infancy stories

Though Luke begins his Gospel with an elegant prologue (1.1–4), he soon drops this and takes up the story-telling style of the scriptures, particularly the phraseology of the LXX. Thus the announcement and birth of John have a number of parallels with the Sarah (Gen 16–17) and Hannah (1 Sam 2) stories. In each, the mothers are old and barren and this is seen as disgrace. A miraculous promise is offered by an angelic messenger, which at least one of the parents finds difficult to believe. And promises are made concerning the significance of the child for Israel. The annunciation of Jesus is somewhat different in that Mary is neither old nor afflicted but her song has a number of parallels with the song of Hannah:

> My heart exults in the Lord; my strength is exalted in my God ... I rejoice in my victory ... There is no Holy One like the Lord ... The bows of the mighty are broken, but the feeble gird on strength ... Those who were full have hired themselves out for bread, but those who were hungry are fat with spoil ... He raises up the poor from the dust; he lifts the needy from the ash heap ... His adversaries shall be shattered; the Most High will thunder in heaven. The Lord will judge the ends of the earth; he will give strength to his king, and exalt the power of his anointed. (1 Sam 2.1–10 abbreviated)

However, though this song offers a model for a hymn of praise following a miraculous conception, Mary's song appears to be an amalgam of scriptural phrases, mostly taken from the Psalms (a significant point for Doble):

My soul magnifies the Lord, and my spirit rejoices in God my Saviour, for he has looked with favour on the lowliness (*tapeinosis*) of his servant (vv. 46b–48a).

O magnify the Lord with me (Psalm 34.3); then my soul shall rejoice in the Lord (Psalm 35.9); I will exult in the God of my salvation (Hab 3.18); look on the misery of your servant (1 Sam 1.11);

Surely, from now on all generations will call me blessed; for the Mighty One has done great things for me, and holy is his name (vv. 48b–49).

Happy am I! For the women will call me happy (Gen 30.13); he is your God, who has done for you these great and awesome things (Deut 10.21); Holy and awesome is his name (Psalm 111.9);

His mercy is for those who fear him from generation to generation. He has shown strength with his arm; he has scattered the proud in the thoughts of their hearts. He has brought down the powerful from their thrones, and lifted up the lowly, he has filled the hungry with good things, and sent the rich away empty (vv. 50–53).

The Lord has compassion for those who fear him (Psalm 103.13); The right hand of the Lord does valiantly (Psalm 117.15); Towards the scorners he is scornful, but to the humble he shows favour (Prov 3.34); For he satisfies the thirsty, and the hungry he fills with good things (Psalm 107.9);

He has helped (*antilambanein*) his servant Israel, in remembrance of his mercy, according to the promise he made to our ancestors, to Abraham and to his descendants for ever (vv. 54–55).

You are my servant, I have chosen you … you whom I took (*antilambanein*) from the ends of the earth (Isa 41.8–9); you will show … unswerving loyalty to Abraham, as you have sworn to our ancestors from the days of old (Mic 7.20).

Is this a translation of Mary's song or a Lukan composition? The use of *antilambanein* is often cited as evidence that the hymn is modelled on the LXX but others have pointed out that unusual Greek phrases like *epoiesen kratos* (lit. 'he made strength') are absent from the LXX and reflect Semitic idiom. More significantly, scholars have asked (1) How could Mary have seen her lowliness as a parallel to Hannah's barrenness? (2) What are the 'great things' (plural) that God has done for her? (3) How has God fed the hungry and brought down the powerful (even by the end of Acts)? Nolland answers these by suggesting that Mary's affliction is not her own lack of a child but Israel's lack of that particular child who is to be the messianic deliverer. Nevertheless, he acknowledges that the hymn has probably been through several stages of development and in its present form, reflects a Christian worship setting.

A rather different view is offered by Jane Schaberg (1995). She notes that unlike Matthew, Luke does not connect the conception of Jesus with Isa 7.14. Instead, the words, 'a virgin engaged to a man' (1.27), are most probably an allusion to the regulations concerning the violation of a 'virgin already engaged to be married' in Deut 22.23–29. This then explains Mary's words that God has helped her in her lowliness (the Greek is *tapeinosis*, 'humiliation') and the use of the term 'mercy', which has always seemed odd as a description of a miraculous conception. Such an interpretation goes against nearly 2000 years of Christian tradition and most scholars think she is making too much of the (possible) allusion to Deut 22.23–29. However, it has to be said that none of the other authors of the New Testament show any knowledge of a virginal conception and Gal 4.4–5 seems to imply that Paul thought of Jesus' birth as the same as the rest of us.

Travel narrative

Evans (1990 pp. 34–36) thinks the inspiration for presenting teaching within the framework of a journey comes from the book of Deuteronomy. He notes that the journey begins with Jesus sending disciples to go before him, as did Moses (Luke 10.17–30; Deut 1). He gives them the double commandment to love God and neighbour, just as Moses gave the Ten Commandments (Luke 10.25–27; Deut 5). He tells them how he has bound the stronger one, just as Moses gave instructions about defeating stronger nations (Luke 11.14–26; Deut 9–10). And he gives instructions about clean and unclean (Luke 11.37–12.12; Deut 12). Few have found this hypothesis entirely convincing but if the sequence is continued, Deut 21–22 (a discussion of inheritance rights for good and bad sons) does form an interesting background for the parable of the prodigal son (Luke 15.11–32).

Passion narrative

After the entry into Jerusalem, Pharisees in the crowd ask Jesus to order his disciples to be quiet. He replies with a prophecy of the destruction of Jerusalem. The words echo a number of Old Testament texts, for example Hab 2.1 (stones crying out), Isa 29.3 (siege) and Hos 10.14 (destruction of women and children). This emphasis is also present in an addition to Mark's apocalyptic discourse, that they will 'fall by the edge of the sword and be taken away as captives' (21.24, alluding to Deut 28.64 and perhaps Ezra 9.7). Luke also adds a reference to those who are weighed down with 'dissipation and drunkenness', a probable allusion to Isa 5.11–13, where the pursuit of strong drink and extravagant living are one of the causes of the exile. Such allusions can never be deemed certain but taken together, they bring to mind Israel's experience of exile, suffering and deportation.

Luke alone has the obscure verse, 'Simon, Simon, listen! Satan has demanded to sift all of you like wheat' (22.31). The metaphor of sifting is a common one (Amos 9.9) but the *locus classicus* of Satanic temptation is the first chapter of Job. Though the portrayal of Satan in the Gospels is that of an evil force, in Job, Satan is amongst the heavenly attendants and can dispute with God. This appears to be the background of 'Satan has demanded' and may have consequences for how Jesus' words are to be understood.

Conclusion

In his Gospel, Luke has not greatly added to Mark's quotations, though the explicit use of Isa 53 ('God's servant') and Isa 61 ('God's anointed') are important. He is thoroughly at home with the language of the LXX and if Kimball is correct, he is familiar with the structure of homiletic sermons and patterns of exegesis. Catch-word links are evident in the combination of Isa 61.1–2 and Isa 58.6 in the synagogue reading and the 'stone' passages of Psalm 118.22 and Isa 8.14. With one exception (8.32), all the quotations in Acts are found in the speeches. On the analogy of the Gospel, one might suggest that these are included because Luke found them in his sources. Most scholars, however, think that variations from the Hebrew text and catch-word links (that depend on the Greek) show that Luke's exegetical hand is evident. Some of the traditional texts have been lengthened (Isa 6.9–10; 40.3–5), suggesting perhaps that Luke had access to certain scrolls (so Steyn, 1995). Older scholarship tended to see Luke's use of the Old Testament as 'apologetic' (proof from prophecy) but more recent work has found this description too narrow. The vocation of Jesus and his disciples is strongly influenced by Isaiah, while the defence of Jesus' death, resurrection and ascension draws mainly on the Psalms. It remains a matter of debate as to whether his suffering is best explained by reference to Isa 53 (and Isaiah himself) or the Psalms (and David himself). Both positions can claim that preliminary allusions appear in the Gospel and are then supplemented by explicit quotations in Acts. Statistics might seem to favour David and the Psalms but as many scholars have pointed out, it is far more likely that narrative would form the framework for the speeches rather than the other way around. As Litwak notes, Luke's emphasis is on the totality of Scripture's witness ('everything written about me in the law of Moses, the prophets, and the psalms must be fulfilled' – 24.44) and so it is probably pointless to try and decide who is the winner. Indeed, one of the main insights of recent studies is the way that Luke not only applies servant texts and suffering texts to Jesus but also applies them to the mission of the Church (Mallen).

Further reading

Peter Doble has written the chapter in the Moyise and Menken volume on the *Psalms in the New Testament* (2004) and Bart Koet (2005) in the Isaiah volume. For the importance of Isaiah, see particularly the monographs of David Pao (2000) and Peter Mallen (2008) and for Luke's use of Deuteronomy and the Minor Prophets, see the chapters by Dietrich Rusam (2008) and Huub van de Sandt (2009) in the respective volumes of the Moyise and Menken series. The chapter in the Beale and Carson Commentary was a collaboration between David Pao and Eckhard Schnabel (2007). Also important is the monograph of Kenneth Litwak, *Echoes of Scripture in Luke-Acts: Telling the History of God's People Intertextually* (2005) and although some twenty years old, Robert Brawley's *Text to Text Pours Forth Speech: Voices of Scripture in Luke-Acts* (1995) was ground-breaking in its day and still has much to offer.

Questions

1. Why is the Nazareth sermon (Luke 4) regarded as important for understanding Luke's use of scripture?
2. What are the main scriptural themes in Peter's speeches (Acts 2, 3, 4, 5)?
3. What are the pros and cons of regarding either the servant of Isaiah or the servant of the Psalms (David) as the model for Jesus in Luke–Acts?

5

The Old Testament in John

Though John only shares a few stories with the Synoptic Gospels, he does use a number of the same Old Testament quotations. For example, after the Priests and Levites question John the Baptist as to whether he is the Christ, Elijah or the Prophet (1.23), he replies in the words of Isa 40.3: 'I am the voice of one calling in the desert, "Make straight the way of the Lord."' (cf. Mark 1.3). During the triumphal entry (11.12-16), John has the crowd uttering the words of Psalm 118.25–26 (cf. Mark 11.9) and like Matthew (21.5) points out that riding on the donkey is a fulfilment of Zech 9.9. John also uses the blindness saying of Isa 6.9-10, though he gives it a different setting. In the Synoptic Gospels, it is linked with Jesus teaching in parables (Mark 4.12) but John links it with his deeds for, 'Although he had performed so many signs in their presence, they did not believe in him' (12.37).

John adds about ten more Old Testament quotations, making a total of around fourteen. Two of these represent explicit quotations where the Synoptic Gospels only have allusions. Thus at the last supper, Jesus refers to Judas as 'the one who has dipped his hand into the bowl with me' (Matt 26.23), an allusion to Psalm 41.9. In John 13.18, the text is explicitly quoted. Similarly, the Synoptic Gospels use the language of Psalm 22.18 to refer to the casting of lots for Jesus' garments (Mark 15.24). In John 19.24, the text is explicitly quoted. This raises interesting questions about the function of quotations and allusions. For example, some have argued that quotations are used for more obscure texts which the reader might otherwise miss. But if John's readers do not recognise the 'voice of one crying out in the wilderness' as a quotation from Isaiah, it is difficult to imagine how they would have understood the prologue (1.1–18) or the 'bread of life' discourse (6.25–59). On the other hand, some have argued that the explicit quotations represent the most important texts. But is a text like Psalm 69.9 ('zeal for your house will consume me') more important for understanding Jesus than the allusions to Gen 1 and Prov 8 in the prologue?

Around half of the quotations are drawn from the Psalms (22, 35, 41, 69, 78, 82, 118) and are distributed throughout the Gospel (2.17; 6.31; 10.34; 12.13; 15.25; 19.34). This is a much higher proportion than in the other Gospels, where according to Daly-Denton (2004, p. 121), they constitute 18 per cent in Matthew, 21 per cent in Mark and 31 per cent in Luke. On the other hand, although there are only four quotations from Isaiah in John's Gospel (6.10; 40.3; 53.1; 54.13), which all occur in the first half of the Gospel (1.23; 6.45; 12.38; 12.39), Isaiah is mentioned four times by name, compared with only one mention of David. The distribution of the Isaiah quotations appears to be deliberate, since the first and the last are introduced with similar words ('as the prophet Isaiah said'/'Isaiah also said'). The other quotations come from Zechariah (9.9; 12.10) and Exodus (12.46 and possibly 16.4).

Introductory formulae

The way that quotations are introduced in John's Gospel is interesting: (1) He prefers a verb of *writing* in the first half of the book; (2) He prefers a verb of *fulfilment* in the second half of the book; and (3) He begins and ends with a verb of *speech*.

John	OT	Introductory formula
1.23	Isa 40.3	… as the prophet Isaiah *said*
2.17	Psalm 69.9	His disciples remembered that it was *written* …
6.31	Psalm 78.24	as it is *written* …
6.45	Isa 54.13	It is *written* in the prophets …
7.38	???	As the scripture has *said* …

10.34	Psalm 82.6	Is it not *written* in your law … ?
12.13	Psalm 118.26	None
12.14	Zech 9.9	as it is *written*
12.38	Isa 53.1	This was to *fulfil* the word spoken by the prophet Isaiah …
12.39	Isa 6.10	Isaiah also said …
13.18	Psalm 41.9	But it is to *fulfil* the scripture …
15.25	Psalm 35.19	It was to *fulfil* the word that is written in their law …
19.24	Psalm 22.18	This was to *fulfil* what the scripture says …
19.36	Exod 12.46	These things occurred so that the scripture might be *fulfilled* …
19.37	Zech 12.10	And again another passage of scripture *says* …

There are two further instances where the actual text is either not quoted (17.12) or obscure (19.28). Both are in the latter half of the Gospel and both use a fulfilment word in the introductory formula. Thus the pattern is maintained. Carson suggests that the 'evangelist particularly wishes to stress the fulfilment of scripture in connection with the passion of Jesus and the obduracy motif with which he links it,' and that this implies, 'an audience that needs a rationale, a biblical rationale, for the substantial rejection of Jesus by his fellow Jews' (1988 p. 248).

Quotations

The temple saying in 2.17

Though John includes a version of the so-called 'cleansing of the temple', he places it at the beginning of his narrative and offers a different scriptural background. In the Synoptic Gospels, Jesus makes a protest using the words of Isa 56.7 and Jer 7.11. In John's account, Jesus says, 'Take these things out of here! Stop making my Father's house a market place!' (2.16). There then follows a quotation from Psalm 69.9 ('Zeal for your house will consume me') but it is not spoken by Jesus.

It is a text which John says the disciples *remembered*. The dialogue continues with the Jews demanding a sign, to which Jesus says, 'Destroy this temple, and in three days I will raise it up' (2.19). They complain that the temple has taken 46 years to build but the narrator then informs us that 'he was speaking of the temple of his body.' This allows John to make a significant point about understanding the scriptures. Understanding depends on knowledge of the resurrection: 'After he was raised from the dead, his disciples *remembered* that he had said this; and they believed the scripture and the word that Jesus had spoken' (2.22).

Hanson (1991 p. 43) thinks that John understood the words of Psalm 69.9 as the literal utterance of the pre-existent Christ. He also suggests that Jesus' words contain an allusion to Zech 14.21 ('And there shall no longer be traders in the house of the Lord') and that the mention of driving out 'sheep and the cattle' (John 2.15 – not mentioned in the Synoptics) might be an allusion to Psalm 8.8. Thus according to Hanson, the emphasis is not on Jesus' protest against temple abuses but the replacement of the earthly temple by his risen body. Daly-Denton argues that the quotation functions programmatically within the Gospel and suggests that the reader is urged to think of the whole of Psalm 69. The line before Psalm 69.9 has the psalmist lament that, 'I have become a stranger to my kindred, an alien to my mother's children', which parallels Jesus' experience (cf. John 7.5) and in John 15.25, Jesus will quote from Psalm 69.4 ('More in number than the hairs of my head are *those who hate me without cause*'). We know that Psalm 69 was important in the early Church (Mark 15.23; Acts 1.20; Rom 15.3) and so 'it is logical, in terms of John's plot, that David's words in Psalm 69:10 would occur to the disciples as appropriate to Jesus' (2004, p. 123).

The bread of life discourse in 6.25–59

The fullest treatment of this passage is found in the monograph by Peder Borgen (1966), who compares it with homilies on Exod 16 found in Philo and the *haggada* (e.g. *Mek. Exod* 16.4). The pattern of these homilies is the exposition of words from the quotation with the help of one of more prophetic texts. In this instance, the text (Exod 16.4) is quoted by the crowd, 'He gave them bread from heaven to eat' (6.31). The exposition is in two parts. In 6.32–48, Jesus clarifies who gave the bread (God not Moses), the nature of the bread (it gives life to the world) and the meaning of 'from' (that which has come down). The quotation, he claims, refers to himself. The Jews object with the words, 'Is not this Jesus, the son of Joseph, whose father and mother we know' (a parallel to Mark 6.3). Jesus then quotes a prophetic text (Isa 54.13), 'And they shall all be taught by God,' and makes the point that anyone who has learned from the father (i.e. 'been taught') comes to him.

In 6.49–58, the meaning of 'to eat' is then expounded. At one level, of course, the people in the wilderness are the ones that ate the manna. But they all died so the manna could not have been the true bread from heaven that gives life to the world. According to John, the true bread is Jesus and whoever eats this bread will live for ever (6.51). But how can one eat Jesus? The rest of the exposition answers this using the eucharistic language of eating his body and drinking his blood and concludes by returning to the original quotation and summarizing the exposition: 'This is the bread that came down from heaven, not like that which your ancestors ate, and they died. But the one who eats this bread will live for ever' (John 6.58).

Not all scholars have accepted Borgen's homiletic theory. Maarten Menken (1996, pp. 47–65), for example, argues that the cited text does not come from Exod 16.4 but Psalm 78.24 ('he rained down on them manna to eat, and gave them the grain of heaven'). He points out that the background for understanding the discourse is the belief that Moses was responsible for the manna miracle. This is only explicitly attested in later sources (*b. Sota* 35a has Caleb say, 'He led us out of Egypt, he cleft for us the sea, and he made us eat the manna') but is in line with the growing exaltation of Moses (e.g. Philo). In the Exodus text ('I am going to rain bread from heaven for you') the use of the first person leaves no doubt that God is the subject. But in Psalm 78.24, the third person 'he' is ambiguous and thus more likely to have led to the misunderstanding.

The connection between the original feeding and this story is not confined to food and drink. In John 6.41, Jesus' hearers are accused of 'grumbling' (*gongyzo*), a term that is particularly associated with the Israelites' rebellion in the wilderness (Exod 17.3; Num 11.1; 14.27; 17.5). As Andreas Köstenberger says (2007, p. 447):

> By linking the response of the Jews in Jesus' day to the Israelites' response to Moses in the wilderness, the Fourth Evangelist establishes a typology that associates Jesus' opponents with a trajectory of unbelief that sets up both the Jews' rejection of Jesus as the Messiah in the passion narrative and the evangelist's concluding indictment of the Jews at the end of chapter 12.

The promise that 'they shall all be taught by God' was understood by later rabbinic writers to mean that God himself will teach the Torah in the age to come (*Pes. R.* 32.3–4). Catrin Williams thinks this is important for understanding the claim that John wants to make in this passage, for Jesus himself has been taught by God (John 7.16–17) and so those who receive Jesus' teaching are fulfilling the promise of Isa 54.13: 'John's definition of the lineage and descent of believers in terms of their divine rather than physical birth (cf. 1.12–13; 3.3), means that only those of heavenly origin can, by coming to Jesus and accepting his word, also be truly taught by God' (2005, pp. 107–8).

Defence of calling Jesus the Son of God in 10.34

In answer to the accusation that he is committing blasphemy by making himself equal to God (10.33), Jesus is said to reply: 'Is it not written in your law, "I said, you are gods"? If those to whom the word of God came were called "gods" – and the scripture cannot be annulled – can you say that the one whom the Father has sanctified and sent into the world is blaspheming because I said, "I am God's Son"?' Some scholars think this is an example of a 'loose' or 'ad hoc' use of Psalm 82.6. Bultmann contends that it is simply playing the Rabbis at their own game. But Hanson insists that the interpretative background makes the meaning clear. He notes that rabbinic tradition links this psalm with the giving of the law at Sinai and gave the Israelites a quasi-divine status. If it was appropriate to call them 'gods' because they were recipients of God's word, how much more is it appropriate for the Word incarnate to be called 'God's Son'? More controversially, Hanson thinks that John had the whole Psalm in mind and it is the final line ('Rise up, O God, judge the earth; for all the nations belong to you!') that is meant when Jesus says, 'and the scripture cannot be annulled'. Interestingly, this text offers a parallel to Jesus' statement in the Sermon on the Mount:

> Do not think that I have come to abolish (*kataluo*) the law or the prophets. (Matt 5.17)

> the scripture cannot be annulled (*luo*). (John 10.35)

Unbelief in 12.38–40

Prior to the quotation of Isa 6.10 in John 12.40, John says that although 'he had performed so many signs in their presence, they did not believe in him'. He then says:

> This was to fulfil the word spoken by the prophet Isaiah: 'Lord who has believed our message, and to whom has the arm of the Lord been revealed?' And so they could not believe, because Isaiah also said, 'He has blinded their eyes and hardened their heart, so that they might not look with their eyes, and understand with their heart and turn – and I would heal them'. (12.38–40)

The quotations appear to raise more questions than they answer. For example, why choose a passage that emphasizes 'believing the message' (Isa 53.1) to support the statement that Jesus 'performed so many signs'? And why ask sorrowfully, 'who has believed our message?' when the next quotation says, 'He has blinded their eyes and hardened their heart', so they cannot believe? And thirdly, having emphasised 'message' rather than 'deeds', why does he preserve Isaiah's references to 'eyes' and 'heart' but omit the two references to 'ears'? Menken thinks the answer lies in how John understood Isa 53.1. First, it is to be noted that the word for 'message' (*akoe*) could equally be rendered 'report' and so the Greek of Isa 53.1 could be translated, 'who has believed our report?' or 'who has believed the report about us?' If Jesus is understood as the speaker, then the 'report about us' can be understood as a reference to the works that God has given Jesus to do. On the other hand, nowhere else does Jesus refer to God as 'Lord' (*kyrie*) and the second part of the quotation ('and to whom has the arm of the Lord been revealed?') can be understood as a reference to signs (of power).

The two quotations are followed by the intriguing statement that 'Isaiah said this because he saw his glory and spoke about him' (12.41). This is most likely a reference to Isaiah's throne vision, which comes immediately before the quoted words in Isa 6.10. The LXX of Isa 6.1 speaks of the glory of God and Jewish tradition generally refers to Isaiah seeing God's glory. Hanson thinks that John is making the claim that what Isaiah actually saw was the pre-existent Christ. This is supported by the dialogue in John 8, where Jesus claims to exist before Abraham (8.58) and indeed that Abraham desired to see Jesus' day and did see it (8.56). On the other hand, the quotations are introduced as 'fulfilment' and so John's meaning may be that Isaiah *foresaw* the glory of the earthly Jesus, in contrast to Jesus' contemporaries, who saw signs but failed to perceive his glory (Williams, 2005, pp.108–15).

Judas's betrayal in 13.18

In Luke, Jesus only signals his betrayer by saying that he is 'with me, and his hand is on the table' (Luke 22.21). Matthew says it is 'the one who has dipped his hand into the bowl with me' (Matt 26.23), whilst Mark 14.20 includes a reference to 'dipping bread into the bowl with me'. Scholars have debated whether any or all of these might be an allusion to Psalm 41.9 ('my bosom friend in whom I trusted, who ate of my bread, has lifted the heel against me') but John makes it explicit:

But it is to fulfil the scripture, 'The one who ate my bread has lifted his heel against me.' ... 'It is the one to whom I give this piece of bread when I have dipped it in the dish.' So when he had dipped the piece of bread, he gave it to Judas son of Simon Iscariot. After he received the piece of bread, Satan entered into him. Jesus said to him, 'Do quickly what you are going to do.' (John 13.18, 26–27)

John's quotation differs considerably from all known versions of Psalm 41.9. Menken suggests that John is making his own translation from the Hebrew, since the LXX uses the word *pternismon* ('craft' or 'cunning') instead of 'heel'. Had John quoted from this version, the meaning would be that Jesus was betrayed by Judas's cunning, which is clearly unacceptable. However, John also differs from the Hebrew text, which speaks of 'magnifying' the heel rather than 'lifting' or 'raising' the heel. This could be stylistic adjustment but Menken thinks John has been influenced by the language of 2 Sam 18.28 ('Blessed be the Lord your God, who has delivered up the men *who raised* their hand against my lord the king'). The context is the betrayal of David by Ahithophel, which Jewish tradition (*b. Sanh* 106b) associates with Psalm 41. Menken suggests that the following parallels show that the early Church saw this as a pattern for Jesus' own betrayal:

- Judas and Ahithophel both hang themselves after the deed (2 Sam 17.23/Matt 27.5).
- They both plan to do the deed at night (2 Sam 17.1/John 13.30).
- David and Jesus both pray for deliverance on the Mount of Olives (2 Sam 15.31/Mark 14.26ff.).
- David and Jesus both cross the Kidron (2 Sam 15.23/John 18.1).
- It is claimed that the death of one man will bring peace to the people (2 Sam 17.3/John 11.50).

Hatred of Jesus in 15.25

This verse is remarkable in that John has Jesus introduce a scriptural quotation with the words, 'It was to fulfil the word that is written in *their* law' (see also 8.17; 10.34). Not only does this make Jesus sound like a non-Jew, it also seems to set a chasm between John and the Jewish scriptures. And since the following verses speak of the Holy Spirit coming to reveal truth, it could be seen as an antithesis – they have the scriptures, we have the Spirit. The source of the quotation is probably Psalm 69.4 ('More in number than the hairs of my head are those *who hate me without cause*'). Daly-Denton denies that it involves any denigration of the scriptures. Indeed:

> The recourse to a scriptural antecedent is intended to encourage a community now experiencing persecution to see a parallel between their situation and the events of Jesus' hour which were also foretold in scripture. It does this by giving them a sense of having a superior insight into the scriptures to that of their opponents and an entitlement to claim as their own the heritage which their persecutors would wish to deny them. (2000 pp. 207–8)

Divided garments in 19.24

As with the 'traitor' saying in 13.18, John has an explicit quotation where all three Synoptic Gospels have an allusion. The quotation agrees exactly with the LXX of Psalm 22.18 ('they divide my clothes among themselves, and for my clothing they cast lots'). Hebrew parallelism would suggest that the two clauses refer to the same thing but John notes that having first divided his garments between them, they did not wish to tear the tunic and so cast lots for it. John took Psalm 22.18 as predicting two separate actions and Barrett (1978) believed that John misunderstood the nature of Hebrew poetry (the same accusation is made about Matthew when he assumes Zech 9.9 is speaking about a donkey and a colt). More likely, however, is the view that John wanted to stress the untorn garment and regards the Hebrew parallelism as providential. Indeed, Hanson notes that later rabbinic tradition did likewise, applying it to the story of Esther. Why John should want to stress the untorn garment is unclear. One suggestion, which goes back at least to Cyprian, is that it represents the unbroken unity of the

Church, though it is problematic that this garment is taken away from Jesus by the soldiers.

No bones broken in 19.36

John has a number of unique features in his description of the crucifixion. First, he tells us that the soldiers broke the legs of those either side of Jesus to hasten their death. Second, when they found that Jesus was already dead, one of the soldiers pierced his side with a spear and out came blood and water. Third, he draws attention to two quotations to explain this: 'These things occurred so that the scripture might be fulfilled, "None of his bones shall be broken." And again another passage of scripture says, "They will look on the one whom they have pierced."' Scholars are divided as to whether the source text for the first quotation is Exod 12.10,46 or Psalm 34.21. In favour of the first is the Passover context, where the sacrificial lamb had to be unblemished ('you shall not break any of its bones'). In favour of Psalm 34.21 is the fact that like John, the verb is in the passive ('not one of them *will be broken*'). Menken thinks that John had both in mind and that John thought of Jesus as both sacrificial lamb and righteous sufferer. Schuchard (1992) agrees, though he wishes to give priority to the Exodus text, believing that the allusion to the Psalm prepares the way for the quotation of Zech 12.10:

> And I will pour out a spirit of compassion and supplication on the house of David and the inhabitants of Jerusalem, so that, when they look on the one whom they have pierced, they shall mourn for him, as one mourns for an only child, and weep bitterly over him, as one weeps over a firstborn.

The combination of 'looking on' and 'pierced' confirms this as the source text but John has not taken it from the LXX, which reads 'danced' instead of 'pierced' (probably through reading the Hebrew consonants *dqrw* as *rqdw*). The Greek version known as Theodotion has 'corrected' this and it may be that John is using such a 'corrected' text, perhaps a proto-Theodotion. Menken notes that a version of Zech 12.10 is quoted in Matt 24.30 and Rev 1.7 and so points to a specifically Christian revision rather than a general (Jewish) revision of the LXX.

> Then the sign of the Son of Man will appear in heaven, and then *all the tribes of the earth will mourn*, and *they will see* 'the Son of Man coming on the clouds of heaven' with power and great glory. (Matt 24.30)

> Look! He is coming with the clouds; *every eye will see* him, even those who pierced him; and on his account *all the tribes of the earth will wail.* So it is to be. Amen. (Rev 1.7)

In terms of the fulfilment, it is clear that John understands the soldier's spear to fulfil the 'piercing' but who are the ones who will 'look on the one whom they have pierced'? Both Matt 24.30 and Rev 1.7 give it a future eschatological reference but this does not appear to be John's meaning. Menken thinks the clue is in the previous verse where it is said, 'He who saw this has testified so that you also may believe' (19.35). Thus the beloved disciple 'represents all believers, and his looking on the pierced Jesus is a representative fulfilment of Zechariah's prophecy' (1996, p. 185).

Allusions

We have noted several incidents where the Synoptic Gospels are content to allude to scripture, whereas John draws attention to it by explicit quotation. Some have deduced from this that quotations are more important to John than allusions. On the other hand, much of John's text is richly allusive, as the following two examples show.

The Prologue (1.1–18)

It can hardly be coincidence that John's Gospel begins with the opening words of the Bible ('In the beginning') and then goes on to speak about light and darkness, the emergence of life and its dependence on God. What is different, of course, is that whereas Genesis simply spoke of God creating the heavens and the earth, John speaks of all things coming into existence through the Word, who was 'with God' and 'was God' (1.1–3). No doubt John saw the mysterious plural of Gen 1.26 ('Let *us* make humankind in our image') as confirmation of this. Many scholars have also pointed to wisdom motifs where God accomplishes his purposes through wisdom, who was with God from the beginning. According to Prov 8, those who find wisdom find life:

> When he established the heavens, I was there … when he marked out the foundations of the earth, then I was beside him, like a master worker; and I was daily his delight, rejoicing before him always … Happy is the one who listens to me, watching daily at my gates, waiting beside my doors. For whoever finds me finds life and obtains favour from the Lord. (Prov 8.27–35 abbreviated)

In addition, Hanson draws attention to an important Sinai background. In Exod 33.14, God says to Moses, 'My presence will go with you.' Moses replies, 'Show me your glory' (33.18). So Moses ascends the mountain and God reveals himself as 'merciful and gracious' (34.6). John writes, 'And the Word became flesh and lived among us, and we have seen his glory, the glory as of a father's only son, full of grace and truth' (1.14). Though the scriptures are never denigrated in John's Gospel as such, there is clearly a polemical edge to 1.17, that no one has ever seen God (not even Moses, from whom came the law) but Christ has made him known.

Jacob's ladder in 1.51

The story of Philip bringing Nathaniel to Jesus ends with the somewhat enigmatic promise, 'Very truly, I tell you, you will see heaven opened and the angels of God ascending and descending upon the Son of Man' (1.51). Most commentators link this with Jacob's vision in Gen 28.12–15:

And he dreamed that there was a ladder set up on the earth, the top of it reaching to heaven; and the angels of God were ascending and descending on it. And the Lord stood beside him and said, 'I am the Lord, the God of Abraham your father and the God of Isaac; the land on which you lie I will give to you and to your offspring, and your offspring shall be like the dust of the earth ... and all the families of the earth shall be blessed in you and in your offspring.

Jesus has just called Nathaniel a true Israelite (1.47) and here we have a reference to Jacob, who was renamed Israel (Gen 32.28). The promise therefore recalls the hopes of Israel and the covenant to Abraham. But Nathaniel will not see angels ascending and descending on a ladder but the Son of Man. This elaborate typology (Hanson) is not entirely clear but the meaning seems to be that Jesus is the bridge between heaven and earth. He is the 'place' where God is to be found, just as in John's next chapter, Jesus is the one who replaces the temple, the 'place' where God is to be worshipped.

Conclusion

Compared with the synoptic Gospels, John has a relatively small number of explicit quotations. This is somewhat akin to his concentration on seven miracle stories (which he calls 'signs') rather than the much larger number found in the other Gospels. The quotations he does include have a strong Christological focus, demonstrating that Jesus is the bread of life, the living water, the paschal lamb, the righteous sufferer and the new temple. Other quotations point to the obduracy of the Jews and the betrayal by Judas. His text is the LXX though he has 'added, omitted, or changed elements on the basis of analogous OT passages' (Menken, 1996, p. 207) and perhaps knowledge of the Hebrew text. He is familiar with patterns of homiletic exegesis (John 6), Jewish *haggada* (exaltation of Moses) and typology (lifting the serpent). One is tempted to say that John's use of the Old

Testament is more profound than the synoptic Gospels but that is probably misleading. Like Matthew, he can also quote texts that are difficult to locate and can appear pedantic in the presence of Hebrew parallelism.

Further reading

Margaret Daly-Denton has written a significant monograph (*David in the Fourth Gospel. The Johannine Reception of the Psalms*, 2000) and has also contributed the chapter on John's use of the Psalms (2004) in the Moyise and Menken volume. We have made frequent reference to Maarten Menken's monograph (*Old Testament Quotations in the Fourth Gospel: Studies in Textual Form*, 1996) and he has also contributed the chapters on Genesis (2012) and the Minor Prophets (2009) in the same series. The chapter in the Beale and Carson commentary was written by Andreas Köstenberger (2007), who has also written a fine commentary on the Gospel in the Baker Exegetical series (2004). Andrew Brunson has written a monograph on the use of Psalm 118 in the Gospel (2003), while Stan Harstine has written on the figure of Moses (2002) and Gary Manning on the allusions to the prophet Ezekiel (2004). Although now somewhat dated, Anthony Hanson's book (*The Prophetic Gospel: A Study of John and the Old Testament* 1991) has many insights, including his view that the 'theophanies under the old dispensation afford him the opportunity of claiming that the appearance of the Word in Jesus Christ was no bolt from the blue, but was the culmination of a series of appearances of the Word in Israel's history' (p. 242).

Questions

1. What are the main themes of John's scriptural quotations?

2. In what ways does John's use of scripture parallel other Jewish writers?

3. In what ways can John's prologue be seen as an interpretation of Gen 1?

6

Jesus' use of the Old Testament

Readers may have begun this book with the view that a chapter on Jesus' use of the Old Testament would simply be the sum total of the chapters on Matthew, Mark, Luke and John. However, there are several reasons why it is more complicated than that: (1) Some of the quotations we have discussed are editorial comments from the evangelists and not ascribed to Jesus (particularly in Matthew); (2) The Gospels are in Greek and so none of the actual quotations were spoken by Jesus – they have already been translated and hence interpreted; (3) Sometimes the Gospels differ among themselves as to how they present a particular quotation and so a decision needs to be made on which is closest to what Jesus might have said; (4) Some stories seem to reflect the interests of the early Church more than the historical Jesus and may need to be discounted (or used more subtly). Not surprisingly, scholars differ in their assessment of these points and in my book, *Jesus and Scripture* (2010), I discuss three broad positions: minimalist, moderate and maximalist.

Minimalists only accept those sayings that are attested in the earliest sources (usually Mark and Q – some add the *Gospel of Thomas*) and show no influence of later Christian disputes (such as divinity, messiahship or atonement). Thus in his book, *The Authentic Gospel of Jesus* (2003), Geza Vermes only considers eleven quotations to be authentic, nine of which are to do with the interpretation of the law (divorce, retaliation, oaths etc.). The other two are the forsaken saying (Psalm 22.1), which he thinks the early Church would hardly have invented (the so-called criterion of embarrassment), and Jesus' reply to

John the Baptist ('the blind receive their sight, the lame walk, the lepers are cleansed ...'). Many would see this as a claim to messiahship, but Vermes thinks that Jesus was not pointing to himself but to God. Jesus was a charismatic prophet who understood that God's kingdom was imminent. He used scripture in debates about the law but in general, preferred to speak on his own authority ('You have heard ... but I say to you' – Matt 5.22, 28, 32, 34, 39, 44).

John Dominic Crossan (1991) and Marcus Borg (1998) are particularly critical of the view that Jesus used scripture to talk about his 'second coming' and the end of the world. This 'apocalyptic' Jesus was popular in the first half of the twentieth century (following Albert Schweitzer) because it was thought to be extremely unlikely that the later Church would invent something that had clearly not happened. For example, in Mark 13.24–30, Jesus appears to claim that the universe will collapse ('the sun will be darkened, and the moon will not give its light, and the stars will be falling from heaven') and that it will happen in 'this generation' (13.30). However, Crossan and Borg argue that such a view is incompatible with the moral and social teachings of Jesus, which show a strong respect for the earth, and is more likely to have arisen through the early Church's belief that Jesus had risen from the dead. Thus we see Paul advising the Christians in Corinth not to marry because time is short and the gospel must be proclaimed (1 Cor 7.29–40). To those in Thessalonica, he urges them not to grieve for those who have died because 'we who are alive, who are left until the coming of the Lord' (1 Thess 4.15) will soon be joining them. This apocalyptic fervour was not part of Jesus' teaching but arose in the early Church. When the Gospels were written, it was assumed that such teaching must go back to Jesus and so an apocalyptic discourse was invented (Mark 13), even though it is quite out of keeping with the rest of Jesus' teaching.

Moderates acknowledge that we cannot simply take the Gospels at face value, especially John, but think that the general picture of Jesus as an *interpreter* of scripture is correct. For example, Tom Wright (1996) argues that the so-called apocalyptic sayings are in fact predictions of the destruction of Jerusalem and the temple. To us, the language of stars falling and the sun turning black sounds like the end of the universe but Israel's prophets used such language to predict forthcoming disasters (Isa 13.10). Thus Wright thinks it is more likely that Jesus' hearers would have understood him to be talking about a future disaster and this appears to be confirmed by the context of Mark 13:

> As he came out of the temple, one of his disciples said to him, 'Look, Teacher, what large stones and what large buildings!' Then Jesus asked him, 'Do you see these great buildings? Not one stone will be left here upon another; all will be thrown down.' (Mark 13.1–2)

This is undoubtedly a neat solution, allowing the sayings to be regarded as authentic (contrary to the minimalists) but not in error about the end of the world (contrary to Schweitzer). But is it too neat? Scholars such as Dale Allison (2010) and Eddie Adams (2007) believe it is, arguing that the finality of Jesus' sayings is one of the most characteristic features of his teaching. Sayings like Matt 13.49 ('So it will be at the end of the age. The angels will come out and separate the evil from the righteous') certainly sound rather more final than the destruction of Jerusalem.

The parable of the vineyard has often been regarded with suspicion because of such allegorical features as the father sending his 'beloved son' (Mark 12.6) and then giving the vineyard to others (Mark 12.9). However, there are good reasons for thinking that the basic parable goes back to Jesus, even if it has been embellished. First, as Stephen Bryan points out, Jesus was rather fond of referring to vineyards (workers in the vineyard, barren fig tree planted in a vineyard) and any Jewish hearer would automatically think of the comparison between Israel and a vineyard in Isa 5. Second, the connection between the murdered son and the rejected stone of Psalm 118.22 can plausibly be explained by the similarity of the Hebrew words *ben* ('son') and *eben* ('stone'), which is not the case in Greek (*huios/lithos*). Third, the parable is found in a simpler form in *Gospel of Thomas* 66, and the very next saying is a quotation from Psalm 118.22. Bryan (2002, p. 86) concludes:

Unlike many of his contemporaries whose understanding of Israel's situation was shaped by biblical traditions which anticipated Israel's restoration and the judgement of the nation's Gentile oppressors, Jesus' expectations were heavily informed by traditions which declared that the heat of God's wrath would be vented on Israel for covenant unfaithfulness.

Neither do we need to reject Jesus' reply to the high priest in Mark 14.62 ('I am; and "you will see the Son of Man seated at the right hand of the Power," and "coming with the clouds of heaven"') because it uses Dan 7.13 to predict Jesus' second coming. This objection would only be convincing if Dan 7.13 actually spoke about a journey from heaven to earth 'on the clouds' but it does not. Daniel is talking about a human-like figure ('one like a son of man') *going* to heaven to receive a kingdom. The meaning of Jesus' reply to the high priest is not that he will return to earth 'on the clouds' (as if this were a mode of transport!) but that God will vindicate him and grant him a kingdom.

Another example is when Jesus' challenges the scribes on their understanding of Psalm 110.1 (Mark 12.35–37). If we understand Jesus to be saying that the 'son of David' can indeed be 'David's Lord' because he is divine and the second person of the Trinity, then of course the saying looks suspicious. But there is no hint in the story that Jesus is claiming to be this 'son of David'; he is simply challenging their self-assurance that they have the correct understanding of scripture. Thus there is no reason to doubt that a Jewish teacher like Jesus (who was sometimes addressed as rabbi) could enter into such debates, though we should note that we cannot have it both ways. If we accept the authenticity of sayings such as these because (when properly understood) they are not making explicitly Christian claims, they also become rather less interesting. This is why most moderates argue that Jesus is often making implicit or subtle claims, which the later Church made explicit because of its knowledge of what came next (or what it believed came next).

For example, there are good reasons for doubting the authenticity of the so-called Nazareth sermon in Luke 4. Not only does it appear to be based on a later incident when Jesus was rejected in his home town (Mark 6.1-6/Matt 13.54–58), the text from which Jesus is said to have read is actually a combination of Isa 61.1–2 and Isa 58.6 and shows a number of distinctive LXX characteristics. Thus Jesus could not have read from such a scroll and the whole incident looks like the work of Luke or one of his sources. On the other hand, there are two other passages which may contain a hint that Jesus did identify with the anointed prophet of Isa 61. The first has already been mentioned, namely, Jesus' reply to John the Baptist, which even Vermes accepts as authentic. Among the snippets of Isaiah is the phrase, 'the poor have good news brought to them' (Luke 7.22), an echo but not a quotation of Isa 61.1. In addition, some scholars have seen an echo of Isa 61 in the beatitudes aimed at the poor (61.1), those who mourn (61.3) and those who will inherit the earth (61.7). Dunn (2003, pp. 516–17) offers this opinion:

> Even if Luke's portrayal of Jesus reading the passage and explicitly claiming its fulfilment (Luke 4.16–21) is an elaboration of the briefer tradition in Mark 6.1–6a, we can still be confident that this elaboration was based on a strong remembrance of Jesus making clear allusion to the passage on more than one occasion.

Perhaps the greatest change in studies of the historical Jesus over the last few decades is the acceptance that Jesus was a law-abiding Jew. How else can we explain the disciples continuing to worship in the Jerusalem temple (Acts 3.1), their reluctance to engage with Gentiles (Acts 11.3) and Peter's declaration in Acts 10.14 that he has never 'eaten anything that is profane or unclean'? This has particular relevance to the debate about Jesus and the food laws. It used to be thought that Jesus regarded such matters as trivial and even if it is Mark rather than Jesus who said, 'Thus he declared all foods clean' (7.19), it is only making explicit what was implicit in Jesus' teaching. However, given that Peter has never eaten anything unclean in his life, including the three years he was with Jesus, and Jesus' warning against those who relax any of the laws in the Sermon on the Mount (Matt 5.19), it is unlikely that Jesus is nullifying the food laws. In fact as James Crossley (2004) points out, it is unlikely that the food laws are in view at all. The issue is whether food that the law declares clean is made unclean by not observing the scrupulous hand-washing rituals of the Pharisees. Jesus says that it is not.

Perhaps even more challenging is the popular view that Jesus had little regard for the Sabbath. For example, Jesus defends his disciples from the accusation of plucking grain on the Sabbath by stating that 'the Son of Man is lord even of the Sabbath' (Mark 2.28). To Christian ears, this sounds like Jesus claiming to be divine and therefore free to suspend the Sabbath but this would directly contradict his claim to uphold the law. A more likely interpretation, therefore, is that Jesus was claiming to know the divine intent behind the Sabbath law and concluded that his disciples' behaviour falls within it (perhaps based on the law of gleaning in Deut 23.25). As in the episode about hand-washing, Jesus challenges the Pharisaic elaborations of the law but not the law itself.

On the other hand, some scholars think the pendulum has swung too far in asserting that Jesus was a law-abiding Jew. Thus while Tom Holmén agrees that Jesus never formally broke the law, he also points out that in a rather conspicuous way, neither did he attempt to demonstrate his loyalty to it. For example, his total prohibition of divorce and the swearing of oaths cannot simply be called an interpretation of the law or even an intensification of it. By forbidding what the law permits, Jesus implied that the law is in some way inadequate as an indicator of God's will (2001, p. 180).

It is clear that there are considerable differences between those whom I have called moderates, but what they have in common is the belief that much of the material in the Gospels (except in John) can be traced back to Jesus in some form or other. They acknowledge that the material has often been embellished and many of the quotations have been conformed to the LXX (e.g. the hypocrisy saying in Mark 7.6–7). However, they differ from maximalists, who are inclined to accept the authenticity of all of the quotations ascribed to Jesus, usually because of a particular church commitment to the authority and inspiration of scripture. When required to defend this on scholarly grounds, the main argument is that this is the best explanation for how the early Church came to believe what it did about Jesus. Thus whereas minimalists cite the use of Psalm 69 in Acts and Romans or Isa 53 in Acts, Romans and 1 Peter as evidence of inauthenticity, maximalists reverse this. Since neither of these texts was being used in a messianic sense in contemporary Judaism, the best explanation for why the early Church adopted them is that Jesus pointed the early disciples in that direction, as Luke 24.25–27 states. Minimalists will see this as special pleading but it has to be said that all things being equal, it is just as logical as the reverse position and it does explain one important phenomenon: the early Church sometimes quotes neighbouring verses to the one that Jesus is said to have quoted. For example, Jesus quotes Isa 53.12 in Luke 22.37 ('And he was counted among the lawless'), which is not overtly theological, but might have been the prompt for the early Church to explore the rest of the chapter and find a deep resonance between 'the suffering servant' and what happened to Jesus.

We have already noted how Kimball argues that the combination of Isa 61.1–2 and 58.6 are a summary of the sermon that Jesus preached in the synagogue rather than the actual text that was read out. He also has an argument for the authenticity of Jesus' replies to the devil in the temptation story. Most scholars think this is a rather obvious expansion of Mark's brief narrative (1.12–13), not only indicating the type of temptations that Jesus faced but also showing him as an expert in biblical interpretation. It is also difficult to imagine a scenario where Jesus conveyed this information to the disciples ('then the devil said to me … and I replied'). Kimball, however, points out that the specific temptations (turning stones into bread, gaining authority over the world by agreeing to worship the devil, and jumping from the temple) are hardly the temptations faced by the early Church. Indeed, there is a rabbinic tradition where the Angel of Death quotes from the Psalms and Moses responds by quoting from Deuteronomy, so such a scenario is not impossible to believe. He summarizes Jesus' use of scripture (1994, p. 197).

In teaching his various Jewish audiences and in debating with the establishment theologians, he employed many of the exegetical methods commonly used by the religious teachers of Judaism. Yet he frequently offered interpretations of Scripture that were radically different from the other teachers of his day because of his superior understanding of Scripture and because of his application of the Old Testament to himself.

The purpose of this short chapter is to indicate the complexity of moving from what the Gospels say to what Jesus might actually have said and thought. It is often referred to as the quest for the historical Jesus, a reference to Schweitzer's famous book (1906). Schweitzer made the point that reconstructions of Jesus are often a thinly veiled reflection of the values of the interpreter, hence the various liberal 'lives of Jesus' produced in the nineteenth century. He was rather less aware of how his own 'apocalyptic' Jesus was influenced by what was going on in pre-war Europe and it is likely that the same thing can be aimed at the twenty-first century interpreters discussed in this book. It is not a reason to abandon the question but it should prompt caution before making definitive statements about what Jesus could or could not have said.

Further reading

Probably because of the complexity of the subject, most of the material on Jesus' use of scripture is found in scholarly journals or collections of essays. Pride of place must go to the four-volume, *Handbook for the Study of the Historical Jesus* (2011), edited by Tom Holmén and Stanley Porter. It runs to 3652 pages and few libraries will be able to afford it, let alone individuals, but its chapters can usually be obtained through inter-library loans. The section on 'Jesus and the Legacy of Israel' contains a number of important studies. Several older studies still have much to offer, such as Richard France, *Jesus and the Old Testament* (1971), Bruce Chilton, *A Galilean Rabbi and His Bible* (1984) and Craig Evans, *To See and Not Perceive: Isaiah 6.9–10 in Early Jewish and Christian Interpretation* (1989). For their more recent views, see France's commentaries on Mark (2002) and Matthew (2007), Chilton's biography of Jesus (2000) and Evans' commentary on Matthew (2012). Michael Bird has written a number of important studies and his, *Are you the One to Come?: The Historical Jesus and the Messianic Question* (2009) is particularly helpful.

Questions

1. Are you more drawn to a minimalist, moderate or maximalist interpretation of Jesus' use of scripture? Can you say why?
2. How has recent work on the 'Jewishness' of Jesus influenced understandings of 'Jesus and the law'?
3. Does Jesus' use of scripture in John's Gospel support the view that his picture of Jesus is significantly different to that of the Synoptic Gospels?

7

The Old Testament in Paul

Paul's letters contain about 100 explicit quotations, concentrated in Romans (60), Corinthians (27) and Galatians (10). There are also five quotations in Ephesians and two in the Pastoral epistles but as many scholars think these were written in Paul's name, they will be treated separately. It is of some interest that there are no explicit quotations in Philippians and Thessalonians, though they are not devoid of allusions (e.g. Phil 2.11). The most frequently quoted books are Isaiah, Psalms, Genesis and Deuteronomy. In the analysis below, I have attempted to group the quotations under the following headings:

- God's plan to include Gentiles
- The faith of Abraham
- Israel's blindness
- The mystery of election
- The character of God
- Jesus Christ
- Adam
- Atonement
- The Christian life
- New and old

This gives a good sense of the themes treated by Paul but it is also important to read through Romans, Galatians and Corinthians to see how they occur sequentially, as the argument unfolds. Because we are dealing with a large number of quotations, we will not have space in this chapter for a separate section on allusions. We will, however, comment on a number of allusions as they effect the argument of particular books (e.g. the references to Adam).

God's plan to include Gentiles

Though himself a Jew of some standing (Phil 3.5–6), Paul was called to be an apostle to the Gentiles (Rom 15.16). His task was to establish churches throughout the world and fight for their right to belong to the people of God. In support of this, he finds in scripture verses that speak of God's intention to include Gentiles. For example, in Rom 9.25, he quotes Hos 2.23 that, 'Those who were not my people I will call "my people", and her who was not beloved I will call "beloved"'. God's purpose is that the 'Gentiles might glorify God for his mercy' (Rom 15.9) and this is supported by a string of texts, all of which contain the word 'Gentiles' (2 Sam 22.50; Psalm 18.49; Deut 32.43; Psalm 117.1; Isa 11.10):

> 'Therefore I will confess you among the Gentiles, and sing praises to your name'; and again he says, 'Rejoice, O Gentiles, with his people'; and again, 'Praise the Lord, all you Gentiles, and let all the peoples praise him'; and again Isaiah says, 'The root of Jesse shall come, the one who rises to rule the Gentiles; in him the Gentiles shall hope.' (Rom 15.9–12)

Paul's burning passion is to preach Christ where he has not been preached before. In Rom 15 he outlines his travel plans to reach Spain because there is 'no further place for me in these regions'. Texts like Isa 52.15 ('Those who have never been told of him shall see, and those who have never heard of him shall understand') echo his burning sense of mission (Rom 15.21).

Not all of these texts are as explicit about God's plan to include Gentiles as Paul makes them seem. For example, Hos 2.23 is a promise that the apostate northern tribes will be reunited with Judah. It is possible that Paul sees an analogy between the 'not my people' of Hosea's day and the 'not my people' (Gentiles) of his own, but most scholars think there is more to it than this. Mark Seifrid, for example, argues that the apostasy of the northern tribes effectively put them in the same position as Gentiles and so the promise of restoration includes within it a promise for the Gentiles (2007, p. 648). Mitchell Kim (2012, pp. 115–29) speaks of the text's 'latent' meaning, a meaning which only becomes available when large numbers of Gentiles turn to God. On the other hand, Christopher Stanley (2004) regards such explanations as special pleading. Paul's use of scripture is 'rhetorical' and aims to persuade readers to accept his theological point of view; it is of no interest to him what the text would have meant prior to the coming of Christ.

The faith of Abraham

The crux of Paul's argument for the admission of Gentiles to the people of God revolves around Abraham. In a detailed and sometimes difficult passage (Gal 3–4), Paul makes the following points. First, Gen 15.6 says that Abraham 'believed God, and it was reckoned to him as righteousness'. Those that were barring Gentiles from full participation in the people of God were probably saying that they had to be 'sons of Abraham', that is direct descendants. But 'son of' is a common idiom for 'shares the characteristics of' (cf. Bar-nabas = 'son of encouragement' – Acts 4.36) and so Paul declares that the true sons of Abraham are those that share his faith (Gal 3.7).

Second, when God called Abraham (Gen 12.3) he gave him the promise that, 'All the Gentiles shall be blessed in you'. Putting these two points together, Paul can deduce that 'those who believe are blessed with Abraham who believed' (Gal 3.9). He then offers an extremely complex explanation of Jesus' death on the cross (to be considered later) and concludes that this took place, 'in order that in Christ Jesus the blessing of Abraham might come to the Gentiles' (Gal 3.14). Thus the purpose of Christ's death was so that the promise made to Abraham might at last be realized. Paul can even say that 'the scripture, foreseeing that God would justify the Gentiles by faith, declared the gospel beforehand to Abraham' (Gal 3.8).

Third, having asserted that Gentile Christians who believe like Abraham are properly called 'descendants of Abraham', Paul launches into a peculiar argument that there is actually only one true descendant of Abraham, namely, Christ. The argument runs like this: 'Now the promises were made to Abraham and to his offspring; it does not say, "And to offsprings", as of many, but it says, "And to your offspring", that is, to one person, who is Christ' (Gal 3.16). This is puzzling for two reasons. First, if Paul intends this as a serious linguistic argument, it does not hold up. Both the Greek and Hebrew words for 'offspring' are collective terms, as can be seen from Gen 13.16 (where Abraham's 'offspring' will be a great multitude). As in English, it would simply be ungrammatical to write 'offsprings'. Second, it is a peculiar argument to introduce when he has just demonstrated that 'Abraham's offspring' applies to Gentile Christians, providing they share his faith. His point appears to be that as well as sharing Abraham's faith in a general sense, they must also be 'in Christ'. Christ is the fulfilment of the singular 'offspring', while Gentile Christians share that fulfilment as members of Christ's body. Dunn defends this exegesis by noting that already in the Genesis text, 'offspring' sometimes refers to Isaac and sometimes to a multitude of descendants and so 'a rhetorical play on the ambiguity is invited' (1993, p. 184). Ben Witherington summarizes:

> The Gentiles are blessed in Abraham, but the means of this happening is that they are blessed in the seed of Abraham, which Paul will argue is Christ. The connection between Gentiles and Abraham then is not simply that they both have faith. The Gentiles are connected to Abraham through faith in Christ the 'seed' of Abraham and the benefits they receive from Him. (1998, p. 228)

Some years later, Paul writes to the Church in Rome and explores in more depth the nature of Abraham's faith. He begins by making a point that perhaps only occurred to him after writing Galatians (since it would have been apposite). The promise came before Abraham was circumcised. It could not, therefore, be dependent on circumcision and so the Judaizers are wrong to insist that Gentile Christians must be circumcised. Circumcision was the 'seal' of the righteousness Abraham had by faith, not its basis. But what was the nature of his faith? It was the fact that though he was old and Sarah was barren, he believed that God could give him an heir. And Paul sees this as a parallel to Christian faith, which holds that God raised Jesus from the dead: 'No distrust made him waver concerning the promise of God, but he grew strong in his faith as he gave glory to God, being fully convinced that God was able to do what he had promised. Therefore his faith "was reckoned to him as righteousness"' (Rom 4.20–21).

Israel's blindness

A further use of the Abraham story is the allegory of Sarah and Hagar in Gal 4.21–31. Abraham had two sons. One was through the slave woman Hagar, the other through Sarah, who is called the 'free woman', (4.22) anticipating Paul's conclusion. These two women represents two covenants and two peoples, one characterized by freedom and one characterized by slavery. And since God tells Abraham in Gen 21.10 to 'Drive out the slave and her child; for the child of the slave will not share the inheritance with the child of the free woman', Paul's Gentile Christians ('the free') should have nothing to do with the Judaizers ('the slaves').

The general principle, that those who stand for freedom are often persecuted by those who enslave is well made. But the particular application to Gentile Christians and law-abiding Judaizers is more precarious. Paul says that Hagar represents Mount Sinai (i.e. the law), which corresponds to the present Jerusalem (the custodians of the law), while Sarah (strangely referred to as 'the other woman') represents the 'Jerusalem above; she is free, and she is our mother' (4.26). There then follows a quotation from Isa 54.1 which urges the one who was barren to rejoice, though in the present context, it confusingly contrasts the 'desolate one' with the 'one who is married' (confusing since it was Sarah who was married). Jewish tradition would agree with the association of Sinai and Jerusalem but would of course count Isaac as their founding father and hence Sarah as their mother. On what basis can Paul reverse this and associate Sinai and the law with Hagar?

One clue is that Paul himself says the story is allegorical (4.24), though the exact meaning of this term is disputed (it only occurs here in all of the Bible). In particular, does he think that the story was written as an allegory, which he is now going to decode (for the first time)? Or is he aiming to offer an allegorical reading of the story, even though he knows that it was not originally intended as an allegory? Bruce Longenecker opts for the latter, claiming that:

> the goal of Paul's scriptural interpretation is not the discovery of a text's 'literal' meaning in its original context; instead, scriptural interpretation is here put in the exclusive service of nurturing and enhancing Christian lifestyle, a goal achieved by an imaginative reading strategy that by-passes any concerns for a literal reading. (1998, p. 167)

Who then is it going to convince? Certainly not those who, in Paul's opinion, are advocating a lifestyle of slavery, for they would consider themselves the true Israel, the true descendants of Isaac, whose mother is Sarah. But then Paul is not addressing them. Rather, he is addressing those Christians in Galatia who have already found freedom in the Spirit (3.5) and so he expects them 'to join him in this imaginative reconfiguration of the story in order to nurture their Christian commitment' (Longenecker, 1998, p. 168).

In Rom 9–11, Paul uses a different strategy. He begins by making the same point, that from Abraham came children of promise and children of flesh. He then quotes a number of texts to the effect that those who thought themselves God's people have either stumbled or become blind:

> See, I am laying in Zion a stone that will make people stumble, a rock that will make them fall, and whoever believes in him will not be put to shame. (Rom 9.33 = Isa 8.14; 28.16)

> All day long I have held out my hands to a disobedient and contrary people. (Rom 10.21 = Isa 65.2)

God gave them a sluggish spirit, eyes that would not see and ears that would not hear, down to this very day. (Rom 11.8 = Deut 29.4; Isa 29.10)

Let their table become a snare and a trap, a stumbling-block and a retribution for them; let their eyes be darkened so that they cannot see, and keep their backs for ever bent. (Rom 11.9-10 = Psalm 69.22-23)

However, Paul's point in Rom 9–11 is that this stumbling/blindness is temporary and is indeed part of God's plan for the inclusion of the Gentiles. He uses the image of a wild olive shoot that has been grafted into a natural olive root. Branches of the natural olive (unbelieving Jews) have been stripped off to make way for the grafted branches (Gentile Christians). But just as God has grafted that which is wild into that which is natural, 'how much more will these natural branches be grafted back into their own olive tree' (Rom 11.24). From this, he is able to quote Isa 59.20–21 ('Out of Zion will come the Deliverer; he will banish ungodliness from Jacob') and Jer 31.33–34 ('And this is my covenant with them, when I take away their sins') and conclude that 'all Israel will be saved' (Rom 11.26).

The mystery of election

Paul ends Rom 9–11 with quotations from Isa 40.13 and Job 41.11 to the effect that God's ways are 'unsearchable' and 'inscrutable'. Despite the happy conclusion that 'all Israel will be saved' and God will be 'merciful to all' (Rom 11.32), Paul explores what scripture has to say about God's choices. In the opening chapters of 1 Corinthians, he argues that it is not through human wisdom that God makes himself known. Those who rely on human wisdom are thwarted, for God 'will destroy the wisdom of the wise' (1 Cor 1.19). This is confirmed for Paul by the fact that the rulers of this age crucified Jesus. Indeed, somewhat at odds with his earlier comments that the gospel was revealed beforehand to Abraham, he now says that 'no eye has seen, nor ear heard, nor the human heart conceived, what God has prepared for those who love him' (1 Cor 2.9, perhaps based on Isa 64.4). The section is brought to a close by quotations from Job 5.13 ('He catches the wise in their craftiness') and Psalm 94.11 ('The Lord knows the thoughts of the wise, that they are futile').

However, it is in Rom 9–11 that the theme is explored in depth. We have already seen that Paul can draw the optimistic conclusion that God will be 'merciful to all' and 'all Israel will be saved'. Why then does God make choices? Certainly not because of human merit, as is shown in the case of Jacob and Esau. God decreed that 'the elder shall serve the younger' (Rom 9.12 = Gen 25.23) 'even before they had been born or had done anything good or bad'. Pharaoh is then introduced as the archetypal protagonist whose evil plans are nevertheless used by God to accomplish his own purposes. Indeed, it is more than God providentially using a godless person, for the scripture says to Pharaoh, 'I have raised you up for the very purpose of showing my power in you, so that my name may be proclaimed in all the earth' (Rom 9.17 = Exod 9.16). This is brought to a climax in a question that goes unanswered:

> What if God, desiring to show his wrath and to make known his power, has endured with much patience the objects of wrath that are made for destruction; and what if he has done so in order to make known the riches of his glory for the objects of mercy, which he has prepared beforehand for glory – including us whom he has called, not from the Jews only but also from the Gentiles? (Rom 9.22–24)

The implied answer seems to be, 'it would still be none of your business'. But since the text appears to say that God predestined some to salvation ('objects of mercy') and some to damnation ('objects of wrath'), it is not so easily silenced. C. H. Dodd famously commented, 'the trouble is that man is not a pot ... and he will not be bludgeoned into silence. It is the weakest point in the whole epistle' (1959, p. 171). What is at stake is the very character of God.

The character of God

Though there has been much debate as to why Paul wrote Romans, it is clear that one of his purposes is to defend God's character. His first Old Testament quotation is in 1.17 ('The one who is righteous will live by faith' – Hab 2.4) and is used to support the assertion that in the gospel 'the righteousness of God is revealed'. The next quotation (2.24) indicts Jewish sin because, 'The name of God is blasphemed among the Gentiles because of you' (Isa 52.5). And the third quotation in 3.4 ('So that you may be justified in your words, and prevail in your judging' – Psalm 51.4) is used to counter the accusation that Jewish lack of faith implies God's unfaithfulness. There then follows a long catena or collection of quotations which shows the utter gulf between God's righteousness and all human reasoning (note the emphasis on speaking):

> There is no one who is righteous, not even one; there is no one who has understanding, there is no one who seeks God. All have turned aside, together they have become worthless; there is no one who shows kindness, there is not even one. Their *throats* are opened graves; they use their *tongues* to deceive. The venom of vipers is under their *lips*. Their *mouths* are full of cursing and bitterness. Their feet are swift to shed blood; ruin and misery are in their paths, and the way of peace they have not known. There is no fear of God before their eyes. (Rom 3.10–18)

Those in the Lutheran tradition have seen the purpose of this catena as proving that every single person is wicked and therefore in need of the gospel (3.19–20). This gospel is then announced in 3.23–24, namely, that 'all have sinned and fall short of the glory of God; they are now justified by his grace as a gift, through the redemption that is in Christ Jesus'. But there is more to it than that. As we have seen, the first three quotations in Romans are to do with defending God's righteousness from the attacks of human reason. And here, in this climactic passage, the purpose of the gospel is stated thus: 'He did this to show his righteousness, because in his divine forbearance he had passed over the sins previously committed; it was to prove at the present time that he himself is righteous and that he justifies the one who has faith in Jesus' (3.25–26). This becomes the main theme in Rom 9–11, where Paul makes the following points: (1) God's word has not failed because some Jews have not believed; (2) God is perfectly just in choosing certain individuals to fulfil his purposes; (3) This would be true even if there were some who were destined for destruction; (4) God has not rejected his people Israel; (5) God's purpose is to have mercy on all. Though Paul's Damascus road experience required him to 'reconfigure' much of what he believed, scripture remains a true witness to God's character. Thus he makes the point in 2 Cor 4.6 that 'it is the God who said, "Let light shine out of darkness", who has shone in our hearts to give the light of the knowledge of the glory of God in the face of Jesus Christ'. And Wright thinks the same is true of God's plan. There is no plan B. God's way of saving the world was to enter into covenant with a people, give a law that would focus the consequences of evil there, and deal with it in the person of the Messiah, Israel's representative. Thus according to Wright, Israel is the 'object of wrath' in order to bring salvation to the world: 'Thus the means by which the Torah condemned Israel at this meta-level are vindicated as part of the strange purposes of the creator, that he should have a covenant people who would die and be raised so that the world might be saved' (1991, p. 243).

Jesus Christ

Paul's use of scripture springs from the consequences of Christ's death and resurrection but surprisingly, there are very few quotations that are specifically related to aspects of his life. We have already mentioned the argument in Gal 3.16 that Christ is Abraham's offspring. In the hymn of Phil 2, words from Isa 45.23 ('To me every knee shall bow, every tongue shall swear') are transferred to Christ ('at the name of Jesus every knee should bend … and every tongue confess that Jesus Christ is Lord').

In 1 Cor 15.27, Paul quotes Psalm 8.6 ('God has put all things in subjection under his feet') to support the view that Christ 'must reign until he has put all his enemies under his feet'. However, the argument is not so much about the final Lordship of Christ, for it is careful to say that 'this does not include the one who put all things in subjection under him'. Paul protects God's Lordship by stating that in the end, 'the Son himself will also be subjected to the one who put all things in subjection under him, so that God may be all in all' (1 Cor 15.28).

In Rom 15.3, Christ's character of not pleasing himself is linked with Psalm 69.9 ('The insults of those who insult you have fallen on me'). This is an important verse in Hanson's theory that Paul understood the pre-existent Christ to be active in Old Testament history. It is not that these words can be *transferred* to Jesus. Hanson thinks that Paul and the other New Testament writers believed that scripture records actual dialogue between Jesus and God. He supports this by referring to 1 Cor 10.4, where Paul identifies the rock that sprung water for the wilderness generation as Christ. This is an amazing piece of exegesis, for in his desire to show that the Israelites were sustained by spiritual food and drink (like the early Church), the rock has become a 'moveable feast' ('For they drank from the spiritual rock that followed them'). This is never stated in the Old Testament but it does occur in a Jewish legend (*Sukkah* 3.11):

> And so the well which was with the Israelites in the wilderness was a rock, the size of a large round vessel, surging and gurgling upward, as from the mouth of this little flask, rising with them up onto the mountains, and going down with them into the valleys. Wherever the Israelites would encamp, it made camp with them, on a high place, opposite the entry to the Tent of Meeting. (quoted in Holmgren, 1999, p. 32)

The written form of this legend dates from about 400 CE but Hanson argues that it was hardly borrowed from Paul. It is more likely that Paul has drawn on an existing Jewish tradition.

A more recent development is the view that Paul urges his readers to focus on the faithfulness of Christ. This does not sound very radical but Hays (2002) has argued that a number of texts that have been traditionally translated as 'faith *in* Christ' should be rendered 'faith *of* Christ' or 'faithfulness of Christ'. The issue is that Paul uses a number of prepositions (words like in, through, over, around) in conjunction with Jesus or Christ. Thus in Gal 2.16, the NRSV assumes that this is simply stylistic variation:

> we know that a person is justified not by the works of the law but through faith in Jesus Christ (*dia pisteos Iesou Christou*). And we have come to believe in Christ Jesus (*eis Christon Iesoun*), so that we might be justified by faith in Christ (*ek pisteos Christou*), and not by doing the works of the law, because no one will be justified by the works of the law.

There is no doubt that the middle expression (*eis Christon Iesoun*) understands Christ as the object of the believing and so 'believe in Christ' is the correct translation. But do the other two expressions (using different prepositions and the genitive case) mean the same thing (as NRSV) or do they refer to a quality of Christ, namely, his faithfulness. In other words, does this verse make two points about justification? The first comes from the middle expression and states the need for believing or trusting in Christ. The second comes from the first and third expressions and states that justification comes 'through' (*dia*) or 'out of' (*ek*) the faithfulness of Christ. It is not referring to a human quality (faith) but Christ's faithfulness in fulfilling his mission.

Adam

It is hardly surprising that the creation and fall stories of Gen 1–3 would be the subject of speculation. The stories raise many questions: What does it mean to be in the image of God (Gen 1.27)? What is the nature of humanity (Gen 2.7)? What are the consequences of Adam's disobedience (Gen 3.14–19)? Is it possible to return to the garden of Eden (Gen 3.24)? Writers such as Philo and works such as the *Life of Adam and Eve* and the Wisdom of Solomon explore many of these themes. Thus Philo uses the two creation stories to distinguish between those who live by reason (or philosophy) and those who live by pleasure and sensual experience. In the *Life of Adam and Eve* (date unknown), Satan transforms himself into an angel of light and 'desire' leads to the couple's downfall. As a consequence, death comes to all people. In the Wisdom of Solomon, idolatry leads to immorality. Those who worship beasts not only become futile in their thinking but take on the characteristics of the very thing they worship. Many scholars believe that Paul is drawing on such traditions when he writes to the Romans:

> Ever since the creation of the world his eternal power and divine nature, invisible though they are, have been understood and seen through the things he has made. So they are without excuse; for though they knew God, they did not honour him as God or give thanks to him, but they became futile in their thinking, and their senseless minds were darkened. Claiming to be wise, they became fools; and they exchanged the glory of the immortal God for images resembling a mortal human being or birds or four-footed animals or reptiles. Therefore God gave them up in the lusts of their hearts to impurity, to the degrading of their bodies among themselves, because they exchanged the truth about God for a lie and worshipped and served the creature rather than the Creator, who is blessed for ever! Amen. (Rom 1.20–25)

The theme of Adam's disobedience is explicitly taken up in Rom 5.12–21, where Paul says that Adam 'is a type of the one who was to come' (5.14). This is surprising since one would have expected Paul to say that Christ was the very opposite of Adam. Indeed, most of the exposition says just that. Adam disobeyed but Christ was obedient. Adam brought death to humanity but Christ brought grace. Adam brought condemnation on all people but Christ brought justification and life. The 'typology' is not that Adam and Christ are alike in what they did or in the consequences that followed. They are alike in that they are both representative or incorporative figures. Their actions affect those who identify with them and hence one is either 'in Adam' or 'in Christ'.

In 1 Cor 15, Paul explains the nature of the resurrection body by drawing on the Adam story. Gen 2.7 calls Adam 'a living being' but Paul says that Christ is a 'life-giving Spirit' (1 Cor 15.45). Adam is a 'man of dust' but Christ is 'from heaven'. Thus there is a body/form that is appropriate for physical existence and a body/form that is appropriate for spiritual existence. Paul comes perilously close to the Gnostic view that Christ's body was unreal but avoids this by stressing temporal sequence. We have bodies of dust now but will 'bear the image of the man from heaven' when 'death has been swallowed up in victory' (1Cor 15.54, perhaps based on Isa 25.8). He concludes with a creative rendering of Hos 13.14:

Hos 13.14	1 Cor 15.55
O Death, where are your plagues?	Where, O death is your victory?
O Sheol, where is your destruction?	Where, O death is your sting?

Thus the figure of Adam is important to Paul in understanding the nature of humanity's predicament, the effects of Christ's death and the nature of the resurrection body. In the light of these parallels, scholars such as Dunn (1997, pp. 281–93) have argued that the hymn in Phil 2.5–11 is also about Adam. Most scholars have taken phrases like 'though he was in the form of God' and 'emptied himself, taking the form of a slave' as references to the incarnation. Form of God means divine existence as opposed to human existence. But seen in the light of the Adam tradition, it might have a more 'earthly' meaning. Paul's purpose in quoting the hymn is to give an example of humility rather than selfishness (2.1–4). Thus in contrast to Adam, who was also in the form/image of God, Christ did not seek something higher but emptied himself, taking the form of a slave. In other words, it is not about a divine choice to become human but a human choice to become a slave. But perhaps these interpretations are not mutually exclusive. As Dunn reminds us, we are dealing here with poetry and evocative allusions, not doctrinal formulae.

The theme of the restoration of the original purposes of creation is central to Beale's recent work, *A New Testament Biblical Theology*.

He argues that the Old Testament views Adam as both king and priest in the temple-like Eden and was given the task to extend this to the whole of the earth: 'Adam would have experienced heightened conditions of a permanent and irreversible nature if he had been faithful to the covenant obligations imposed on him by God' (2012, p. 45). He failed as king (he was subdued by the serpent) and priest (he should have expelled the serpent) and so the task passed to Noah, Abraham and later Israel. Thus Christ came as 'the end-time Adam to do what the first Adam should have done and to reflect his Father's image perfectly and to enable his people to have that image restored in them. In doing so, Christ is restarting history, which is a new-creational age to be successfully consummated at his final coming' (2012, p. 465).

Atonement

It is widely agreed that Gal 3.10–14 is one of Paul's most difficult passages. It consists of quotations from Deut 27.26, Hab 2.4, Lev 18.5 and Deut 21.23, in a highly compressed argument. The quotations are linked by certain catch-words. Deut 27.26 and 21.23 both contain the word *epikataratos* ('cursed'). Hab 2.4 and Lev 18.5 both contain the word *zesetai* ('shall live'), giving the sequence cursed/live/live/cursed. And though it is unclear in the NRSV translation, both Deut 27.26 and Lev 18.5 contain the words *poiein auta* ('to do them'):

> For all who rely on the works of the law are under a curse; for it is written, 'Cursed is everyone who does not observe and obey all the things written in the book of the law.' Now it is evident that no one is justified before God by the law; for 'The one who is righteous will live by faith.' But the law does not rest on faith; on the contrary, 'Whoever does the works of the law will live by them.' Christ redeemed us from the curse of the law by becoming a curse for us – for it is written, 'Cursed is everyone who hangs on a tree' – in order that in Christ Jesus the blessing of Abraham might come to the Gentiles, so that we might receive the promise of the Spirit through faith. (Gal 3.10–14)

What is difficult about this argument is that it would seem to make better sense if the word 'not' were omitted from Deut 27.26 ('Cursed is everyone who does observe and obey') and included in Lev 18.5 ('Whoever does the works of the law will not live'). As it is, these two quotations seem to say the opposite of what Paul requires and in order to make sense of it, many commentators have suggested a hidden premise. The one most commonly suggested is that no one can keep the law perfectly. The logic of the passage would then be this. Lev 18.5 promises life to all who keep the law perfectly but since no one can, all are under the curse pronounced by Deut 27.26. But when Christ died on the cross, the curse of Deut 21.23 (a curse on criminals left hanging on a tree) fell on him and this had the effect of redeeming us from the curse of the law, providing that we now live by faith, as scripture already indicates (Hab 2.4).

However, there are at least three problems with this interpretation. First, the law does not require everyone to be perfect in order to be acceptable to God. Indeed, the law contains the God-given instructions to make atonement for sin. This is why Paul can still regard his former life as a Pharisee as 'blameless' (Phil 3.6). Since such a view would be highly controversial, it can hardly function as an unstated and unsupported premise. Second, if Paul's argument is that Christ bore the curse of the law on our behalf (i.e. substitution), it is not helped by citing Deut 21.23 that suggests that Christ was *rightly* cursed for hanging on a tree/cross. For example, when Paul wishes to argue that Christ bore our sins, it is important to establish that Christ himself was without sin (2 Cor 5.21). One would therefore have expected the argument to assert that Christ bears the curse on our behalf because he himself was not under a curse. Kim suggests that Paul's meaning is that the law has now been shown to have *wrongly* cursed Christ and is thus discredited (1981, pp. 274–5). But if that is so, then perhaps it wrongly cursed us as well, in which case there was no need for Christ to die.

Third, the universal indictment has lost sight of the ethnic debate being conducted in Galatians. Paul's conclusion to the argument is that the blessing of Abraham can now come to the Gentiles. What was stopping that was a problem related to the Jewish law, which has now been sorted. Paul does not begin his argument by saying 'all are under a curse' but 'all who rely on the works of the law are under a curse'.

Dunn's solution is that the phrase, 'all who rely on the works of the law' is Paul's shorthand for what we have been calling 'Judaizers', those who insist that Christians must show their obedience to God by keeping the (Jewish) law. 'In continuing to insist on Israel's privilege and separation from other nations', Dunn says, 'they were resisting the manifest will of God in the gospel' (1998, p. 362). Thus despite their apparent zeal for the law, they were actually going against God's will and thus come under the curse of Deut 27.26. But the curse of the law has been absorbed by Christ and 'with it both the misunderstanding of the law's role and its effect in excluding Gentiles from the promise, which had brought the curse into effect, have been declared null and void. The result is that the promised blessing can now be freely offered to the Gentiles' (p. 375).

Wright thinks this view is too narrow. For him, the reference to blessing and curse from Deuteronomy is a link to Israel's experience of exile. Because of national disobedience (not necessarily every individual), Israel went into exile and though now physically back in Palestine, their subjugation under the Romans shows that they are still in exile and therefore under the curse of the law. This came to a climax when Christ died on a Roman cross and took upon himself Israel's curse. But Deuteronomy also envisaged restoration (what Jeremiah calls new covenant) and that has been inaugurated in Christ's resurrection and the outpouring of the Spirit:

> Because the Messiah represents Israel, he is able to take upon himself Israel's curse and exhaust it. Jesus dies as the King of the Jews, at the hands of the Romans whose oppression of Israel is the present, and climactic, form of the curse of exile itself ... Christ, as the representative Messiah, has achieved a specific task, that of taking upon himself the curse which hung over Israel and which on the one hand prevented her from enjoying full membership of Abraham's family and thereby on the other hand prevented the blessing of Abraham from flowing out to the Gentiles. (1991, p. 151)

It is perhaps easier to understand what Paul is trying to say in this passage than follow his actual argument. In Jewish tradition, the promise of life for those who are faithful to the law (Lev 18.5) is synonymous with the promise of righteousness for those who live by faith(fulness). Thus the Qumran commentary says on Hab 2.4, 'Interpreted, this concerns all those who observe the Law in the House of Judah, whom God will deliver from the House of judgement because of their suffering and because of their faith in the Teacher of Righteousness.' But Paul has played off one against the other by the statement, 'But the law does not rest on faith.' Furthermore, it is unclear how Deut 21.23 helps his case. Must we assume a hidden premise that coming under the curse of one particular law (to be left hanging on a tree) implies coming under the whole curse and hence Christ is able to absorb/neutralize Israel's curse? In which case, does the whole doctrine of salvation depend on the particular mode of execution?

Another difficult but significant passage for Paul's understanding of atonement is Rom 3.21–26. It does not contain an Old Testament quotation but the background of *hilasterion* has been crucial for understanding the passage. In Greek literature, the word would normally be translated 'propitiation' and the KJV renders, 'Whom God hath set forth to be a propitiation.' However, it is used in the LXX to translate the Hebrew *kipper*, meaning 'atonement' or 'expiation'. God does not propitiate his own wrath but provides atonement for human sin, hence the NRSV renders Rom 3.25, 'whom God put forward as a sacrifice of atonement by his blood', with no mention of 'propitiation.'

Wright notes that the theme of the 'unveiling of God's righteousness' occurs five times in Rom 3:21–26 and so 'the obvious thing to do is to look for a biblical passage with a similar concentration of the same theme; and the obvious candidate is Isaiah 40–55' (2013, p. 998). He concludes that 'when Paul describes the death of Jesus in sacrificial language … he is deliberately setting up a complex chain of allusion and echo in which Isaiah 40–55 in general, the figure of the servant in particular and the fourth servant song climatically, are central and loadbearing' (2013, p. 999). As with Gal 3.10–14, the exact meaning is still a matter of debate among scholars, particularly as some Christian traditions hold 'propitiation' (or penal substitution) as a central tenet of their beliefs (see John Piper, 2007).

The Christian life

Paul's well-known chapter on love (1 Cor 13) is not itself supported by scripture but Lev 19.18 ('You shall love your neighbour as yourself) is quoted in Gal 5.14 and Rom 13.9. In the former, it occurs in a section where Paul is trying to show that freedom from the law should not be an 'opportunity for self-indulgence'. Rather, love should lead to serving one another. The whole law, he says, is summed up in this single commandment. In Rom 13.8, the one who loves has fulfilled the law. There then follows an abbreviated list of commandments (adultery, murder, stealing, coveting) and 'any other commandment', which are 'summed up in this word, "Love your neighbour as yourself."' As in Jesus' preaching, the real test of this is the ability to love one's enemies (Rom 12.14–21). Paul uses two quotations here. The first says that vengeance belongs to God (Deut 32.35). Christians are not to take the law into their own hands. The second urges positive action: 'if your enemies are hungry, feed them; if they are thirsty, give them something to drink; for by doing this you will heap burning coals on their heads' (Prov 25.21–22). The meaning of the last phrase is debated. Some think the context requires a positive meaning, that they will see the error of their ways and repent. Others suggest a negative meaning, that their judgement will be greater because they have spurned your kindness, though this seems an unworthy motive for the actions.

Perhaps because arrogance was a particular problem in Corinth, Paul quotes Jer 9.24 ('Let the one who boasts, boast in the Lord') in each of his letters to the Corinthians (1 Cor 1.31; 2 Cor 10.17). They are not to work to boost their own glory or reputation but God's. Above all, they are to live lives of faith. They are to be generous in their giving, knowing that God 'scatters abroad, he gives to the poor; his righteousness endures for ever' (2 Cor 9.9 = Psalm 112.9). They are to recognize that the text which says, 'At an acceptable time I have listened to you, and on a day of salvation I have helped you' (Isa 49.8) is for them, the present moment.

All this does not mean that the Christian life is easy. Paul frequently cites his difficulties and sees them as sharing in the sufferings of Christ. In the climax of Rom 8, where he confidently asserts that 'all things work together for good for those who love God' (8.28), he nevertheless sees Psalm 44.22 ('For your sake we are being killed all day long; we are accounted as sheep to be slaughtered') as describing his lot. Indeed, the scriptures contain warnings for the early Church. The purpose of citing the 'rock' passage in 1 Cor 10 is to make the point that God punishes disobedience, both then and now. According to Paul, the wilderness generation were guilty of idolatry, sexual immorality, putting the Lord (some manuscripts have 'Christ') to the test and complaining. In an important saying for understanding Paul's use of the Old Testament, he says, 'These things happened to them to serve as an example, and they were written down to instruct us, on whom the end of the ages have come' (1 Cor 10.11).

New and old

Paul's exposition of Exod 34 in 2 Cor 3 has been the subject of a number of important studies. Paul begins by claiming that God has 'made us competent to be ministers (*diakonoi*) of a new covenant' (3.3). There then follows a series of contrasts. The old covenant 'chiselled in letters on stone tablets' kills but 'the Spirit gives life' (3.6). The old was a ministry of condemnation but the new is a ministry of justification (3.9). Moses put a veil over his face but we act with boldness (3.13). When Moses is read, a 'veil lies over their minds' but we see the glory of the Lord with 'unveiled faces' (3.18). Paul acknowledges that glory was associated with Moses and the law (vv. 7, 9, 10) but claims that this has been put in the shade by the greater glory of Christ. He justifies this with what looks like a novel reading of the Exodus story:

As he came down from the mountain with the two tablets of the covenant in his hand, Moses did not know that the skin of his face shone ... When Aaron and all the Israelites saw ... they were afraid to come near ... But Moses called to them and ... gave them in commandment all that the Lord had spoken ... When Moses had finished speaking with them, he put a veil on his face; but whenever Moses went in before the Lord to speak with him, he would take the veil off ... when he came out, and told the Israelites what he had been commanded, the Israelites would see ... the skin of his face shining; and Moses put the veil on his face again. (Exod 34.29–35 abbreviated)

Since, then, we have such a hope, we act with great boldness, not like Moses, who put a veil over his face to keep the people of Israel from gazing at the end (*telos*) of the glory that was being set aside (*katargoumenou*). But their minds were hardened. Indeed, to this very day, when they hear the reading of the old covenant, that same veil is still there, since only in Christ is it set aside. Indeed, to this very day whenever Moses is read, a veil lies over their minds; but when one turns to the Lord, the veil is removed. (2 Cor 3.12–16)

From the Exodus story, it would seem that Moses veiled himself to protect the Israelites from seeing God's glory, either because of their human frailty or their sinful state (cf. Isaiah's reaction to the throne vision in Isa 6). Paul suggests that Moses put on a veil in order to hide or obscure something. What that something was depends on the translation of the two italicized Greek words. The NIV renders *katargoumenou* as 'fading', implying that Moses veiled himself to protect the Israelites from disappointment: 'We are not like Moses, who would put a veil over his face to keep the Israelites from gazing at it while the radiance was fading away.' Belleville has a more positive explanation. She suggests it was to keep Israel from 'becoming so fascinated with the splendor of the covenant that they would obstinately fix their gaze right down to the last glimmer and thereby miss the significance of this fading' (1991, p. 295).

Hays, on the other hand, translates *katargoumenou* as 'nullified' and *telos* as 'goal'. He points out that there is nothing in the story or Jewish tradition to suggest a 'fading glory.' The glory of Moses was transitory *only* when seen in the light of the greater glory, namely, Christ. It is not a description of what was actually happening at the time. Hindsight allows Paul to understand the veiling of Moses as pointing forward to the greater revelation, of which he is a minister. Thus Hays paraphrases:

> But if the ministry of death, chiseled in stone script, came with such glory that the sons of Israel were not able to gaze upon the face of Moses because of the glory of his face (a glory now nullified in Christ), how much more will the ministry of the Spirit come with glory. (1989, p. 135)

The passage becomes even more complicated when Paul says, 'Indeed, to this very day whenever Moses is read, a veil lies over their minds; but when one turns to the Lord, the veil is removed.' Does this mean that true biblical interpretation was impossible before Christ? Some scholars avoid this conclusion by visualizing the veil as opaque and thus speak of 'obscuring' the meaning. But Belleville is more forthright. Paul is saying that their understanding 'is enveloped in an impenetrable veil of darkness' (1991, p. 296), citing 1 Cor 2.7–9 ('what no eye has seen') and Rom 16.25 ('the revelation of the mystery that was kept secret for long ages'). She notes that such a view is characteristic of the Qumran documents. For example, 4QpIsa 5.1–14 says that those in Jerusalem 'are quite oblivious to what the Lord is about, too blinded ever to see what he is actually doing.'

However, a different conclusion is possible if the phrase, 'Moses went in before the Lord' is equivalent to 'when one turns to the Lord.' Moses put on a veil in front of the people but he met with God with an unveiled face, just as Christians 'with unveiled faces, seeing the glory of the Lord ... are being transformed' (3.18). Thus Hays says that Moses is 'both the paradigm for the Christian's direct experience of the Spirit and the symbol for the old covenant to which that experience is set in antithesis' (1989, p. 144). He calls this a *dissimile* for it allows 'Paul to appropriate some of the mythical grandeur associated with the Sinai covenant – particularly the images of glory and transformation – even while he repudiates the linkage of his ministry to that covenant'

(p. 142). If Paul were asked to justify his exegesis, his answer would not be to quote exegetical rules but to point to living communities who are a 'letter of Christ, prepared by us, written not with ink but with the Spirit of the living God, not on tables of stone but on tablets of human hearts' (2 Cor 3.3). Thus according to Hays, Paul 'seems to have leaped – in moments of metaphorical insight – to intuitive apprehensions of the meanings of texts without the aid or encumbrance of systematic reflection about his own hermeneutics' (1989, p. 161).

Paul and the law

Closely connected to Paul's use of scripture is a series of studies on Paul and the law, largely initiated by the publication of *Paul and Palestinian Judaism* (1977) by E. P. Sanders (see Horrell, 2006, Ch. 6). Sanders notes that despite centuries of Christian propaganda, Jewish texts of the first century do not regard the law as a way of earning salvation. Far from it. The Jews are the people of the covenant, of whom the law is the gift of a gracious God (as in the Old Testament). Obedience to the law is a response to God's favour, not a means of earning it. And the same is true of Paul, for while he vigorously proclaims that salvation is by faith not works, he also exhorts his hearers to live lives worthy of the gospel. Indeed, he even warns that certain types of sinners will be excluded. Thus Sanders issues a challenge – either Paul has misrepresented Judaism or Christian scholars have misrepresented Paul.

Sanders' own view, articulated particularly in his later book, *Paul, the Law and the Jewish People* (1983) is that Paul gives different answers to different questions. To the question of how one joins the people of God, Paul answers, 'by faith not works of the law'. But to the question of what sort of behaviour is appropriate for the people of God, his answer is to fulfil the law, though his emphasis is more on the command to love one's neighbour (from Lev 19) than the specific requirements of circumcision and food laws. Thus for Sanders, obedience to the law is not about 'getting in' but 'staying in'. And the importance of good works for those who are 'already in' (Judaism or Christianity) is that 'great is your reward in heaven' (Matt 5.12,19; 6.4, 6,18).

Dunn congratulates Sanders on opening up a 'new perspective' on Paul but understands 'the works of the law' differently. Paul's dispute, he says, is not with Judaism as such but Jewish Christians who insist that Gentile Christians show their membership of the people of God by exhibiting the traditional 'boundary markers', namely, circumcision, food laws and the observance of special days. Thus Paul is not attacking those who think that salvation comes from keeping the law but those who insist on maintaining those aspects of the law that separate Jews from Gentiles. That is why Gal 3.10–14 ends with the words, 'in order that in Christ Jesus the blessing of Abraham might come to the Gentiles'.

This overturning of the traditional Protestant position has convinced many (see the articles on the website 'The Paul Page') but it is not without its opponents. In his book, *Paul and the Hermeneutics of Faith* (2004), Watson agrees that Judaism has been falsely caricatured as 'legalistic' but does not think that the 'New Perspective' emphasis on continuity is the answer. Paul clearly thinks that there is a dichotomy between faith and works ('But the law does not rest on faith' – Gal 3:12) but this is not his own invention. It lies at the heart of the Old Testament itself, for some texts focus on God's covenant faithfulness, while other texts focus on the necessity of Israel's obedience. Paul did not impose this dichotomy on the Old Testament but drew on it to explain the difference between faith in Christ and continuing to follow the Jewish law. In terms of Jewish tradition, it is a radical interpretation but one that attends very closely to the contours of scripture:

> Paul practices a consecutive reading of his texts from Leviticus and Deuteronomy, in which the latter effectively cancels out the former. In doing so, he identifies a severe internal tension within the crucial closing chapters of Deuteronomy: the tension between conditional statements, which imply that the choice between blessing and curse, life and death is genuinely open, and statements of prophetic denunciation, in which the realization of the curse has become a certainty. (2004, p. 429)

Colossians, Ephesians and the Pastoral Epistles

For a variety of reasons (see Horrell, 2006, Ch. 8), many scholars do not think some or all of these epistles come directly from the Apostle. In particular, the Pastoral Epistles (1 and 2 Timothy, Titus) are widely regarded as post-Pauline, written in Paul's name for a much later situation (perhaps incorporating some genuine fragments). Colossians contains no explicit quotations though Beetham finds a number of significant allusions. For example, the hymn of Col 1.15–20 draws on Gen 1.26 (image of God), Psalm 68.16 (God pleased to dwell), Psalm 89.27 (firstborn) and Prov 8.22–27 (creation through an agent): 'The rhetorical aim of this exalted portrayal was to strengthen the confidence of the Colossians in Christ's sufficiency as God's revelation, in his preeminence over the spirit world, and in his superiority over anything the false "philosophy" could offer, so that they would entrust themselves to him alone' (Beetham, 2008, p. 156). The error of the Colossians is that they are following 'human commands and teachings' (2.22), an allusion to Isa 29.13 (LXX), which is explicitly quoted in Mark 7.7/Matt 15.9. A more puzzling allusion is detected by Beale (2007, p. 868) in Col 4.5 ('Conduct yourselves wisely toward outsiders, making the most of the time'). The last phrase is literally 'buying back the time' (using the verb *exagorazo* and the noun *kairos*), a combination which only occurs in the LXX at Dan 2.8. However, the contexts are very different (in Daniel the king is accusing the soothsayers of 'trying to gain time') and it may be that the author of Colossians (Beale and Beetham think it is Paul) simply liked the phrase.

The use of the Old Testament in Ephesians has a number of interesting features. For example, all the explicit quotations occur in the latter half of the letter (4.8; 5.31; 6.3), along with what are probably the clearest allusions (Zech 8.16 in 4.25; Psalm 4.4 in 4.26). Indeed, the author says in 3.5–9 that the inclusion of the Gentiles is a 'mystery' that has been hidden in times past and only now revealed to the apostles and prophets. In Romans and Galatians, Paul goes to great lengths to show that the Old Testament prophets *did* know about the inclusion of the Gentiles and is one reason why some scholars doubt the Pauline authorship of the letter. It is also why some scholars have questioned whether the Old Testament plays a significant role in Ephesians. After all, the quotations at 5.31 and 6.3 are simply reminders of the law concerning marriage (Gen 2.24) and the duty of children to obey parents (Exod 20.12) and the quotation in 4.8 (Psalm 68.18) has been so rewritten as to say something quite different from its original meaning. A case can be made that Ephesians is a freestanding theological discourse that is only minimally influenced by the Old Testament.

On the other hand, others have argued that there are significant allusions in Eph 1–3 and the author appears to be deliberately expanding sections of Colossians by including biblical material. For example, the claims in 1.20 ('God put this power to work in Christ when he raised him from the dead and *seated him at his right hand* in the heavenly places') and 1.22 ('And he has *put all things under his feet*') are clearly allusions to Psalm 110.1 and Psalm 8.6 respectively. It could be argued that the author is simply drawing on Christian tradition (1 Cor 15.25–27; Heb 1.3,13; 2.6–8; 1 Pet 3.22) but Thorsten Moritz (2004, p. 187) sees this as 'one of a number of passages where Ephesians goes well beyond Colossians in underpinning a major theological argument by appealing to a crucial Old Testament precedent'.

Frank Thielman (2007, pp. 817–18) sees an allusion to Isa 57.19 ('Peace, peace, to the far and the near') in Eph 2.17 ('So he came and proclaimed *peace* to you who were *far* off and peace to those who were *near*'). Indeed, the proclamation of peace is probably an allusion to Isa 52.7 ('How beautiful upon the mountains are the feet of the messenger who *announces peace*'), a text that Paul quotes in Rom 10.15. If this is accepted, then it is likely that the earlier statement in Eph 2.13 ('But now in Christ Jesus you who once were *far* off have been brought *near* by the blood of Christ') is an echo of Isa 57.19, preparing for the fuller allusion in 2.17. This at least offers a caution before concluding that the Old Testament is not a significant influence in Ephesians.

We thus come to the extremely difficult quotation of Psalm 68.18 in Eph 4.8. Paul wishes to assert that Christ has given gifts to his church so that 'some would be apostles, some prophets, some evangelists, some pastors and teachers, to equip the saints for the work of ministry, for building up the body of Christ' (4.11–12). He supports this by a quotation which appears to be taken from Psalm 68.18, though there are significant differences:

You ascended the high mount, leading captives in your train and *receiving gifts* from people, even from those who rebel against the Lord God's abiding there. (Psalm 68.18)

When he ascended on high he made captivity itself captive; he *gave gifts* to his people' (Eph 4.8).

The author follows the rather literal rendering of the LXX ('captivity itself captive') but changes to the third person ('he ascended') and reverses the direction of the giving. The Greek and Hebrew both speak of *receiving* gifts whereas Ephesians speaks of *giving* gifts. Solutions fall broadly into three categories: (1) Readers would know the Jewish tradition that associates Psalm 68 with the receiving of the Torah by Moses and by implication (explicit in the Targum), his giving of it to the Israelites; (2) Readers would know from the impersonal introductory formula ('Therefore *it* says') that this is not intended to be an exact quotation but a Christian reflection (the same formula introduces the words, 'Sleeper, awake! Rise from the dead, and Christ will shine on you' in 5.14); (3) Readers would understand it as a deliberate change in order to make a Christological point. Moritz (2004, p. 194) attempts to do justice to all three solutions when he says:

The point of 4:9f is to remind the implied Christian audience of their common descent-ascent Christology, but to do so in a way which tacitly brings out Christ's superiority over the Law of Moses. This is done not by interpreting Psalm 68 itself, but by utilizing an early Christian tradition which polemically emulates the Jewish reinterpretation of Psalm 68 in the context of Jewish Pentecost.

In short, the author's 'misuse' of the Psalm is a deliberate polemic against the Jewish 'misuse' of it and it is not a Christological interpretation of the actual words of the Psalm.

There are only two explicit quotations in the Pastoral epistles. In 1 Tim 5.18–19, the text, 'You shall not muzzle an ox while it is treading out the grain' (Deut 25.4) is quoted with respect to Christian workers (as in 1 Cor 9.9) and combined with what appear to be a saying of Jesus, 'The labourer deserves to be paid' (cf. Matt 10.10). The quotation of Deut 25.4 is often cited as an example of a New Testament author taking a text out of context, either because there is no intrinsic link between care for oxen and payment of Christian ministers or because it is drawing on Christian tradition – though probably not the actual text of 1 Cor 9.9, which uses a different verb for 'muzzle'. Others note that Jewish tradition also expands the reference, so that God's concern for oxen becomes God's concern for humanity and according to Philip Towner (2007), it is not an enormous step to apply it to Christian ministers.

In the following verse, the author offers another admonition: 'Never accept any accusation against an elder except on the evidence of two or three witnesses' (5.19). This ultimately goes back to Old Testament law (Deut 19.5; cf. Deut 17.6; Num 35.30) but the principle is well known in the New Testament (Matt 18.19–20; John 8.17; cf. Heb 6.18; Rev 11.3–4) and it is likely that the author is simply drawing on this, rather than expecting readers to consult the Old Testament relevant passages (Häfner, 2007, pp. 144–47).

The second quotation occurs in 2 Tim 2.19: 'But God's firm foundation stands, bearing this inscription: "The Lord knows those who are his," and, "Let everyone who calls on the name of the Lord turn away from wickedness." The first phrase could be an echo of the famous stone passage in Isa 28.16 ('See, I am laying in Zion a foundation stone, a tested stone, a precious cornerstone, a sure foundation'), which is quoted in Rom 9.33 and 1 Pet 2.6. The assertion that 'The Lord knows who are his' is generally recognised as a quotation of Num 16.5 because of the parallel contexts (rebels leading God's people astray) and the close agreement with the language of the LXX. Towner says (2007, pp. 904–5): 'The OT story serves as a paradigm that acknowledges the rebellion of some within the church and God's continued presence within it; however, the statement is both a consolation and a warning that God will distinguish between those who are his and those who are not.' The final phrase ('Let everyone who calls on the name of the Lord') could have many sources and is indeed common in the New Testament (Acts 2.21; Rom 10.13; 1 Cor 1.2). However, the Greek is more literally 'naming the name of the Lord' and probably points to the LXX of Isa 26.13, which literally translated says: 'O Lord our God, take possession of us: O Lord, we know not any other beside you: we name your name'.

Towner discusses a number of other allusions from 1 Timothy (2.5; 2.8; 2.13–14; 4.3–4; 6.1), 2 Timothy (2.7; 3.8, 11, 15; 4.8, 14, 16–18) and Titus (2.14; 3.4–6), which we do not have space to discuss, but one passage has become notorious:

> I permit no woman to teach or to have authority over a man; she is to keep silent. For Adam was formed first, then Eve; and Adam was not deceived, but the woman was deceived and became a transgressor. Yet she will be saved through childbearing, provided they continue in faith and love and holiness, with modesty. (1 Tim 2.12–15)

The surprise here is not so much the command to silence, which we find in 1 Cor 14.34, or the tradition that Eve was deceived, which occurs in 2 Cor 11.3, but the apparent exoneration of Adam. In Rom 5, Paul contrasts the effects of Adam's disobedience with the effects of Christ's obedience by repeatedly stressing Adam's role ('by the trespass of the one man'; 'the result of one man's sin'; 'disobedience of the one man'). For Houlden, it is further evidence that Paul did not write the Pastoral epistles and is indeed 'another example of the relative theological shallowness of our writer' (1976, p. 72). Other scholars have tried to understand the passage (all regard the phrase about being saved through childbearing as obscure) by suggesting that the author is combating the practice of certain women who were ignoring authority and being disrespectful to men and were justifying this by claiming that Christianity had made the Genesis stories redundant. In response, the author suggests that such women are deceived, just as Eve was deceived.

Also of interest is the mention of Jannes and Jambres opposing Moses in 2 Tim 3.8. This is not recorded in the canonical scriptures but there is a reference in the Qumran literature (CD 5.19) to Satan raising up 'Jannes and his brother' to oppose Moses and Aaron. This legend is greatly elaborated in later rabbinic writings and the author can apparently assume that it was well known among his readers.

Conclusion

It will be apparent that we have been able to give a substantial account of Paul's theology by summarizing his use of scripture. Romans has the greatest density of quotations (60 in 16 chapters) in the New Testament and is especially important for understanding Paul's thought. Paul focuses on Adam, Abraham and Moses to articulate the divine plan to include Gentiles into the people of God. How this was accomplished is argued in such passages as Gal 3.10–14 and Rom 3.21–26 and the relationship between new and old in Rom 9–11 and 2 Cor 3. Also important are the themes of exile and restoration from the book of Isaiah. As Ross Wagner (2002, p. 41) says:

> By adopting as his own the stories Isaiah and his fellow scriptural witnesses tell about God's unquenchable love for his people, Paul is able to maintain confidently that the God who is now embracing Gentiles as his own will be faithful to redeem and restore his covenant people Israel as well, so that Jew and Gentile can with one voice laud the incomparable mercy of their God.

We have seen that Paul uses many of the techniques found at Qumran, such as typology, allegory, catch-word links, altering texts, reading texts in an unusual manner and borrowing from Jewish *haggada* legends. However, it is unclear whether this actually 'explains'

Paul's use of scripture or merely shows that he was a first century Jew. Hays, for example, argues that Paul did not set out to 'apply' exegetical techniques but grasped the meaning of texts with intuitive leaps. Watson thinks that Paul has discerned a fundamental antithesis in scripture between conditional and unconditional promises and uses it to explain the current situation. Contrary to most 'New Perspective' scholars (Sanders, Dunn, Wright, Hays), Watson does not think that a focus on 'continuity' (understandable in the light of past carica-tures) should mask the very real differences between Paul and his contemporaries. Finally, Stanley's work highlights a key dilemma in Pauline scholarship: should Paul be seen primarily as an exegete or an apologist? In other words, is he more influenced by the rhetorical needs of his readers or the main themes of scripture? Most scholars suggest that the interaction is mutual (scripture sheds light on the present just as the present sheds light on scripture) and some use literary terms like 'intertextuality' to describe this (see Moyise, 2008, pp. 125–41). However, it remains a debate as to which is dominant in any particular instance.

Further reading

Since Paul's letters occupy nearly a quarter of the New Testament, there is a vast literature that is either explicitly about Paul's use of scripture or makes a significant contribution to particular passages (e.g. major commentaries). For a brief summary of this literature and key themes, see my *Paul and Scripture* (2010). If Sanders (1977) initiated a fresh look at Paul's relationship with the law, Hays (1989) initiated a fresh look at Paul's use of scripture and is fundamental to what has followed. Particular works that acknowledge their debt to Hays are Roy Ciampa's, *The Presence of and Function of Scripture in Galatians 1 and 2* (1998), Sylvia Keesmaat's, *Paul and his Story: (Re)Interpreting the Exodus Tradition* (1999), Timothy Berkeley's, *From a Broken Covenant to Circumcision of the Heart. Pauline Intertextual Exegesis in Romans 2.17–29* (2000), Ross Wagner's, *Heralds of the Good News: Isaiah and Paul 'In Concert' in the Letter to the Romans* (2002) and Douglas Campbell's *The Deliverance of God: An Apocalyptic Rereading of Justification in Paul* (2009). Hays has also written a further book and the title captures his approach: *The Conversion of the Imagination: Paul as Interpreter of Israel's Scripture* (2005). We have already noted Stanley's rhetorical approach (*Arguing with Scripture: The Rhetoric of Quotations in the Letters of Paul* – 2004) and we should also mention John Paul Heil's, *The Rhetorical Role of Scripture in 1 Corinthians* (2005). The most significant book of the last decade must go to Francis Watson's, *Paul and the Hermeneutics of Faith* (2004) and perhaps the most significant commentary is Anthony Thiselton on 1 Corinthians (2000). What promises to be the most significant book of this decade is Tom Wright's *Paul and the Faithfulness of God* (2013), which runs to 1658 pages.

8

The Old Testament in Hebrews

Introduction

The Letter to the Hebrews contains around 36 explicit quotations, drawn mainly from the Psalms (14) and the Pentateuch (13), with comparatively few from the Prophets (5). In the light of the rest of the New Testament, it is surprising that there is only one quotation from Isaiah, albeit split into two (Isa 8.17–18/Heb 2.13). The author is particularly fond of using quotations in pairs: 1.5–6 (Psalm 2.7/2 Sam 7.14); 1.8–12 (Psalm 45.6–7/Psalm 102.25–27); 2.12–13 (Psalm 22.22/ Isa 8.17–18); 5.5–6 (Psalm 2.7/Psalm 110.4); 13.5–6 (Deut 31.6, 8/ Psalm 118.6), perhaps because of the biblical principle of confirming a case with two witnesses (Deut 19.5). Other quotations are closely linked in his exegesis ('subjection' in Psalm 110.1 and Psalm 8.6; 'rest' in Psalm 95.11 and God 'resting' in Gen 2.2; 'divine appointment' in Psalm 2.7 and Psalm 110.4). Gert Steyn (2010, pp. 25–27) extends this pattern to cover all of the quotations (omitting texts that occur more than once) and finds fourteen pairs. If this is correct, it is interesting that the first seven pairs begin with a Psalm (1.5; 1.6 [text uncertain]; 1.7; 1.13; 2.12; 3.7; 5.5), while the latter seven begin with a text from the Pentateuch (6.13; 8.5; 9.20; 10.30; 11.18; 12.21; 13.5). However, the repetitions of Psalms 2, 95, 110 and Jer 31, the extended discussion of Melchizedek in Chapter 7, and the heroes of faith in Chapter 11, make it difficult to believe that the author intended his readers to discern this pattern, though it may be evidence of an earlier source.

God has spoken

> Long ago God spoke to our ancestors in many (*polumeros*) and various
> (*polutropos*) ways by the prophets, but in these last days he has spoken
> to us by a Son. (Heb 1.1–2a)

For Graham Hughes, this opening sentence is the key to the author's
use of scripture, affirming as it does, both continuity and discontinuity.
The subject matter is God's word, for God spoke to Israel in the past
and he speaks to the Church now. It is the same God, the same voice
that offers promise, rebuke, guidance and challenge. Frequently in this
letter the author (who is not named and remains unknown) invites
his readers to see their situation as parallel to that of the Israelites.
Heb 11 lists a 'cloud of witnesses' who by their faith 'conquered
kingdoms, administered justice, obtained promises' (11.33). But there
is also contrast. The word spoken 'by the prophets' is contrasted with
the word spoken 'by a Son'. The adverb *polumeros* is better translated
'fragmentary' (so NEB). As our author will go on to show, some of the
words belonging to the old covenant are now redundant 'because it was
weak and ineffectual' (7.18). Hughes says:

> the revelation of the Word of God is seen as a continuous activity,
> stretching right across the boundaries of its various economies, and
> binding the members of the covenants into a single history of salvation.
> At the same time it is abundantly clear that in its dispensation through
> the Son it has achieved a clarity and finality not possible for those who
> received it through Moses. (1979, p. 12).

The catena of 1.5–14

It would appear that the purpose of this collection of seven quotations
is to support the view announced in 1.4, that Jesus is superior to the
angels. He does this in three ways. In 1.5–6 and 1.13, he asks rhetori-
cally whether God ever said to an angel such exalted things as Psalm
2.7, 2 Sam 7.14, Deut 32.43 and Psalm 110.1. In 1.8–12, he quotes
Psalm 45.6–7 ('Your throne, O God, is for ever and ever') and Psalm

102.25–27 ('In the beginning, Lord, you founded the earth') and claims that they are addressed to the Son. Finally, in 1.7, he quotes Psalm 104.4 to show that angels are simply God's messengers, concluding the collection with the rhetorical question, 'Are not all angels spirits in the divine service, sent to serve for the sake of those who are to inherit salvation?' (1.14) Herbert Bateman (1997, p. 241) thinks the catena revolves around the twin themes of Jesus as Davidic King and Jesus as God, forming a conceptual chiasm:

A The Son's Status as Davidic King (1.5)
  B The Son's Status as God (1.6–7)
    C The Son's Status as Divine Davidic King (1.8–9)
  B' The Son's Status as God (1.10–12)
A' The Son's Status as Davidic King (1.13–14)

As Bateman demonstrates, the author's exegesis has parallels in rabbinic and Qumran literature but it does raise a number of issues. First, the point that God has never used such exalted language of angels would appear to be contradicted by Gen 6.2, where they are called 'sons of God', and Psalm 82.6, where they are called 'gods' (the verse quoted in John 10.34). However, it is the case that no *individual* angel is ever called 'Son' or 'God'. Second, on any straight-forward reading of Psalm 104.4, the Psalmist is clearly addressing God ('you founded the earth') not Jesus. Similarly, Psalm 45 specifically states, 'I address my verses to the king', which is confirmed by the next line, 'You are the most handsome of men.' How then can the author claim that these verses are addressed to the Son? Indeed, the only quotation that specifically compares the Son with angels ('Let all God's angels worship him') is not only missing from the Hebrew text of Deut 32.43 but reads in the LXX, 'Let all sons of God worship him'. It is not a problem taking 'sons of God' to mean 'angels' and the author might have been influenced by Psalm 97.7, where the Hebrew ('worship him, all gods') was rendered by the LXX, 'worship him, all angels'. But the 'him' of both Deut 32.43 and Psalm 97.7 refers to God, not the Son.

One explanation is that the author of Hebrews did not select these texts for himself but used an already existing collection. Hugh Montefiore (1964) thought the collection was obviously designed for another purpose since it only mentions 'angels' in passing. He thinks that purpose was to illustrate the various stages of Christ's life. Thus it begins with testimonies to his pre-existence and eternity (Psalm 2; 2 Sam 7). It then moves to his incarnation (Deut 34), baptism (Psalm 45 speaks of 'anointing') and resurrection (Psalm 104 speaks of his 'indestructibility'), concluding with the Church's standard proof-text for the ascension, Psalm 110 ('Sit at my right hand until I make your enemies a footstool for your feet.') Few have found this convincing, though Harold Attridge (1989, pp. 50–51) is open to the possibility that some of these texts might have been linked prior to the writing of Hebrews.

Susan Docherty notes that the rabbis were often drawn to texts which contained first person speech, especially if the speaker was not named. Thus the debate in Mark 12.35–37 about the identity of 'the Lord' in the opening words of Psalm 110.1 ('The Lord said to my Lord') is quite plausible in a Jewish setting and is not necessarily a case of imposing a Christological interpretation (there is no attempt to identify Jesus as the 'Lord' of the psalm). Similarly, the identity of the 'son' addressed in Psalm 2 or the 'king' addressed as God in Psalm 45 are genuine exegetical questions. The frequency of first person speech in the Psalms is probably why they figure so much in Hebrews and it is likely that the author understood them as divine speech between Father and Son. Paradoxically to us, the author appears to believe that texts can be 'excerpted from their context' and read in isolation, as well as being part of an interconnected whole, so that the links created between 'originally separate and independent passages of scripture' can speak in unison:

> The author of Hebrews as much as any ancient Jewish exegete … regarded it as legitimate interpretation to seek out what scriptural texts imply as much as what they actually say, presumably believing

that the new meaning he gave them was inherent in the original revelation, which he regarded as having endless depths of meaning and real contemporary relevance. (2009, p. 181).

Hughes thinks there is more to the catena than simply showing that the Son is greater than the angels. The readers already believe that Jesus is God's Son (Psalm 2; 2 Sam 7) and seated at his right hand (Psalm 110) and so can hardly think that he is less than the angels. Rather, the point is that Jewish tradition held that the law was delivered via angels (Gal 3.19; Acts 7.53) and so the author is supporting his statement in 1.1–2, that the revelation that comes through Jesus is superior to the revelation that came through the law. That is why he goes on to argue that Jesus is superior to Moses (the human agent of the law) and the priesthood (the system prescribed by the law), which would have been obvious if Jesus is divine.

Psalm 8.4–6 in 2.6–8

If the quotations in Chapter 1 are largely illustrative, our author seems to feel that Psalm 8.4–6 needs careful exposition. A footnote in the NRSV tells us that the Hebrew of the psalm uses 'man' and 'son of man' generically of all humankind, and so translates Heb 2.6–8 as:

What are human beings that you are mindful of them,
or mortals, that you care for them?
You have made them for a little while lower than the angels;
you have crowned them with glory and honour,
subjecting all things under their feet.

Read like this, the psalm states that though human beings are lower than the angels 'for a little while', God has bestowed on them 'glory and honour' and given them dominion (perhaps a reference to Gen 1.28). The exposition would then mean that while we do not yet see everything in subjection to humanity at present, we do see Jesus, who had to become human like us in order to be our high priest and offer a sacrifice for our sins. Thus it offers a rationale for why Christ was made lower than the angels 'for a little while'. This is the anthropological interpretation. Alternatively, it may be that the author did not read the psalm generically but as directly speaking about Christ. Thus the NIV translates Heb 2.6–8 as follows:

> What is *man* that you are mindful of *him*,
> the *son of man* that you care for *him*?
> You made *him* a little lower than the angels;
> you crowned *him* with glory and honour
> and put everything under *his* feet.

There is debate as to whether readers would have linked 'son of man' with the title used in the Gospels, especially as the Greek lacks the definite article ('the'), but the important point is the use of the singular. Having just been told that the promise of subjection of enemies (underfoot) in Psalm 110.1 has never been applied to an angel but (by implication) to the son, why would the author now wish to state that subjection (underfoot) was in fact given to humankind at creation? It seems more likely that readers would assume that the 'man'/'him' of the psalm is also a reference to the son, especially as the words, 'You made him a little lower than angels', could easily be taken as a reference to the incarnation. Thus according to George Guthrie, what we have here is a classic example of rabbinic exegesis where two texts that appear to contradict one another are resolved: Psalm 110.1 says that the subjugation of the Messiah's enemies is in the future, while Psalm 8.4–6 says it is a present fact (2007, p. 946). They are resolved in what follows:

> Yet at present we do not see everything subject to him. But we see Jesus, who was made a little lower than the angels, *now crowned with glory and honour* because he suffered death, so that by the grace of God he might taste death for everyone. (Heb 2.8–9 NIV)

The quoted text differs from the Hebrew in two important ways. First, the Hebrew says that humanity has been made lower than God (*elohim*) but our author quotes from the LXX, which says 'lower than angels', presumably because it took *elohim* to be a genuine plural ('gods') and then interpreted it as 'higher beings'. Second, the Hebrew text means 'a little lower', not 'for a little while'. The LXX rendered 'a little lower' by *brachu ti*, which opens up the possibility of a temporal contrast. Many commentators, therefore, argue that the author of Hebrews takes his quotations from a Greek translation similar to the LXX and shows little, if any, knowledge of the Hebrew text. The identification between Jesus and humanity is further supported by quotations from Psalm 22.22 ('I will proclaim your name to my brothers and sisters') and Isa 8.17–18 ('Here am I and the children whom God has given me'). This close connection between Jesus and humanity perhaps suggests that the anthropological and Christological interpretations of Psalm 8 are not necessarily mutually exclusive.

Psalm 95.7–11 in 3.7–11

Chapter 3 opens with a paragraph that begins with a parallel between Jesus and Moses (they were both faithful over God's house) followed by a contrast ('Jesus is worthy of more glory than Moses'). The passage draws on Num 12.6–8, where God rebukes Aaron and Miriam for criticizing Moses, declaring that 'my servant Moses ... is entrusted with all my house. With him I speak face to face – clearly, not in riddles; and he beholds the form (LXX 'glory') of the LORD'. The author does not wish to denigrate Moses (see Heb 11.23–28) but as in Heb 1.1–4, he sets up a contrast: Moses was God's servant, Jesus is God's son. He is thus worthy of more glory – perhaps suggesting that Moses only *beheld* God's glory whereas Jesus *shares* it (Heb 1.3).

There then follows a quotation from Psalm 95 concerning the rebellion of the wilderness generation, ending with God's pronouncement that, 'They will not enter my rest'. This is used as a warning to the readers, repeating key parts from the psalm, such as, 'Today, if you hear my voice, do not harden your hearts as in the rebellion' (3.14; 4.7). The threat is that since the 'good news came to us just as to them' (4.2) and the wilderness generation fell through disobedience and unbelief (3.17–19), then the same could happen to the readers. But there is also the promise of rest. This is brought out by the connection between the 'rest' (*katapausin*) of Psalm 95 and God's 'resting' (*katepausen*) on the seventh day in the creation story (Gen 2.2). As well as the similarity of the Greek words (the Hebrew is quite different), it may be that Psalm 95 suggested a connection with the Sabbath because it was read in the light of the title given to Psalm 92 ('A Song for the Sabbath Day'). The 'rest' was not fulfilled in the conquest of Canaan since the psalm was spoken 'through David much later' (4.7). The author of Hebrews concludes:

> So then, a sabbath rest still remains for the people of God; for those who enter God's rest also cease from their labours as God did from his. Let us therefore make every effort to enter that rest, so that no one may fall through such disobedience as theirs. (4.9–11)

Melchizedek in 5.5–7.28

Chapter 4 ends with an exhortation to approach the throne of grace with boldness because Jesus is their high priest and fully understands the situation. High priests do not take this role upon themselves and neither did Jesus. He was called by God in the words of Psalm 2.7 ('You are my Son, today I have begotten you') and Psalm 110.4 ('You are a priest for ever, according to the order of Melchizedek'). The phrase immediately before this ('The Lord has sworn and will not change his mind') is not quoted until 7.20 but is anticipated in 6.13–20. When human beings utter an oath, they swear by one greater than themselves, namely God. But when God utters an oath, he can only swear by himself, as when he said to Abraham, 'I will surely bless you and multiply you' (6.14). Chapter 7 is then an exposition of the meeting between Abraham and Melchizedek (Gen 14) and its implications for an alternative priesthood.

The exposition makes the following points. First, as is frequent in Jewish exegesis, etymology is used to give meaning to names and titles. Melchizedek comes from two words, *melek* meaning 'king' and *sedek* meaning 'righteousness'; Gen 14.18 also calls him king of 'Salem', which means 'peace'. Surprisingly, no further use is made of these derivations. Second, since in Gen 14, Melchizedek simply appears on the scene and then disappears, our author draws the conclusion that, 'Without father, without mother, without genealogy, having neither beginning of days nor end of life, but resembling the Son of God, he remains a priest for ever' (7.3). It is not quite clear if this is a claim to pre-existence but it is certainly a claim to an everlasting priesthood. Third, the story of Abraham giving Melchizedek a tenth of his belongings is linked to the regulation that the levitical priests are to receive a tithe. The argument is as follows: (1) Abraham's gifts to Melchizedek were the equivalent of paying tithes; (2) Levi paid tithes to Melchizedek because Levi was in a sense 'in the loins of his ancestor' at the time; (3) Scripture therefore knows of two priesthoods; (4) Jesus belongs to the priesthood of Melchizedek since he was manifestly not of the tribe of Levi. This is somewhat different from Paul's Adam typology since the author's main point is not that Christ supersedes or undoes the work of Melchizedek but that he belongs to the same order. Paul Ellingworth calls Melchizedek an 'anti-antitype', since like Jesus, he also 'has no place in the levitical system' (1993, p. 49).

What are we to make of this exegesis? At first sight it seems fanciful and unconvincing but two factors should be borne in mind. First, as demonstrated by Bateman, the techniques can easily be paralleled in the Qumran literature and later rabbinic exegesis. They might not have agreed with his conclusions but they would not have despised his methods. Second, we know from the Qumran literature (and *1 Enoch*) that the figure of Melchizedek was already a subject of speculation. As we saw in Chapter 2, the Qumran document known as 11QMelch speaks of Melchizedek as a heavenly figure who acts as judge at the end times and by association with Psalm 82.1, is even called *elohim*.

For this is the moment of the Year of Grace for Melchizedek. [And h]e will, by his strength, judge the holy ones of God, executing judgement as it is written concerning him in the Songs of David, who said,

'*Elohim has taken his place in the divine council; in the midst of the gods he holds judgement.*' (11QMelch 9–10)

Psalm 110 in Hebrews

It is clear that Psalm 110.1 and 4 play a pivotal role in Hebrews. The first verse is quoted or alluded to in Chapters 1, 2, 8, 10 and 12, while the fourth verse appears in Chapters 2, 3, 5, 6, 7, and 10. This led George Buchanan (1972) to suggest that the whole of Hebrews is in fact a Christian homily based on Psalm 110, with the other quotations used to explain or clarify its meaning. The weakness of this view is that the author appears to show no interest in the intervening verses (italics):

¹The LORD says to my lord,
'Sit at my right hand until I make your enemies your footstool.'
²*The LORD sends out from Zion your mighty scepter.*
Rule in the midst of your foes.
³*Your people will offer themselves willingly*
on the day you lead your forces on the holy mountains.
From the womb of the morning, like dew, your youth will come to you.
⁴The LORD has sworn and will not change his mind,
'You are a priest for ever according to the order of Melchizedek.'
⁵*The Lord is at your right hand; he will shatter kings on the day of his wrath.*
⁶*He will execute judgment among the nations, filling them with corpses;*
he will shatter heads over the wide earth.
⁷*He will drink from the stream by the path;*
therefore he will lift up his head. (Psalm 110)

However, Gert Jordaan and Pieter Nel (2010, pp. 229–40) argue that the *themes* of the intervening verses are 'victory on the day of battle' (vv. 2–3) and 'victory on the day of wrath' (vv. 5–7) and these can be correlated with Heb 2–4 and 8–10 respectively, leading to the following structure of Hebrews:

Jesus the appointed King superior even to angels (1)
Jesus in battle for the eternal rest of believers (2–4)

Jesus appointed as Priest-King for ever (5–7)
Jesus the atonement for God's wrath to believers (8–10)
Jesus the victorious King-Priest in glory (11–12)

It is by no means impossible that the military imagery of the psalm would have been interpreted as Christ's victory through his death and exaltation but it does not answer why there are around 20 recognizable references to Psalm 110.1 and 4 but none to the rest of the psalm. It seems more likely that Hebrews draws on these two verses, just as he draws on specific verses from Psalms 2, 8, 22, 40, 45, 95 and 104.

Jer 31.31–34 in 8.8–12 and 10.16–17

This is the longest quotation in the New Testament (131 words). Because Jesus is a priest for ever and is 'seated at the right hand of the throne of the Majesty in the heavens' (8.1), he is the mediator of a better covenant. Why do we need a better covenant? Because Israel did not continue in the old and so God promised a new one through Jeremiah:

> This is the covenant that I will make with the house of Israel after those days, says the Lord: I will put my laws in their minds, and write them on their hearts, and I will be their God, and they shall be my people. And they shall not teach one another or say to each other, 'Know the Lord,' for they shall all know me, from the least of them to the greatest. For I will be merciful toward their iniquities, and I will remember their sins no more. (Heb 8.10–12)

This is not interpreted immediately, except to say that talk of a 'new covenant' implies the previous one is 'obsolete' (8.13). What the author wants to say is that this promised forgiveness comes through the sacrificial death of Christ. But before he can do that, he needs to establish that, although 'without the shedding of blood there is no forgiveness of sins' (9.22), 'it is impossible for the blood of bulls and goats to take away sins' (10.4). Having done that, he can then assert that Christ has 'offered for all time a single sacrifice for sins' (10.12) and hence the prophecy of Jer 31 (which is substantially repeated in 10.16–17) has been fulfilled.

According to Paul, Jesus spoke of a 'new covenant' at the last supper (1 Cor 11.25; cf. Luke 22.20) and there are possible allusions to Jer 31.31–34 in 2 Cor 3.6 ('who has made us competent to be ministers of a *new covenant*') and Rom 11.27 ('And this is my *covenant* with them, *when I take away their sins*'). But it does not appear to be present in Mark's version of the supper ('This is my blood of the covenant, which is poured out for many') and is not picked up in the rest of the New Testament. Thus like his use of Psalm 110.4, the author of Hebrews appears to draw on early Christian tradition and then take it in new directions. He is both a traditionalist and an innovator.

The word 'covenant' (*diatheke*) occurs 33 times in the New Testament, 17 of them in Hebrews (14 in Chapters 8–10). Ellingworth (1993, p. 413) points out that there is a parallel here with the way that the author deals with the theme of Christ's high priesthood, for he first introduces it in passing, then quotes the key text, confirms it with other texts, discusses its exegesis in detail and then applies it to his readers:

	The Priesthood	The Covenant
Introduced in passing	2.17	7.22
Supported by an OT text	5.6	8.8–12
Confirmed by further texts	7.1f.	9.20; 10.5–7
Discussed in detail	7.15–25	10.11–18
Applied to the readers	7.26–8.2	10.19–39

Psalm 40.6–8 in 10.5–7

That sacrifices and offerings are to come to an end is confirmed by deduction and quotation. For the author, the sheer repetition of the sacrifices is itself a sign that they are unable to 'make perfect those who approach' (Heb 10.1) for 'every priest stands day after day at his service, offering again and again the same sacrifices that can never take away sins' (Heb 10.11). Indeed, the very details of the tabernacle, where Moses was instructed to make everything according to the 'pattern' (*typos*) of what he was shown, indicates that something better was to come. Drawing on ideas found in Philo (and Plato), the earthly tabernacle is but a 'sketch' or 'shadow' of the heavenly reality (Heb 8.5), just as the law is only a 'shadow of the good things to come and not the true form of these realities' (Heb 10.1). It is because Christ's sacrifice took place in a *heavenly* sanctuary that it can have eternal consequences. The transitory nature of the sacrificial system is also confirmed by a quotation from Psalm 40.6–8 in the form:

> Sacrifices and offerings you have not desired,
> but a *body you have prepared for me*;
> in burnt offerings and sin offerings you have taken no pleasure.
> Then I said, 'See, God, I have come to do your will, O God'
> (in the scroll of the book it is written of me).' (Heb 10.5–7)

The author of the psalm claims in v. 8, 'I delight to do your will, O my God; your law is within my heart,' which might explain the link with Jer 31. In addition, v. 9 ('I have told the glad news of deliverance in the great congregation') is close to the quotation of Psalm 22.22 in Heb 2.12 ('I will proclaim your name to my brothers and sisters, in the midst of the congregation I will praise you'). Once again we have an example of first-person speech understood as words between Christ and God. Martin Karrer not only sees this as an important exegetical principle but also a contrast with the Gospels: 'the Jesus of Hebrews differs in a double sense from the Jesus of the gospels. He speaks only words of scripture ... and he speaks these words relating to his pre-existence' (2010, p. 130).

There is a textual conundrum in the quotation. According to the NRSV, Psalm 40.6 makes no mention of a 'prepared body' but reads: 'Sacrifice and offering you do not desire, but you have given me an *open ear*'. The last phrase translates two Hebrew words, the noun 'ears' and the verb 'dug out', a graphic description of 'unblocked ears', presumably referring to ears that are 'open' or 'attentive'. However, it is likely that the author is simply following the LXX text before him, which also reads 'body' (now confirmed by the discovery of Bodmer Papyrus 24), either through a misreading of the Hebrew text or more likely, a deliberate interpretation where a part of something ('ears') is taken as a reference to the whole ('body'). It has to be said that the author's aim is not primarily to offer a proof-text for the incarnation but to show that the sacrifices offered 'again and again … can never take away sins' (Heb 10.11). But he does draw on the word 'body' when he says: 'And it is by God's will that we have been sanctified through the offering of the *body* of Jesus Christ once for all' (Heb 10.10). If the author of Hebrews was aware that this differs from the Hebrew text, he would probably have concluded that the LXX was the first stage in making clear the true meaning of the text.

Hab 2.3–4 in 10.37–38

In Hab 2, God promises a vision that 'will surely come, it will not delay' (2.3) and then contrasts the proud whose 'spirit is not right in them' with the 'the righteous [who] live by their faith' (2.4). The LXX has 'live by *my* faith', presumably in the sense of 'my faithfulness'. Paul, when he quotes this verse in Rom 1.17 and Gal 3.11, omits the pronoun altogether ('the righteous will live by faith'). Hebrews retains the pronoun 'my' but applies it to 'my righteous' rather than 'live by my faith'. There are two more important changes. The first is to do with context; it is no longer the vision that 'will surely come' but Christ. As elsewhere in the New Testament, the participle of 'to come' (*erchomenos*) is used as a noun (*ho erchomenos*) and is virtually seen as a title ('the coming one'). This interpretation is aided by an ambiguity in the LXX where the form of the pronoun could be neuter ('it', referring to the vision) or masculine ('him', referring to a person). Second, the quotation opens with a few words ('in a very little while') which are not from Habakkuk but appear to come from Isa 26.20, a chapter full of warning. Thus the form of the quotation in Heb 10.37–38 acts as a summary of the argument so far and prepares for the cloud of witnesses in Chapter 11. Although the exegesis may appear somewhat arbitrary to us, Radu Gheorghita (2003, p. 224) concludes that the author's changes are 'not only a legitimate rearrangement of the text intended to untangle the meaning of Habakkuk 2.2–4 LXX, they are also congruent with and supported by the overall message of the LXX Habakkuk'.

Hab 2.3–4 (NRSV)	Hab 2.3–4 (LXX)	Heb 10.37–38 (NRSV)
		For yet 'in a very little while,
For there is still a vision for the appointed time; it speaks of the end, and does not lie.	For there is still a vision for an appointed time, and it/he will rise up at the end and not in vain.	
If it seems to tarry, wait for it; it will surely come, it will not delay.	If it/he should tarry, wait for *him*, for when *he* comes it/he will come and not delay.	the one who is coming will come and will not delay;
Look at the proud! Their spirit is not right in them, but the righteous live by their faith.	If it/he draws back, my soul is not pleased in it/him. but the righteous shall live by my faith.	but my righteous one will live by faith. My soul takes no pleasure in anyone who shrinks back.'

Cloud of witnesses in Chapter 11

Similar lists of biblical saints are common in writings between the testaments (Sirach 44; 1 Macc 2; 4 Macc 16; Wisdom 10; Philo) and one also occurs in Stephen's speech (Acts 7) and the early Christian writing known as 1 Clement. Here, most space is given to Abraham (11.8–19) and Moses (11.23–29) but mention is also made of Abel, Enoch, Noah, Isaac, Jacob, Joseph and Rahab, while the author confesses that 'time would fail me to tell of Gideon, Barak, Samson, Jephthah, of David and Samuel and the prophets' (11.32); other individuals are alluded to without being named (11.35–38). It is clear that the Old Testament narrative (usually the Greek) is the source of the material but there are some interesting interpretative features. For example, Gen 4 does not say why God accepted Abel's sacrifice but rejected Cain's. Our author claims that Abel was righteous and made his offering in faith. This appears to be a deduction based on (1) The author's belief that 'without faith it is impossible to please God' (11.6) and (2) righteous people live by faith (10.38).

The author's comments on Abraham have parallels with Acts 7, Rom 4 and Jas 2 but his particular focus is the *aqedah* or 'binding' of Isaac. What is of particular interest is that both Paul and the author of Hebrews deduce from the Genesis narratives that Abraham believed that God could bring life out of death. For Paul, this comes from Abraham's willingness to believe that God could give a son to parents whose bodies were as good as dead (Rom 4.19). In Hebrews, having quoted Gen 21.12 ('It is through Isaac that descendants shall be named after you' – Heb 11.18), the writer deduces that Abraham's willingness to sacrifice Isaac was because he 'considered the fact that God is able even to raise someone from the dead – and figuratively speaking, he did receive him back' (Heb 11.19). Abraham not only looked forward to a heavenly home, he also believed in resurrection.

Hebrews 11	Acts 7	Romans 4	James 2
		Righteous by faith (Gen 15.6)	Righteous by works (Gen 15.6)
Left his homeland	Left his homeland		
Stayed in a foreign land	Stayed in a foreign land		
	Received circumcision	Received circumcision	
	Accepted land was not for him		
Believed he and Sarah could have a child		Believed he and Sarah could have a child	
Willing to sacrifice Isaac			Willing to sacrifice Isaac
Sacrifice of Isaac was like believing God can bring life out of death		Birth of Isaac was like believing God can bring life out of death	

The summary of Moses' life has also received enhancements. For example, despite the fact that Exod 2.14 states that Moses was afraid of the Pharaoh, Hebrews praises him for being 'unafraid of the king's anger' (11.27). His identification with the people of Israel is said to have been a choice to share ill-treatment rather than the 'fleeting pleasures of sin'. Most significant of all, Moses' willingness to suffer with the Israelites is because he 'considered abuse (*oneidismos*) suffered for the Christ to be greater wealth than the treasures of Egypt' (11.26). The particular word used for abuse here is found in Psalms 69.9 and 89.51 and is associated with the crucifixion in Mark 15.32 and Rom 15.3. Thus not only does Moses trust God in a general sense, his faith is even said to be cruciform in nature.

Miscellaneous quotations in Chs. 12–13

As the letter draws to a close, the author uses quotations to show that hardship and persecution can be seen as training for righteousness (Prov 3.11–12), to bolster confidence ('The Lord is my helper; I will not be afraid' – Psalm 118.6–7), and to leave them with an image of an awesome God who will 'shake not only the earth but also the heaven' (Hag 2.6). The writer's use of scripture in the latter text is particularly interesting. He begins by describing the awesome scene at Sinai ('blazing fire, and darkness, and gloom, and a tempest') only to tell them that this is not what they have come to. Instead, he tells them that they have come to 'the city of the living God, the heavenly Jerusalem, and to innumerable angels in festal gathering' (12.22). But he then uses the fiery images of Sinai (which they have not come to) as a warning, since 'if they did not escape when they refused the one who warned them on earth, how much less will we escape if we reject the one who warns from heaven!' (12.25). This is similar to what George Lord observed about Milton: 'Milton repeatedly denies the beauty of countless pagan paradises in comparison with Eden, while tacitly employing their strong legendary associations to enhance and embellish its incomparable perfections' (quoted in Hays, 1989, p. 142).

In contrast to the 'heroes' cited in Hebrews 11, the author urges the readers not to be like Esau, 'an immoral and godless person, who sold his birthright for a single meal' (Heb 12.16). The adjective 'immoral' (*pornos*) usually refers to sexual sin and the author may be drawing on traditions such as Philo, who spoke of Esau 'indulging without restraint in the pleasures of the belly and the lower lying parts' (quoted in Attridge, 1989, p. 369). Alternatively, his meaning might be a metaphorical reference to apostasy (unfaithfulness to God), especially as he concludes by stating that Esau 'found no chance to repent' (Heb 12.17). This is not stated in the biblical story (Gen 27.30–40) but corresponds to the author's view that 'it is impossible to restore again to repentance those who have once been enlightened … and then have fallen away' (Heb 6.4–6). Esau was desperate to change his father's mind but there is no hint of repentance for his former actions. It would appear that the author's understanding of idolatry and repentance for Christians has influenced his reading of the Genesis story.

Conclusion

Hebrews is the only New Testament book to make use of Melchizedek traditions and the discovery of 11QMelch shows that he was not alone. The difference between Hebrews and 11QMelch is that Hebrews does not assign Melchizedek a future role in the plan of salvation. However, it is interesting that he is never denigrated in Hebrews and indeed Jesus belongs to his priesthood, not vice versa. We meet many of the exegetical techniques that are now becoming familiar. In particular, we note the ease at which the author changes the reference of texts so as to apply them to Christ or the readers and Docherty is probably correct that their frequent use of the first person pronoun ('I') is responsible for this. The rabbis also thought that such pronouns required clarification and the author of Hebrews offers it by interpreting words spoken *by* God or addressed *to* God as a divine exchange between God and Jesus. Guthrie is also of the view that many of the techniques used by the author can be paralleled in Rabbinic writings, and he sees the apparent contradiction between Psalm 8.6 (everything is subject to the messiah) and Psalm 110.1 (everything *will be* subject to the messiah) as a good example of resolving two apparently contradictory texts. Hebrews contains the longest quotation in the New Testament (Jer 31.31–34) and the longest catena (1.5–13). The issue of continuity and discontinuity is present in all of the New Testament books but is at its starkest in Hebrews. Thus on the one hand, figures such as Abraham and Moses are treated as 'Christians before Christ'. On the other, some parts of scripture are declared obsolete. According to Hughes, it is the need to distinguish between these that has prompted the writing.

Further reading

Although written over thirty years ago, the monograph by Hughes (*Hebrews and Hermeneutics*, 1979) remains an important work, as do the commentaries by Attridge (1989) and Ellingworth (1993). More recent monographs include Bateman (*Early Jewish Hermeneutics and Hebrews 1.5–13*, 1997), Gheorghita (*The Role of the Septuagint in Hebrews*, 2003), Allen (*Deuteronomy and Exhortation in Hebrews*, 2007) and Docherty (*The Use of the Old Testament in Hebrews*, 2009). The chapter in the Beale and Carson Commentary is written by Guthrie (2007, pp. 919–95) and the chapters on Hebrews in the Moyise and Menken series were written by Docherty (Genesis), Steyn (Deuteronomy), Attridge (Psalms), McCullough (Isaiah), Gheorghita (Minor Prophets). We have quoted from a number of the contributors to the Human and Steyn collection (*Psalms and Hebrews. Studies in Reception*, 2010) and Steyn has written the most detailed study to date on the textual form of the quotations (*A Quest for the Assumed LXX Vorlage of the Explicit Quotations in Hebrews*, 2011).

9

The Old Testament in 1 and 2 Peter, Jude

For its size, 1 Peter is second only to Romans for its density of Old Testament quotations (eighteen in five chapters). The author generally follows the LXX, though variations in the 'stone' passages (that appear also in Paul) has been one of the strongest arguments for a testimony source. Jude and 2 Peter are quite different, preferring a more allusive style and drawing on a range of Jewish *haggada*. In particular, the only explicit quotation in Jude is from *1 Enoch*. He also draws on traditions that were later incorporated into a work known as the *Assumption of Moses*.

Quotations

Lev 19.2 in 1 Pet 1.16

It might come as a surprise that the first quotation in 1 Peter is from Leviticus but it should be remembered that Jesus' command to 'love your neighbour as yourself' is from this same chapter (19.18). It comes from that section of Leviticus which scholars call the 'Holiness Code' (17–26) and Selwyn thinks that 1 Peter is probably using a baptismal catechism which understands the Church as a 'neo-Levitical community, at once sacerdotal and sacrificial' (1947, p. 460). On the other hand, although much of Leviticus is aimed at the priests, this particular section is aimed at the whole people of God. It is thus truer to say that the parallel is between Israel and the Church, though the focus is certainly on its priestly nature. What is of note is the ease at which statements about Israel are assumed to apply to the Church.

Isa 40.6–8 in 1 Pet 1.24–25

This is one of four quotations (1.24–25; 3.10–12; 4.18; 5.5) that Hanson suggests is 'simply illustrative' (1983, p. 147). The author wishes to contrast the new life given 'through the living and enduring word of God' (1.23) to that which is perishable. He finds such a contrast in Isa 40.6–8 ('The grass withers and the flower falls but the word of the Lord endures for ever.') The change from 'our God' to 'the Lord' facilitates the application to Jesus and the mention of glory (from the LXX; the Hebrew has 'constancy') anticipates the glory to be revealed, mentioned in 4.13. Interestingly, though the quotation does not include verse 9, his conclusion that this 'word is the good news that was announced to you' (1.25b) appears to echo the heralding of good news in Isa 40.9. One might therefore question Hanson's judgement that the author's use of Isa 40.6–8 is 'simply illustrative'. Indeed, Karen Jobes (2005, p. 126) highlights the contextual similarity between the two writings: both are addressed to exiles facing persecution and are tempted to doubt the veracity of God's promises. In both cases, the author's response is that the 'word of God' can be trusted because it abides for ever.

The 'living stone' in 1 Pet 2.6–8

As we have already seen, Mark's identification of Christ with the 'stone that the builders rejected' (Psalm 118.22) was extended by Luke to include other 'stone' passages, certainly Isa 8.14 ('a stone that makes them stumble') and possibly the stone that crushes (Dan 2.34–35). In Rom 9.33, Paul explains Israel's rejection of the gospel by quoting Isa 8.14, along with Isa 28.16 ('I am laying in Zion a stone that will make people stumble'). Here in 1 Peter, both Isaiah passages are quoted, along with Psalm 118, to support the positive statement that Christ is the precious corner stone and the negative statement that they 'stumble because they disobey the word, as they were destined to do'. There are a number of differences from the LXX, some of which are shared by Paul (*tithemi, skandalou*). It would appear, therefore, that they are both drawing on a common tradition, either a specific source or perhaps a revised version of the LXX.

Old Testament	1 Pet 2.6–8	Rom 9.33
See, I am laying (*embalo*) in Zion a *foundation* stone, a tested stone, a precious cornerstone, a sure foundation:	'See, I am laying (*tithemi*) in Zion a stone, a cornerstone chosen and precious;	'See, I am laying (*tithemi*) in Zion a stone that will make people stumble, a rock that will make them fall (*skandalou*),
'One who trusts will not panic.' (Isa 28.16)	and whoever believes in him will not be put to shame.'	and whoever believes in him will not be put to shame.'
	To you then who believe, he is precious; but for those who do not believe,	
The stone that the builders rejected has become the chief cornerstone. (Psalm 118.22)	'The stone that the builders rejected has become the very head of the corner', and	
He will become a sanctuary, a stone one strikes against; for both houses of Israel he will become a rock one stumbles over (*ptomati*) – a trap and a snare for the inhabitants of Jerusalem. (Isa 8.14)	'A stone that makes them stumble, and a rock that makes them fall (*skandalou*).'	

Isa 53.4–12 in 1 Pet 2.22–25

In the context of an exhortation to slaves (1 Pet 2.18), 1 Peter finds a number of important themes in Isa 53. First, although Christ's suffering was unjust ('He committed no sin, and no deceit was found in his mouth'), he did not retaliate or utter abuse. Isaiah says that the servant was 'oppressed, and he was afflicted' but 'there was no deceit in his mouth'. Second, both Isaiah and 1 Peter use the metaphor of 'straying sheep' to describe the situation of the readers. 1 Peter adds, 'but now you have returned to the shepherd and guardian of your souls'. This is probably drawn from Christian tradition, although it might have been suggested by the link between 'turning' and 'healing' found in Isa 6.10 or perhaps the 'going astray' and 'returning' of the sheep in Ezek 34.4 and 16. Third, Jesus' suffering was not simply the product of injustice and abuse but accomplished something for others: 'He himself bore our sins in his body on the cross … by his wounds you have been healed'. Here and perhaps here alone in the New Testament we have a vicarious role ascribed to Jesus' death based on Isa 53.

Isa 53.4, 5, 6, 7, 9, 12	1 Pet 2.22–25
(A) Surely he has borne our infirmities …	(E) 'He committed no sin, and no deceit was found in his mouth.'
(B) upon him was the punishment that made us whole, and by his bruises we are healed…	(D) When he was abused, he did not return abuse; when he suffered, he did not threaten;
(C) All we like sheep have gone astray …	
(D) He was oppressed, and he was afflicted, yet he did not open his mouth …	(F) but he entrusted himself (*paredidou*) to the one who judges justly.
(E) he had done no violence, and there was no deceit in his mouth …	(A, G) He himself bore our sins in his body on the cross, so that, free from sins, we might live for righteousness;
(F) he poured out (*paredothe*) himself to death …	(B) by his wounds you have been healed.
(G) he bore the sin of many …	(C) For you were going astray like sheep, but now you have returned to the shepherd and guardian of your souls.

Psalm 34.12–16 in 1 Pet 3.10–12

The familiar dictum, 'Do not repay evil for evil' (Matt 5.44; Rom 12.17; 1 Thess 5.15) is here supported by a quotation from Psalm 34.12–16, which states that 'the eyes of the Lord are on the righteous' but 'the face of the Lord is against those who do evil'. The psalm is important for the author, as can be seen from 2.3 ('if indeed you have tasted that the Lord is good',) a clear allusion to verse 8 of the psalm ('O taste and see that the Lord is good'). Boring (1999, p. 94) suggests that this might have been facilitated by the fact that the word for 'good' is *chrestos*, which in Hellenistic Greek, would have been pronounced the same as *christos*, thus achieving the pun, 'The Lord is Christ'/'The Lord is good'. Jobes goes further. She thinks that the themes of the psalm, namely, deliverance from shame (34.5), affliction (34.6) and want (34.9–10) are precisely what the readers of 1 Peter are facing:

> His logic appears to be that just as God delivered David from his sojourn among the Philistines, God will deliver the Asian Christians from the afflictions caused by their faith in Christ, because they are no less God's covenant people than was David. (2005, p. 223)

Isa 8.12 in 1 Pet 3.14

The encouragement offered by the psalm leads the author to ask, 'Now who will harm you if you are eager to do what is good?' But his readers are suffering and so he changes his approach: 'But even if you do suffer for doing what is right, you are blessed.' He then quotes words from Isa 8.12, 'Do not fear what they fear, and do not be intimidated.' By themselves, these words could come from Christian tradition or Gospel sayings but (1) The use of the cognate 'fear what they fear' agrees with the LXX of Isa 8.12; (2) The next verse in 1 Peter ('sanctify Christ as Lord') echoes the next verse in Isaiah ('the Lord of hosts, him you should regard as holy'); (3) He has already quoted Isa 8.14. It would appear that this section of Isaiah was of particular importance to the author.

Prov 11.31 in 1 Pet 4.18

As well as the promise that bearing unjust suffering will lead to blessing (3.14) and glory (4.13), the author reminds his readers that the coming judgement will 'begin with the household of God'. He then reflects that 'if it begins with us, what will be the end for those who do not

obey the gospel of God?' The answer is given in the form of a verbatim
quotation from the LXX of Prov 11.31: 'If it is hard for the righteous
to be saved, what will become of the ungodly and the sinners?' The
Masoretic Hebrew text says something quite different and would not
have supported his argument ('If the righteous are repaid on earth,
how much more the wicked and the sinner!') Hanson notes the ease at
which our author gives the text an eschatological interpretation.

Prov 3.34 in 1 Pet 5.5

Prov 3.34 is also quoted in Jas 4.6 and 'shows that it had become an
element in stock Christian tradition' (Boring, 1999, p. 174). Perhaps it
suggested itself to the early Church because the LXX rendered the Hebrew
'to show favour' with *charis* ('grace'), a word that had become important to
Christians. Thus Jas 4.6 reads, 'But he gives all the more grace; therefore it
says, "God opposes the proud, but gives grace to the humble."'

Peter does not have this emphasis but focuses on showing humility
to one another. However, it is clear that they are drawing on common
traditions since they both follow the quotation with the exhortation to
submit to God so that he might exalt you.

Jas 4.6–10	1 Pet 5.5–6
But he gives all the more grace	Cloth yourselves with humility
God opposes the proud,	God opposes the proud,
but gives grace to the humble.	but gives grace to the humble.
Submit to God … Resist the devil	
Humble yourselves before the Lord, and he will exalt you	Humble yourselves therefore under the mighty hand of God, so that he may exalt you in due time.

Prov 26.11 in 2 Pet 2.22

The only explicit quotation in 2 Peter is the somewhat distasteful
proverb, 'The dog turns back to its own vomit' and 'The sow is

washed only to wallow in the mud.' Only the first part is from the Old Testament. The saying about the sow appears to derive from an ancient tradition called the *Story of Ahikar*. The Arabic version runs, 'thou hast been to me like the pig who went into the hot bath with people of quality, and when it came out of the hot bath, it saw a filthy hole and it went down and wallowed in it' (quoted in Bauckham, 1983, p. 279). It is possible that the saying from Proverbs suggested the other saying but given the differences from the LXX, it is more likely that the author of 2 Peter derived them both from a common collection.

1 Enoch 1.9 in Jude 14

Jude alludes to Jewish apocryphal works and traditions as much as he does to the Old Testament (Bauckham, 1983, p. 7). He is familiar with most of the books of Enoch, from which comes his only explicit quotation. He is also familiar with traditions that were to be incorporated into the *Assumption of Moses* (see below). The text of *1 Enoch* 1.9 is known from an Aramaic fragment discovered at Qumran (4QEn), a Greek translation in Codex Panopolitanus (C), a Latin version in Pseudo-Cyprian and also a version in Ethiopic. Jude's quotation is similar to the Greek but has some agreements with the other versions, perhaps indicating that he knew the original Aramaic. He seems to have been attracted to the text by its repetition of the word 'ungodly', which he claims is a prophecy about the fate of his 'ungodly' opponents.

> It was also about these that Enoch, in the seventh generation from Adam, prophesied, saying, 'See, the Lord is coming with tens of thousands of his holy ones, to execute judgement on all, and to convict everyone of all the deeds of ungodliness that they have committed in such an ungodly way, and of all the harsh things that ungodly sinners have spoken against him.' (Jude 14)

Allusions in Jude and 2 Peter

Jude 6	2 Pet 2.4
And the angels who did not keep their own position, but left their proper dwelling, he has kept in eternal chains in deepest darkness for the judgement of the great day.	For if God did not spare the angels when they sinned, but cast them into hell and committed them to chains of deepest darkness to be kept until the judgement;

In the first century, the story in Gen 6 that the 'sons of God' took wives and gave birth to a race of warriors, was almost universally understood to be a reference to 'fallen angels' (so *Enoch, Jubilees, Targum, Damascus Rule, Testament of Reuben*). The earliest form of this tradition is found in *1 Enoch* 6–19 (early second century BCE), where two hundred angels ('Watchers') descended from Mount Hermon, took wives and gave birth to a race of giants. The fallen angels taught the human race all manner of wickedness and forbidden knowledge and were thus responsible for the Flood. Their punishment was to be chained under the earth until the day of judgement, when they would be thrown into Gehenna.

Older commentators took these passages in Jude and 2 Peter to be a reference to a fall of angels prior to the creation of Adam and Eve and thus an explanation for the presence of the serpent. But the close parallels with *1 Enoch* and the fact that Jude 7 speaks of their sexual immorality confirms that it is the Gen 6 incident that is in mind. Although 2 Peter is dependent on Jude his use of the verb *tartaroun* shows that he was also drawing on a source other than *1 Enoch*. Tartarus is where the Cyclopes and the Titans were imprisoned in Greek mythology and the verb means literally, 'to be thrown into Tartarus'. This is its only occurrence in the Old or New Testament. Later Rabbinic tradition became unhappy with this explanation of Gen 6 and took 'sons of God' to mean 'men'.

Jude 9	2 Pet 2.10b–11
But when the archangel Michael contended with the devil and disputed about the body of Moses, he did not dare to bring a condemnation of slander against him, but said, 'The Lord rebuke you!'	Bold and wilful, they are not afraid to slander the glorious ones, whereas angels, though greater in might and power, do not bring against them a slanderous judgment from the Lord.

This strange reference is dependent on Jewish *haggada* that the devil disputed Moses' right to burial because he murdered an Egyptian (Exod 2.12). The words, 'The Lord rebuke you!' are taken from Zech 3.2, where Satan brings an accusation against the high priest Joshua (cf. Job 1). The theme of demonic opposition was then read back into Israel's earlier history. Thus a document found at Qumran (4QAmram) tells of Moses' father (Amram) having a dream where the Prince of darkness and the Prince of light argue over Amram's destiny. In the Book of Jubilees, the devil (called Mastema) is on the side of Pharaoh and the magicians against Moses. In the Damascus Rule (CD 5.17–18), Satan raises up Jannes and his brother to oppose Moses and Aaron (cf. 2 Tim 3.8). And more specifically, in the Slavonic *Life of Moses,* Satan disputes Moses' right to burial because he murdered the Egyptian and so, 'Michael prayed to God and there was thunder and lightning and suddenly the devil disappeared; but Michael buried him with his (own) hands' (text in Bauckham, 1983, p. 69). Other forms of the story concern the fate of Moses' soul after death.

Bauckham thinks these traditions ultimately derive from a lost work known as the *Testament of Moses*, which formed the basis of the *Assumption of Moses*, a work known to us from a seventh century Latin manuscript. Jude uses the tradition to show that Michael condemned the devil on God's authority, not his own. But the author of 2 Peter appears to have misunderstood this and takes Jude to mean that angels (in general) know it is not their place to slander beings greater than themselves (unlike the false teachers).

In 2 Pet 3, the author seeks to answer a specific accusation of the scoffers: 'Where is the promise of his coming? For ever since our ancestors died, all things continue as they were from the beginning of creation!' (2 Pet 3.4). His answer is twofold. First, they should understand that everything happens by God's command, as is seen in the creation story ('by the word of God heavens existed long ago and an earth was formed out of water and by means of water') and the flood ('through which the world of that time was deluged with water and perished'). Equally certain is the fact that 'the present heavens and earth have been reserved for fire, being kept until the day of judgement and destruction of the godless' (2 Pet 3.7). Various texts threaten judgement by fire (Isa 30.30; 66.15; Mal 4.1) but in the light of the rest of 2 Peter, it is just as likely that he is drawing on other traditions.

Second, God does not operate with the same timescale as humans for 'with the Lord one day is like a thousand years, and a thousand years are like one day' (2 Pet 3.8). This draws on Psalm 90.4 ('For a thousand years in your sight are like yesterday when it is past, or like a watch in the night'), which also follows a comment about creation ('Before the mountains were brought forth, or ever you had formed the earth and the world, from everlasting to everlasting you are God' – Psalm 90.2). Ultimately, the author shares the hope of Isaiah that there will be 'new heavens and a new earth, where righteousness is at home' (2 Pet 3.13/Isa 65.17; 66.22) but his main point is that this will happen in God's timing.

Conclusion

For a number of reasons, most scholars think that 2 Peter was written by a different author to that of 1 Peter and their use of scripture would support such a conclusion. Scripture in 1 Peter is essentially traditional, drawing on key psalms (34; 40; 118), key chapters of Isaiah (8; 40; 53) and wisdom sayings, some of which are found elsewhere in the New

Testament (Prov 3.34). Hanson thinks it lacks the profundity of Paul but it appears to be of the same general type. Jude and 2 Peter, however, are quite different, favouring a more allusive style and dependent on more obscure sources. They seem to have a fascination with traditions about angels and demons and thus have more in common with the book of Revelation than the rest of the New Testament. It is no coincidence that Jude, 2 Peter and Revelation all experienced some opposition before finally being accepted into the canon.

Further reading

There have not been many books dedicated to the study of the Old Testament in these books and so Schutter's monograph (*Hermeneutics and Composition in 1 Peter*, 1989) remains important. There have, however, been a number of important commentaries which offer many insights into the use of the Old Testament: 1 Peter (Elliott, 2000; Jobes, 2005); 2 Peter and Jude (Bauckham, 1983; Green, 2008). The chapters in the Beale and Carson Commentary were all written by Carson and the chapters in the Moyise and Menken volumes were written by Woan (Psalms), Moyise (Isaiah) and Jobes (Minor Prophets).

10

The Old Testament in James and 1–3 John

Although James is best known for his use of Gen 15.6 to argue that 'a person is justified by works and not by faith alone' (Jas 2.24), it is important to see this in the light of his rich understanding of the first five books of the Bible. Thus in his discussion of the huge damage that can be done by the tongue, he says that even though 'every species of beast and bird, of reptile and sea creature, can be tamed' (Jas 3.7), no one can tame the tongue. On its own, this might not be a specific reference to the creation story but two verses later, he says that the tongue curses 'those who are made in the *likeness* of God' (Jas 3.9). This makes it probable that he has Gen 1.26 in mind, where God says: 'Let us make humankind in our image, according to our *likeness*; and let them have dominion over the *fish* of the sea, and over the *birds* of the air, and over the *cattle*, and over all the *wild animals* of the earth.' James's point is that although humankind was given dominion over the animal kingdom ('tamed'), it has little control over its own desires and his description of how this leads to death appears to owe something to the Adam and Eve story: 'But one is tempted by one's own desire, being lured and enticed by it; then, when that desire has conceived, it gives birth to sin, and that sin, when it is fully grown, gives birth to death' (Jas 1.14–15).

Exodus is represented by a discussion of two of the Ten Commandments. James wishes to establish the point that 'whoever keeps the whole law but fails in one point has become accountable for all of it' (Jas 2.10). He illustrates this by observing that the one who gave the commandment against adultery also gave the commandment against murder (Jas 2.11). This seems a rather obvious point but Scott McKnight thinks the choice of commandments is deliberate; his opponents are not committing adultery but they are committing murder (Jas 4.2; 5.6). Most commentators take this figuratively but McKnight thinks it might be more than that: 'Perhaps … oppression was leading to the death of poor members of the messianic community, and complicity with the rich on the part of some was contributing to those deaths' (2011, p. 218). In making such a point, James affirms the unity of the law and the seriousness of transgressing any part of it (cf. Matt 5.19).

There is a specific quotation of Lev 19.18 ('you shall love your neighbour as yourself') in Jas 2.8, which probably derives from the Jesus tradition (Matt 5.43; 19.19; 22.39). But what is of particular interest is that just prior to this command, Leviticus is concerned with two things that very much concern James: 'you shall not keep for yourself the wages of a labourer until morning' and 'you shall not be partial to the poor or defer to the great' (Lev 19.13, 15). The context of Jas 2.1–7 is precisely that of showing partiality to the rich against the poor and in Jas 5.4, he issues this warning: 'Listen! The *wages of the labourers* who mowed your fields, *which you kept back* by fraud, cry out, and the cries of the harvesters have reached the ears of the Lord of hosts.' The latter phrase probably draws on Isa 5.9 but the warnings of Lev 19 are the key text. James is following the teaching of Jesus in elevating Lev 19.18 to a hermeneutical principle but, more than any other New Testament writer, he has also drawn on its surrounding context.

There do not appear to be any allusions to Numbers in James but the statement that 'God is one' in Jas 2.19 ultimately goes back to Deut 6.4. This was part of the *Shema* ('Hear, O Israel') that Jews recited daily, a form of which occurs in the Jesus tradition (Mark 12.29–30). Interestingly, Jesus combined this with Lev 19.18 ('love your neighbour') and we find all three elements in Jas 2: God is one (2.19); love God (2.5); love neighbour (2.8).We might also mention the definition of true religion in Jas 1.27, which includes looking after 'orphans and widows'. This is a particular concern of Deuteronomy (10.18; 14.29; 16.11; 24.17 etc.), as it was for Jesus (Luke 7.12; 18.3; 21.2).

As well as specific references to the Pentateuch, James has some important things to say about the law. Its importance is clear from the statement that 'whoever keeps the whole law but fails in one point has become accountable for all of it' (Jas 2.10). Indeed, to criticize the law is to criticize the one who gave the law (Jas 4.11–12) and to 'hear the law' without actually 'doing the law' is as incongruous as looking in a mirror and immediately forgetting what you look like (Jas 1.22–24). James's concern is with consistency. Thus if a 'brother or sister is naked and lacks daily food, and one of you says to them, "Go in peace; keep warm and eat your fill", and yet you do not supply their bodily needs, what is the good of that?' (Jas 2.15–16). From James's point of view, if people are using the slogan 'justification by faith' to indicate that 'works of mercy' are not necessary, they deceive themselves. This was not the teaching of Jesus or the law and so James concludes that 'faith by itself, if it has no works, is dead' (Jas 2.17).

Finally, before we discuss his controversial claim that 'a person is justified by works and not by faith alone' (Jas 2.24), it should be noted that, like Jesus and Paul, he can summarize the law in terms of the love command: 'You do well if you really fulfil the royal law according to the scripture, "You shall love your neighbour as yourself"' (Jas 2.8). The primary meaning of 'royal' here is 'preeminent', though it might also carry a connotation of 'kingly' in the sense of pertaining to the kingdom. He can also refer to the law as the 'perfect law' (cf. Psalm 19.7) and the 'law of liberty' (Jas 1.25), which the NIV renders, 'the perfect law that gives freedom'. Indeed, James says that his readers will be judged by the law that gives liberty/freedom (Jas 2.12). There is no exact parallel to this expression but the thought comes close to what Paul says in Gal 5.13: 'For you were called to freedom, brothers and sisters; only do not use your freedom as an opportunity for self-indulgence'. Although the context of James requires him to major on judgement, he can also say – somewhat enigmatically – that 'mercy triumphs over judgement' (Jas 2.13).

Justification by works

We are now in a position to consider James's scriptural argument that
Abraham was justified by works (Jas 2.14–26). What has perplexed –
and sometimes distressed – commentators is that James uses the very
same text (Gen 15.6) that Paul uses in Gal 3.6 and Rom 4.3 to prove
that Abraham was justified by faith and not by works. James's argument
runs as follows:

> Do you want to be shown, you senseless person, that faith without
> works is barren? Was not our ancestor Abraham justified by works
> when he offered his son Isaac on the altar? You see that faith was
> active along with his works, and faith was brought to completion by
> the works. Thus the scripture was fulfilled that says, 'Abraham believed
> God, and it was reckoned to him as righteousness', and he was called
> the friend of God. You see that a person is justified by works and not
> by faith alone. Likewise, was not Rahab the prostitute also justified
> by works when she welcomed the messengers and sent them out by
> another road? For just as the body without the spirit is dead, so faith
> without works is also dead. (Jas 2.20–26)

There are three main strategies for understanding this text. The
first thinks that James is contradicting Paul's doctrine of 'justification by faith' and thus relegates it to a minor (Jewish) voice in
the New Testament. The best known example is Martin Luther, who
famously described it as an 'epistle of straw' because its message
was in opposition to 'Paul and all Scripture'. Although Paul does
not specifically mention the sacrifice of Isaac, his chronological
argument in Rom 4 that the promise of Gen 15.6 came before the
introduction of circumcision in Gen 17 would be equally applicable
to the offering of Isaac in Gen 22. Abraham was declared righteous
because he trusted in God's promise and so it cannot depend on
any later 'work', whether that is submitting to circumcision or his
willingness to offer Isaac. However virtuous such 'works' might be
(though the latter would be questioned today!) they are not the basis
of the promise in Gen 15.6.

The second strategy seeks to harmonize Paul and James by reading James in the light of Paul (already in Calvin). Thus when James says that 'faith was active along with his works', what he means is that faith was the guiding force behind his works. And when he says that 'faith was brought to completion by the works', what he means is that his faith was thereby shown to be genuine. Thus there is no contradiction with Paul. Abraham's actions show that he was guided by faith and in that sense, one could say that he was 'justified by works', meaning that his works demonstrated the genuineness of his faith. This is why he can also use Rahab as an example. The story in Josh 2 says nothing about her faith but her actions demonstrate that she was motivated by faith in Israel's God; otherwise she would have acted in the interests of her own people. Thus the role of faith is to generate or inspire good works and hence the analogy at the end of the passage: 'For just as the body without the spirit is dead, so faith without works is also dead' (Jas 2.26). The spirit energizes the body just as faith energizes good works. Justification can be said to be 'by works' providing that it is understood as those things that demonstrate the presence of faith.

The third strategy is to 'let James be James' and interpret him in light of his own context and traditions. James is clearly close to the teachings of Jesus and so it is somewhat ironic to accuse him of being sub-Christian. Jesus asserted the importance of the law (Matt 5.17–19), the need to do it as well as hear it (Matt 7.21–27) and the priority of the love command (Matt 22.39). Paul's comments in Gal 3–4 and Rom 4 derive from a particular context where Jewish Christians were forcing Gentile converts to be circumcised. Outside of that context, Paul can also assert the importance of the law (Rom 7.12), the need to do it as well as hear it (Rom 2.13) and the priority of the love command (Rom 13.9). James is not faced with the problem of Gentile circumcision but the problem of those who profess faith but act in ways that are thoroughly inconsistent with it.

1–3 John

The documents traditionally known as the Letters of John consist of a homily of five chapters (1 John), where author and recipients are not named, followed by two short letters (13 and 15 verses respectively) from someone who calls himself 'The Elder', writing to 'the elect lady and her children' (2 John 1) and 'the beloved Gaius' (3 John 1). Church tradition associated this elder with John the apostle, thought to be the author of the Fourth Gospel and the Book of Revelation. Scholars today are more inclined to think of a 'Johannine community' than common authorship, though the issue continues to be debated. There are no explicit quotations in the three works, though the advice not to emulate Cain in 1 John 3.12 is clearly a reference to Gen 4.8 and there is probably an allusion to Prov 28.13 in 1 John 1.8–9.

Cain and Abel in 1 John 3.12

As we have seen, Heb 11.4 offers Abel as an example of faith and righteousness but 1 John 3.12 alludes to Cain as a warning: 'We must not be like Cain who was from the evil one and murdered his brother. And why did he murder him? Because his own deeds were evil and his brother's righteous.' Since Cain is not mentioned again in the Hebrew Bible and only once in the LXX (*4 Macc* 18.11), the author is probably drawing on Jewish tradition. Thus in the *Apocalypse of Abraham* 24.5, Cain's actions are linked with the serpent/adversary of Gen 3 and in the *Testament of Dan* 7.1–5, Cain's envy and hatred is linked to Beliar, an alternative name for the devil. The Genesis story focuses on Cain's choice but the author of 1 John considers choice to be an indicator of character and hence Cain is 'from the evil one'. Similarly, those who took the decision to leave the congregation – to set up rival congregations according to 2 and 3 John – show themselves to be 'antichrists' (1 John 2.18–28), even though they once belonged to the congregation.

Prov 28.13 in 1 John 1.8–9

The most convincing allusion occurs in 1 John 1.8–9, where a negative proposition ('If we say we have no sin, we deceive ourselves') is followed by the positive ('If we confess our sins, he who is faithful and just will forgive us our sins and cleanse us from all unrighteousness'). Some of the language may be drawn from Deut 32.4 ('A *faithful* God, without deceit, *just* and upright is he') and David's confession in Psalm 32.5 ('I will confess my transgressions') but it is Prov 28.13 where we find both aspects: 'No one who conceals transgressions will prosper, but one who confesses and forsakes them will obtain mercy.' Given the nature of the book of Proverbs, it is unlikely that our author intends his readers to look up the passage. It is more that the pattern of negative followed by positive sounds 'biblical' and is therefore more convincing. We might say the same about the verse before (1 John 1.7) where 'walking in the light' and 'cleansing from sin' may allude to Prov 20.9 and Isa 2.5 respectively, but the effect is not dependent on knowing the particular passages.

Further reading

James is well served by commentaries that offer important comments on its use of the Old Testament: McKnight (2011), McCartney (2009), Bauckham (1999), Johnson (1995), and for 1–3 John, see Yarbrough (2008), Lieu (2008) and Brown (1982). The chapters on James and 1–3 John in the Beale and Carson Commentary were both written by Carson (2007). In the Moyise and Menken series, see Jobes on 'The Minor prophets in James, 1 and 2 Peter and Jude' (2009), Allen on 'Genesis in James, 1 and 2 Peter and Jude' (2012) and Menken on Genesis in 1 John (2012).

11

The Old Testament in Revelation

If we were to restrict ourselves to a discussion of explicit quotations, this would be a very short chapter. There aren't any! However, as the lists in *The Greek New Testament* indicate, there are more allusions to scripture in Revelation than any other New Testament book. Even a conservative estimate works out at about one allusion for every verse. No wonder it has a very biblical feel to it. John's favourite books are Isaiah, Ezekiel, Daniel and the Psalms, with comparatively few from the narrative portions of the Old Testament. The sheer density of allusion has led some scholars (Beale, 1984) to call it a 'midrash', though others (Ruiz, 1989) do not think this does justice to the originality of John's composition. We will begin with John's use of Ezekiel, Daniel and Isaiah and then look at some selected passages.

John's use of Ezekiel

According to *The Greek New Testament*, there are 138 allusions to Ezekiel in the New Testament and 84 of them come from the book of Revelation. It is the only New Testament writing that shows a significant interest in this great prophet. What is of particular interest is that John alludes to five major sections of Ezekiel and these occur in the same order in Revelation, raising the question of whether John is in some way modelling his book on Ezekiel.

God on his throne, multi-faced creatures (Rev 4)	Ezek 1
Marking/sealing of the saints (Rev 7–8)	Ezek 9–10
Punishment of the harlot city (Rev 17)	Ezek 16, 23
Lament over fallen city, trading list (Rev 18)	Ezek 26–27
Establishment of the new Jerusalem (Rev 20–22)	Ezek 37–48

God on his throne, multi-faced creatures

John's vision draws on various throne visions in the Old Testament (1 Kgs 22; Isa 6; Ezek 1; Dan 7) but it is the parallels to Ezekiel that are most striking. As well as the imagery of precious stones, a rainbow and a crystal sea, both surround the throne with creatures exhibiting the faces of a man, a lion, an ox and an eagle and use the curious expression 'full of eyes'.

> As I looked … a great cloud with brightness around it … and in the middle of the fire, something like gleaming amber. In the middle of it was something like four living creatures. This was their appearance: they were of human form. Each had four faces, and each of them had four wings … they sparkled like burnished bronze … As for the appearance of their faces: the four had the face of a human being, the face of a lion on the right side, the face of an ox on the left side, and the face of an eagle … I saw a wheel on the earth beside the living creatures … Their rims were tall and awesome, for the rims of all four were full of eyes all round … Like the bow in a cloud on a rainy day, such was the appearance of the splendour all round. (Ezek 1.4–28, abbreviated)

> And the one seated there looks like jasper and carnelian, and around the throne is a rainbow that looks like an emerald … Coming from the throne are flashes of lightning … and in front of the throne there is something like a sea of glass, like crystal. Around the throne, and on each side of the throne, are four living creatures, full of eyes in front and behind: the first living creature like a lion, the second living creature like an ox, the third living creature with a face like a human face, and the fourth living creature like a flying eagle. And the four

living creatures, each of them with six wings, are full of eyes all around and inside. (Rev 4.3–8)

There are also significant differences between the visions. Ezekiel speaks of wheels and appears to be describing a chariot-throne which moves though the heavens. This vision was subject to much speculation at Qumran and was important in what was later called 'merkabah mysticism' (*merkabah* is the Hebrew word for chariot). John would appear to have eliminated this aspect of the vision. He has also changed Ezekiel's four-faced creatures for four separate creatures, each having a different face. Thus John is not slavishly following his model but using it creatively.

Marking/sealing of the saints

Before the demonic beasts are allowed to deceive the world into false worship (Rev 13), the 144,000 (12x12x1000, probably a symbol for the whole Church) receive a seal on their foreheads (Rev 7.3). This is reminiscent of the blood on the doorposts on the night of the Passover but as it is followed by the hurling of fire onto the earth (Rev 8.5), Ezek 9–10 is the more likely influence since it also has such a sequence. Because the 'land is full of bloodshed and the city full of perversity' (Ezek 9.9), God will send judgement in the form of six agents of destruction, but not before he has given the command: 'Go through the city, through Jerusalem, and put a mark on the foreheads of those who sigh and groan over all the abominations that are committed in it' (Ezek 9.4). There then follows another vision where the command is given: 'fill your hands with burning coals from among the cherubim, and scatter them over the city' (Ezek 10.2).

Punishment of the harlot city

One of the more disagreeable features of the book of Revelation is its use of feminine imagery to characterize evil as a harlot, stripped naked and burnt alive (Rev 17.16). However, the imagery did not originate with John. He found it in Ezekiel's description of apostate Jerusalem in Chapters 16 and 23. Both are decked in costly jewels and fine linen (Ezek 16.13/Rev 17.4), both are guilty of shedding blood (Ezek 16.38/ Rev 17.6) and both use the image of drinking a cup of abominations (Ezek 23.33/Rev 17.4). As for their destruction:

> and your survivors shall be devoured by fire. They shall also strip you of your clothes and take away your fine jewels … and they shall deal with you in hatred … and leave you naked and bare, and the nakedness of your whorings shall be exposed. (Ezek 23.25–29, abbreviated)

> And the ten horns that you saw, they and the beast will hate the whore; they will make her desolate and naked; they will devour her flesh and burn her up with fire. (Rev 17.16)

Lament over the fallen city, trading list

Moving from evil as harlot to evil as city, John describes the destruction of Babylon (probably a cypher for Rome), followed by a series of laments from those who once prospered. This is similar to Ezekiel's description of the fall of Tyre. Verbal parallels include people weeping and throwing dust on their head (Ezek 27.30/Rev 18.19), the end of music and dancing (Ezek 26.13/Rev 18.22) and the cry of amazement: 'Who was ever destroyed like Tyre' (Ezek 27.32)/ 'What city was like the great city?' (Rev 18.18). But the major parallel is that each contains a trading list of luxury products and it is this that is being condemned. Among the goods mentioned (gold, silver, jewels, pearls etc), both speak of *psychai anthropon*, literally the 'souls of men', in other words 'slaves'. The interpretation of this passage has been important for determining the purpose of Revelation.

Establishment of the New Jerusalem

The account of the New Jerusalem involves a complex network of allusions but many commentators have been impressed by the way it corresponds to the broad sequence of Ezek 37–48.

Ezekiel	*Revelation*
Revival of dry bones (37.10)	First resurrection (20.5)
Reunited kingdom (37.21)	Saints rule for 1000 years (20.4)
Gog of Magog battle (38.2)	Gog *and* Magog battle (20.8)
Gorging of the birds (39.4)	Gorging of the birds (19.21)
Taken to high mountain (40.2)	Taken to high mountain (21.10)
Temple is measured (40.5)	*City* is measured (21.15)
Temple full of God's glory (43.2)	*City* full of God's glory (21.23)
River of life (47.12)	River of life (22.2)

As well as these parallels, one of the main arguments for John's use of Ezekiel here is that it explains why John envisages a resurgence of evil after the millennial kingdom. Other New Testament writers expect a final battle with evil (Mark 13; 2 Thess 2) but not the defeat of evil, followed by a resurgence and then a further battle. This has been a controversial feature of Revelation right from the start. Justin Martyr (*c.* 150 CE) was one of many who took it literally:

> I and others, who are right-minded Christians at all points, are assured that there will be a resurrection of the dead, and a thousand years in Jerusalem, which will then be built and adorned and enlarged as the prophets Ezekiel and Isaiah and others declare. (*Dial. Trypho*, 80)

However, what is even more surprising is that having borrowed so much from Ezek 37–48, John denies the very thing that these chapters are all about: 'I saw no temple in the city, for its temple is the Lord God the Almighty and the Lamb' (Rev 21.22). So when Ezekiel speaks of measuring the temple (40.5) and the glory of God filling the temple (43.2), John speaks of measuring the city (21.15) and the glory of God filling the city (21.23). Thus John's use of Ezekiel consists both of striking similarities and remarkable differences.

John's use of Daniel

Beale (1998) makes the point that relative to its size, there are more allusions to Daniel than any other portion of scripture. And since nearly half of the allusions come from its seventh chapter, a good case can be made for regarding this as one of John's most important influences. This is signalled at the very beginning where after the greeting, John says, 'Look! He is coming with the clouds' (Rev 1.7/Dan 7.13). He then describes his vision of 'one like the Son of Man', whose hair was 'as white wool, white as snow' (a description of God in Dan 7.9). The chapter has also contributed to John's description of the throne scene, particularly in Rev 5, with its mention of the scroll, the saints reigning in an everlasting kingdom and the myriads of worshipping angels. Correspondingly, the throne scene at the end of Revelation has books being opened and judgement pronounced in favour of the saints (Rev 20.12).

As well as the use of the throne imagery, John models his description of the beast from the sea on Daniel's four beasts. Verbal parallels include their rising from the sea, their appearance, making war with the saints, speaking haughty words and the time of their reign (variously given as 3½ years, 42 months or 1260 days). The major difference is that instead of having a succession of beasts coming from the sea (lion, bear, leopard, beast with ten horns) representing a succession of empires, John combines all these features into a single beast. It is interesting that this is the opposite of what he did with Ezekiel's four-faced creatures, showing how difficult it is to offer a single rationale for John's use of scripture.

> And I saw a beast rising out of the sea, having ten horns and seven heads; and on its horns were ten diadems, and on its heads were blasphemous names. And the beast that I saw was like a leopard, its feet were like a bear's, and its mouth was like a lion's mouth … The beast was given a mouth uttering haughty and blasphemous words, and it was allowed to exercise authority for forty-two months. It opened its mouth to utter blasphemies against God … Also it was allowed to make war on the saints and to conquer them. (Rev 13.1–7 abbreviated)

Also important to John is the Nebuchadnezzar material in Dan 2–4. In Dan 2, the king has a dream which no one can interpret. Daniel is therefore brought in and declares that God has revealed to Nebuchadnezzar, 'what will happen at the end of days'. The Greek phrase *ha dei genesthai* ('what must happen') is used in John's opening sentence ('The revelation of Jesus Christ, which God gave him to show his servants *what must soon take place*') and is repeated in 1.19, 4.1 and 22.6. Beale argues that this divides the book into four sections and that John's replacement of 'end of days' with 'soon' means that 'what Daniel expected to occur in the distant future, the defeat of cosmic evil and ushering in of the kingdom, John expects to begin in his own generation, and perhaps has already been inaugurated (1998, p. 115).

John's use of Isaiah

The highest number of allusions in total come from Isaiah, though they have attracted less attention than John's use of Ezekiel and Daniel. This is perhaps because they are often combined with other texts. For example, in the visionary descriptions of Christ in Rev 1 and 19, the sword that comes from his mouth is almost certainly an allusion to Isa 11.4, but there is no suggestion that John's description is based on that passage. Similarly, the four living creatures in Rev 4 have six wings and sing, 'Holy, holy, holy', undoubtedly a reference to Isa 6.3. But the more significant parallels come from Ezek 1 and Dan 7. Fekkes (1994, p. 282) divides John's uses of Isaiah into four categories:

1. *Visionary experience and language*: Isa 6.1–4
2. *Christological titles and descriptions*: Isa 11.4, 10; 22.22; 44.6; 65.15
3. *Eschatological judgement*:
   a. Holy war and Day of the Lord: Isa 2.19, 10; 34.4; 63.1–3
   b. Oracles against the nations: Isa 13.21; 21.9; 23.8, 17; 34.9-14; 47.7–9
4. *Eschatological salvation*:
   a. Salvation oracles in anticipation: Isa 65.15/62.2; 61.10; 60.14/49.23; 43.4; 49.10; 25.8b

    b. Oracles of renewal: Isa 65.15–20a; 25.8ab; 43.18, 19; 55.1

    c. New Jerusalem oracles: Isa 52.1; 54.11–12; 60.1–3, 5, 11, 19

John's description of the New Jerusalem in Rev 21 is a passage that does draw on Isaiah more than any other source. The passage opens with the statement, 'I saw a new heaven and a new earth,' a reference to Isa 65.17. It is described as 'the holy city' (Isa 52.1). It is a place where there will be no more tears (Isa 25.8). The thirsty will be invited to drink from the water of life (Isa 55.1). It is adorned with every precious jewel (Isa 54.11–12) and the nations will bring their glory into it (Isa 60.3, 5). Its gates are left open (Isa 60.11). Indeed, the one who sits on the throne says, 'See, I am making all things new.' Isa 43.19 says, 'I am about to do a new thing.' Despite the 'gloom and doom' that pervades so much of Revelation, it is Isaiah's universal vision that shines through in the end. As David Mathewson (2003, p. 225) says, 'these texts provide a lens of perception which informs their expectation of how God will act in the future (new creation, new exodus, new covenant, new Jerusalem, restored and new paradise)'.

    Fekkes claims that John's use of the Old Testament shows considerable contextual awareness and he 'expected his readers to appreciate the exegetical foundation of his visions' (p. 290). He 'consistently employs accepted hermeneutical procedures' and indeed from the point of view of technique, 'it would be difficult to distinguish the prophet from his Jewish contemporaries' (p. 285). What makes the difference, he says, are John's Christological presuppositions. He does note, however, that while the exegetical techniques are generally at the service of the Christological presuppositions, the latter does not always dictate the former.

Selected passages

The inaugural vision (Rev 1.12–16)

Matthew, Luke and John all record appearances of the risen Christ but they are nothing like John's description in Rev 1.12–16. Whatever it was that John saw, what he has written down is an amalgam of Old Testament phrases, taken from descriptions of angels (Dan 10.5–6), the one like a son of man (Dan 7.13), the branch of Jesse (Isa 11.4), God (Dan 7.9) and the brilliance of the sun (Judg 5.31). Several explanations have been offered to account for this: (1) John's mind was so full of scripture that his vision naturally took its form in scriptural imagery; (2) John is trying to give the reader an impression of his vision by referring to other well-known visions; (3) John's vision was actually the result of a scriptural meditation; (4) The vision is a literary composition and part of the author's Christology.

> Then I turned to see whose voice it was that spoke to me, and on turning I saw seven golden lampstands, and in the midst of the lampstands I saw one like the Son of Man, clothed with a long robe and with a golden sash across his chest. His head and his hair were white as white wool, white as snow; his eyes were like a flame of fire, his feet were like burnished bronze, refined as in a furnace, and his voice was like the sound of many waters. In his right hand he held seven stars, and from his mouth came a sharp, two-edged sword, and his face was like the sun shining with full force. (1.12–16)

The seven letters (Rev 2–3)

An interesting feature of the seven letters is that the first five all begin with a description of the sender that is taken from the inaugural vision:

> These are the words of him who holds the seven stars in his right hand, who walks among the seven golden lampstands. (Ephesus)

> These are the words of the first and the last, who was dead and came to life. (Smyrna)

> These are the words of him who has the sharp two-edged sword. (Pergamum)

> These are the words of the Son of God, who has eyes like a flame of fire, and whose feet are like burnished bronze. (Thyatira)

These are the words of him who has the seven spirits of God and the
seven stars. (Sardis)

This is so deliberate that one can only speculate as to why it was not
continued for Philadelphia and Laodicea. Farrer (1964) suggests that
the 'key of David' (Philadelphia) refers back to the 'keys of Death and
of Hades' in 1.18 and 'faithful and true witness' (Laodicea) back to the
opening greeting in 1.5. He concludes that the letters are an exposition
of the vision (1.12–18) with the final letter forming an inclusion by
returning to the opening greeting. On this view, the letters have no
particular relevance to the places addressed but were composed as
a unit. The opposite view is espoused by Hemer (1986), who thinks
the descriptions began as local allusions (e.g. the metal industry of
Thyatira suggested the 'flame of fire' and 'burnished bronze') and that
the inaugural vision was constructed out of these, even though it now
comes first in the book. The debate shows something of the complexity
of understanding John's use of scripture.

The Lion and the Lamb in 5.5–6

This has been a key passage for the interpretation of Revelation. In
Rev 4, John has a vision of God on his throne, which he describes in
language drawn from Ezek 1, Dan 7 and Isa 6. In Rev 5, he sees a scroll
and the question is asked, 'Who is worthy to open the scroll and break
its seals?' (5.2) He then hears that only Jesus can open the scroll:

> 'See, the Lion of the tribe of Judah, the Root of David, has conquered,
> so that he can open the scroll and its seven seals.' Then I saw between
> the throne and the four living creatures and among the elders a Lamb
> standing as if it had been slaughtered, having seven horns and seven
> eyes, which are the seven spirits of God sent out into all the earth.
> (5.5–6)

The significance of this passage is that we have the juxtaposition of
two quite different images of Jesus, one violent (Lion) and one gentle
(Lamb). The first is drawn from Gen 49.9 and Isa 11.1 and represents

the messiah as a powerful military figure (as in the Targums and 1QSb 5.21–29). The Lamb is probably the Passover Lamb or perhaps the Lamb of Isa 53.10 (or both) and represents gentleness and self-sacrifice. Thus according to Sweet (1990, p. 125), the 'Lion of Judah, the traditional messianic expectation, is reinterpreted by the slain Lamb: God's power and victory lie in self-sacrifice.' This is an attractive position as it allows the violence of Revelation to be reinterpreted as symbolic of Christ's self-sacrifice. As Mark Bredin (2003, p. 192) says, 'Lamb redefines violent imagery in terms of self-suffering through which victory is gained'. However, it may be more complicated than that. The Lamb of Revelation is not a gentle figure. Even in this passage, the Lamb has seven horns, a symbol of power, and seven eyes, a symbol of omniscience. In the following chapter, the destruction brought about by opening the seals causes the people to seek death rather than face the 'wrath of the Lamb' (6.16). In 17.14, the kings of the earth make war on the Lamb but he conquers them for he is 'Lord of lords and King of kings'. It would appear that as well as the Lion undergoing reinterpretation by being juxtaposed with a Lamb, the Lamb has also picked up characteristics of the powerful Lion. As Resseguie says: 'The Lion of the tribe of Judah interprets what John sees: death on the cross (the Lamb) is not defeat but is the way to power and victory (the Lion) … the Lamb, though not in nature a strong animal, is a being of incontrovertible might in this book' (1998, pp. 34, 129).

War in heaven in Rev 12

Although Gen 3 lays the blame for the first temptation on the serpent, there is very little in the rest of the Old Testament to suggest that human sin is incited by external forces. However, by the time we get to the New Testament period there is a considerable literature on the influence of angels and demons on human affairs. Indeed, in the Gospels, the devil or Satan is seen as the force behind temptation (Matt 4.1–11), demon possession (Mark 3.20–30), certain types of illness (Luke 13.16), unbelief (Luke 8.12) and betrayal (John 13.2). But the book of Revelation is the first to connect this explicitly with the serpent of Genesis:

> And war broke out in heaven; Michael and his angels fought against the dragon. The dragon and his angels fought back, but they were defeated, and there was no longer any place for them in heaven. The great dragon was thrown down, that ancient serpent, who is called the Devil and Satan, the deceiver of the whole world – he was thrown down to the earth, and his angels were thrown down with him. (12.7–9)

There are two main interpretations of this difficult text. The first was popularized in Milton's *Paradise Lost* and suggests that John is offering an explanation for the presence of evil in the garden of Eden. Prior to creation, there was a 'fall from heaven' and this is alluded to in texts like Isa 14.12 ('How you are fallen from heaven, O Day Star, son of Dawn!') and Ezek 28.16 ('you were filled with violence, and you sinned; so I cast you as a profane thing from the mountain of God'). Historically, these texts are referring to the kings of Babylon and Tyre respectively, but the extreme language could suggest that they are modelled on a far greater 'fall from grace'. Osborne (2002, pp. 468–73) is a modern advocate of this position, citing a number of parallel texts (eg. *1 Enoch* 1–6; *2 Enoch* 29.4–5 (J); *Sib. Or.* 5.528–9) to support his position. On this view, John is not only offering an explanation of the serpent in the garden of Eden but the presence of evil throughout world history.

On the other hand, the dragon's fall appears to be the result of Christ's victory (12.5–6) and its purpose in the narrative is to explain the persecution of the Church. This is stated first by saying that the dragon goes in pursuit of the 'woman who had given birth to the male child' (Rev 12.13) and then that it 'went off to make war on the rest of her children, those who keep the commandments of God and hold the testimony of Jesus' (12.17). This latter phrase is almost certainly a reference to the Church at large and not simply to Jesus' siblings. Consequently, many scholars think that the woman is not specifically

Mary but the 'messianic community' that gave birth to Jesus. Be that as it may, the point is that it is Jesus' victory on the cross that triggers the defeat of the dragon and so on this interpretation, John's reference to the serpent is simply to assert its defeat also.

The Song of the Lamb in 15.3–5

Before John begins three chapters of judgement in Rev 16 (seven bowls), 17 (destruction of the harlot and the beast) and 18 (fall of Babylon), he narrates a vision of the saints in heaven who are singing 'the song of Moses, the servant of God, and the song of the Lamb' (15.3). What is puzzling about the song that follows is that it bears no similarity to the song of Moses in Exod 15 but is based on Psalm 86.8–10, supplemented by a number of texts which share common vocabulary (Deut 32.4; Psalm 145.7; Jer 10.6–7). Psalm 86 proclaims the incomparability of God ('There is none like you among the gods … you alone are God'), the greatness of his works ('For you are great and do wondrous things') and the universality of his salvation ('All the nations you have made shall come and bow down before you, O Lord, and shall glorify your name'). Given the fact that 'the nations' have been the subject of judgement in Rev 6–14, the inclusion of a hymn that proclaims their salvation can only be deliberate.

> Great and amazing are your deeds, Lord God the Almighty! Just and true are your ways, King of the nations! Lord, who will not fear and glorify your name? For you alone are holy. All nations will come and worship before you, for your judgements have been revealed. (15.3–4)

Conclusion

The use of the Old Testament in Revelation has many unique features. It is the only book to incorporate allusions in almost every verse, while never explicitly quoting scripture. It is the only book whose structure is modelled on Ezekiel; indeed the only New Testament book to make significant use of this great prophet. And its picture of Jesus seems to owe more to Old Testament theophanies (appearances of God) than resurrection stories. There are some parallels with the so-called apocalyptic discourse in Mark 13 and it may be that both are drawing on a common source (perhaps a midrash on Daniel). It also shares characteristics with Jude and 2 Peter, such as its focus on angels and demons. Richard Bauckham calls his collection of studies on Revelation, *The Climax of Prophecy* (1993). As the last book of the Bible, it certainly calls to mind the rich heritage of Israel's scriptures.

Did John have a vision of the future (and present) and use scripture to describe it (a rhetorical model), or did his vision come from scripture, either by exegesis (a scribal model) or meditation (a mystical model)? Those who are most impressed by the similarities opt for a scribal/ exegetical model, concluding that John's careful study of scripture has enabled him to offer a theological synthesis which captures the true intent of the biblical authors. For example, Bauckham argues that the song to be sung in the new age (Rev 15.3–4) is not simply an amalgam of worship texts but has been derived by careful exegesis of Exod 15. Although there are no words in common, he argues that John was led by verbal association from Exod 15.11 ('who is like you, O Lord, among the nations?') to three other texts (Psalm 86.8–10, Psalm 98.1–2, Jer 10.7) where similar words occur. In this way, John was able to deduce the content of the new song. Beale also thinks that John uses texts with their original context very much in mind.

On the other hand, those who are more struck by the differences between Revelation and scripture opt for either a rhetorical or mystical model. The former begins with an analysis of John's rhetorical purposes and seeks to show how he uses scripture to support his case. This applies both to his choice of scripture – he only alludes to those texts that support the point he is trying to make – and what he does with them. George Caird is a good example of this approach, where the fact of Christ's death and resurrection causes John to reinterpret the biblical texts: 'Wherever the Old Testament speaks of the victory of the Messiah or the overthrow of the enemies of God, we are to remember that the gospel recognizes no other way of achieving these ends than the way of the Cross' (1984, p. 75). Schüssler Fiorenza is also an advocate of a 'rhetorical' model, stating that John 'does not interpret the Old Testament but uses its words, images, phrases, and patterns as a language arsenal in order to make his own theological statement or express his own prophetic vision' (1985, p. 135).

An important advocate of the 'mystical' model is Christopher Rowland (1993). He recognizes that a degree of planning has gone into the structure of the book and that John is certainly harnessing key images from the scriptures to make his point. But Rowland wants to do justice to John's claim to be 'in the spirit' (Rev 1.10; 4.2) and a receiver of visions. Texts and images have come together in John's mind but not through exegesis or attention to original context. They are more like dreams, which jump about without any apparent logic, and yet reveal some of our most basic hopes and fears. Thus before he comments on the text of Revelation in his commentary (1993), he invites us to contemplate some contemporary pictures to get us 'in the mood'. As with Revelation, modern art only 'works' if one has some familiarity with the images (like a political cartoon) but such 'contexts' do not determine their meaning. Indeed, Rowland questions whether 'authorial intention' is the appropriate goal for a work like Revelation. If asked why he has combined images from Isaiah, Daniel and Ezekiel in his inaugural vision, John would most likely have replied, 'I was in the spirit.'

Further reading

Although the use of scripture in Revelation was once seen as a neglected topic, there are now important monographs on the author's use of Daniel (Beale), Ezekiel (Ruiz, Bøe), Isaiah (Fekkes) and Zechariah (Jauhiainen), as well as studies on selected passages, such as Rev 21–22 (Lee, Matthewson) and themes, such as non-violence (Bredin) and intertextuality (Moyise). The chapters in the Moyise and Menken series were written by Moyise (Genesis), Tilly (Deuteronomy), Moyise (Psalms), Mathewson (Isaiah) and Jauhiainen (Minor Prophets). And the chapter on Revelation in the Beale and Carson Commentary was written by Beale and McDonough.

12

Concluding Hermeneutical Observations

Jewish exegesis and the New Testament

Our studies have shown that the use of the Old Testament in the New has many similarities with contemporary Jewish exegesis. In particular, the New Testament authors share with the Qumran writings the presupposition that they are living in the age of fulfilment. This means that scripture can be applied directly to those involved in the final eschatological events. So just as the author of 1QpHab discovered the battle between the Wicked Priest and the Teacher of Righteousness in the book of Habakkuk, the Christian writers found the treachery of Judas and the need to replace him in the Psalms. Both groups saw the establishment of their community as a fulfilment of God's promises to Israel and both thought judgement would soon fall on those who resist.

In some cases, they even use the same texts. The restoration of the fallen tent of David (Amos 9.11) is used in 4QFlor and Acts 15, the proclamation of liberty to the oppressed (Isa 61) in 11QMelch and Luke 4, and the rage of the nations against God's anointed (Psalm 2) in 4QFlor and Acts 4. One might suggest that these are fairly obvious 'messianic' texts and put it down to coincidence. But that can hardly be said of Amos 5.25–26 ('You shall take up Sakkuth your king, and Kaiwan your star-god,') which is quoted in CD 7 and Acts 7. Even more significant is that they use many of the same exegetical techniques. In the course of our study, we have seen examples of typology, allegory, catch-word links, quoting from variant texts, altering the quoted text, reading the text in an unorthodox manner, drawing on *haggada* legends and using homiletic forms of argumentation.

Typology

In Rom 5.14, Paul specifically says that Adam is a 'type of the one to come'. In other passages, the actual word 'type' is not used but it is clear that a 'biblical event, person, or institution' is serving as an 'example or pattern for other events, persons, or institutions' (Baker, 1994, p. 327). Thus eating and drinking in the wilderness corresponds to participation in the Christian Eucharist (both bring 'types' of life). The lifting up of the serpent corresponds to the crucifixion (both bring 'types' of healing). The crossing of the Red Sea corresponds to Christian baptism (both bring 'types' of deliverance). Michael Fishbane says that such 'typological alignments have deep exegetical dimensions, in so far as they "read" one historical moment in terms of another, and thereby project the powerful associations of the past into future images of longing and hope' (1985, p. 371).

Allegory

The word 'allegory' is only found in Gal 4.24 (as a verb), where Sarah and Hagar are identified with two mountains, then with two covenants and finally with those who follow Paul's law free gospel and those who believe Gentiles must be circumcised. In the book of Revelation, a whole host of images (lampstands, stars, beasts, dragons, locusts) and numbers (666, 144,000) are given special symbolic meanings. Payment of those who work in Christ's service is supported by a quotation about not muzzling an ox (Deut 25.4). It is just about impossible to believe that these interpretations were in the mind of the original authors or editors.

Catch-word links

In Rom 4, Paul expounds the meaning of Gen 15.6 ('the Lord reckoned it to him as righteousness') by referring to Psalm 32.1–2 ('blessed is the one against whom the Lord will not reckon sin'). The 'stone' passage quoted in Mark 12.10–11 has generated further 'stone' passages in Luke 20.18, Rom 9.33 and 1 Pet 2.6-8. In Gal 3, the 'curse' of not obeying the law (Deut 27.26) has led Paul to another 'curse' text, one which pronounces a curse on a criminal left hanging on a tree (Deut 21.23). Paul is able to use this connection by asserting that Christ's death on the cross/tree incurred the curse of Deut 21.23, which somehow neutralized the curse of Deut 27.26.

Quoting from variant texts

This is somewhat different from Qumran or the Rabbis in that the New Testament authors generally quote from a Greek translation rather than the Hebrew. Thus in one sense, they are always quoting from a variant text. But of particular interest are those occasions when the Greek text diverges significantly from the Hebrew. In Acts 15.16–17, a text of Amos 9.12 is quoted which read 'Adam' instead of 'Edom'. The author of Hebrews obtains a proof-text for the incarnation by means of a text that read 'body' instead of 'open ear'. In Acts 7.43, Stephen quotes a text of Amos 5.25 that names the foreign gods as 'Moloch' and 'Rephan', instead of 'Sakkuth' and 'Kaiwan'.

Altering the quoted text

In the above example, 'Moloch' and 'Rephan' are changes already found in the LXX but the change from 'Damascus' (Israel's northern exile) to 'Babylon' (Judah's southern exile) has no precedent and appears to be the author's. Matthew inserts *oudamos* ('by no means') in his quotation of Mic 5.2, effectively reversing its meaning. John has Judas betraying Jesus by raising 'his heel' rather than 'by cunning' (13.18), the latter probably being regarded as doctrinally inappropriate.

Reading the text in an unorthodox manner

In Matt 21.5 (donkey and colt) and John 19.24 (clothes and clothing) the Hebrew parallelism is ignored and taken to refer to two different things. It is impossible to believe that this was done in ignorance. One can only suppose that they regarded the parallelism as fortuitous (i.e. planned by God) and chose to exploit it. Paul's linguistic argument concerning the singular 'offspring' is similar. He clearly knows that the original promise refers to a multitude since he speaks of 'Abraham's children and his true descendants' in Rom 9.7. In Gal 3.16, he chooses to exploit a feature of the language to make a Christological point.

Use of *haggada* legends

The extraordinary statement in 1 Cor 10.4, that the rock which supplied water for the wilderness generation followed them in their wanderings, was not original to Paul. It is known from Jewish tradition. Twice in the New Testament (Gal 3.19; Acts 7.53) we hear of the tradition that Moses received the law on Mount Sinai through angels. Jude and 2 Peter make use of the legendary interpretation of Gen 6, that angels had intercourse with women and produced a race of giants. Jude uses the tradition that Michael disputed with Satan concerning the body of Moses. In 2 Tim 3.8 there is a reference to the tradition that Satan raised up Jannes and Jambres to oppose Moses.

Traditional forms of homiletic argumentation

Kimball cites the rabbinic form of debate known as *yelammeddenu* as the explanation for Jesus answering the lawyer's question ('who is my neighbour?') with the parable of the Good Samaritan. This tradition began with a question, cited relevant texts from the law, clarified with a text from the prophets, illustrated the meaning of key terms with a story and closed with a return to the original texts. Borgen does a similar thing for the 'Bread of life' discourse in John 6. Stockhausen argues that Paul often begins his argument with texts (or events) from the law, clarifies with a text from the prophets (or the wisdom writings) and uses *pesher*-type exegesis to bring out their contemporary meaning.

Explaining the Old Testament in the New

Do the parallels set out above 'explain' the use of the Old Testament in the New? Some scholars think so, suggesting that the only difference between the two sets of writings is that each saw their own community as the true fulfilment of scripture. In other words, they applied the same methods and techniques but with different presuppositions. The New Testament authors viewed the scriptures through the lens of the Christ event and the establishment of the Church. The Qumran authors viewed them through the lens of the Teacher of Righteousness and the establishment of the Essenes/Qumran community. If Luke thinks that Jesus opened the minds of the disciples to understand the scriptures (Luke 24.27), the Qumran community believed that the Teacher of Righteousness 'made known all the mysteries of the words of his servants the Prophets' (1QpHab 7.5). This of course raises the question of validity. Did the two communities simply find in the scriptures what they wanted to find? In other words, is ancient exegesis a serious attempt to discover what is in the text or an apologetic strategy to defend views arrived at on other grounds?

Other scholars regard the parallels as superficial and think that the use of the Old Testament in the New is quite different from the Qumran writings. This can take several forms. First, there are those who suggest that the more 'arbitrary' types of exegesis (allegory, altering texts, *haggada*) are rare in the New Testament and should not be seen as parallel to the extensive use of such devices at Qumran. Second, there are those that regard the eschatological orientation of the two communities as quite different. The Qumran community looked forward to a time when Isa 61 (liberty to the oppressed) or Amos 9 (restoration of Davidic dynasty) would come about. The New Testament authors proclaimed that these had been fulfilled in Christ. Third, some argue that christological exegesis is quite different from anything at Qumran. It is not about applying methods but being involved in a type of spiritual transformation. And lastly, we should not forget that scholars themselves have presuppositions. Christian scholars naturally think that the application of the Old Testament to Christ and the Church was correct, while the application to the Teacher of Righteousness and the Qumran community was false. It would be a naive scholar who thought this had no effect on their judgements.

1. Interpretations that emphasize continuity

We have seen a number of these in the course of our study. Moo argues that Jesus' use of the Old Testament is quite different from the arbitrary exegesis of Qumran. Jesus was not interested in bringing new meaning to old texts but aimed to show how the texts, when properly understood, spoke about himself. Kimball is happy to link Jesus with the more acceptable forms of Jewish exegesis but thinks the purpose of the quotations was (1) To claim eschatological fulfilment and (2) To correct traditional Jewish interpretation with his own superior exegesis. Thus he acknowledges that the reading in the synagogue consists of Isa 61.1–2 with a phrase from Isa 58.6 inserted, but believes we are to understand this as a summary of Jesus' sermon rather than the actual reading. He thinks that Jesus chose this combination of texts (not Luke) to assert that he was both the herald of the coming liberation (Isa 61) and its agent (Isa 58).

The most extreme form of continuity is argued by scholars such as Kaiser in his contribution to the Beale collection (1994, pp. 55–69) and in his book (1985). The title of the article ('The Single Intent of Scripture') makes his position clear. The meaning of the Old Testament is no more and no less than the original intention of the authors. This is ascertained by the normal means of understanding texts (genre, grammar, syntax, etc.) and this applies both to our use of scripture and that of the New Testament authors, who did not find some *super-additum* in addition to the original intention of the authors. They simply applied the one single meaning to new situations.

The opposite strategy is found in Beale's contribution to the collection (1994, pp. 387–404) and in his more recent handbook (2012). Beale argues that the single intent of scripture is the meaning that God intended when the writings were inspired. He believes that the New Testament authors had certain presuppositions, among the most important being: (1) Corporate solidarity, the way a person can represent and embody a people; (2) Christ's representation of true Israel in the Old Testament and the Church (the new Israel) in the New; (3) History is unified by a wise and sovereign plan so that the earlier parts are designed to correspond and point to the latter parts; (4) The age of eschatological fulfilment has come in Christ. As a consequence, the fifth presupposition

> affirms that the latter parts of biblical history function as the broader context to interpret earlier parts because they all have the same, ultimate divine author who inspires the various human authors, and one deduction from this premise is that Christ as the centre of history is the *key to interpreting the earlier portions of the Old Testament and its promises.* (1994, p. 392)

Thus Beale can acknowledge that the New Testament applies Old Testament texts in ways that were not necessarily envisaged by their original authors. But he insists that this never involves a change of meaning. Rather, it is drawing out the full potential of the text, now that the age of fulfilment has come. It is like a seed which contains everything that is to develop from it, from an 'acorn to an oak tree, a bud to a flower, or a seed to an apple' (2012, p. 27).

2. Interpretations that emphasize discontinuity

One of the first scholars to compare the Qumran writings with the New Testament was Krister Stendahl (1954). The fact that he based his study on Matthew is significant. Matthew, as we have seen, is most open to the charge of manipulating texts to prove what he wants to prove. Stendahl pointed to the use of variant texts, changing the wording of texts, ignoring the original context and supplying different vowels, in order to make his point. He characterized Matthew's use of the Old Testament as *midrash-pesher*, by which he meant that it strongly resembled the type of interpretation found in 1QpHab. Davies and Allison continue this tradition in their multi-volume commentary, stating, for example, that contrary to Matthew's interpretation, Isa 7.14 only means that 'she who is now a virgin will later conceive and give birth: no miracle is involved' (1988, p. 214).

Interpretations that emphasize discontinuity often stress the apologetic nature of the New Testament use of scripture. The authors did not believe in the death and resurrection of Christ or the birth of the Church through scripture study. They believed in these things because they had experienced them and only turned to scripture in order to convince others. Thus Paul's quotations are mainly concentrated in Galatians and Romans, where the issue of 'works of the law' is uppermost. There are no explicit quotations in Philippians or Thessalonians, where this is not the issue. In the book of Acts, Luke portrays Paul as using scripture when preaching to Jews (Acts 13) but not when preaching to Gentiles (Acts 17). Instead, he has Paul quote from some of their poets. The apologetic interpretation is particularly associated with Barnabas Lindars (*New Testament Apologetic*, 1961), who says that

> The place of the Old Testament in the formation of New Testament theology is that of a servant, ready to run to the aid of the gospel whenever it is required, bolstering up arguments, and filling out meaning through evocative allusions, but never acting as the master or leading the way, nor even guiding the process of thought behind the scenes. (In Beale, 1994, p. 145)

3. Interpretations that emphasize continuity and discontinuity

Not surprisingly, many scholars find the above positions too extreme and so seek to do justice to both continuity and discontinuity. This takes many forms. Some acknowledge that Old Testament texts appear to be taken out of context but appeal either to the surrounding verses or to exegetical developments that took place between the Testaments. Hanson makes this a significant feature of his work. Others seek to show that the Old Testament texts, while not specifically addressing the situation envisaged in the New, nevertheless have a certain 'givenness' to them. The obvious example is Isa 53, which seems to 'cry out' for an individual interpretation/fulfilment.

Joel Marcus argues that Mark modelled his Gospel on the new exodus promised by Isaiah but its application to Christ and the disciples caused a transformation. Yahweh's triumphant march through the wilderness is forced to collide with the reality of Jesus' death and the 'befuddled, bedraggled little band of disciples'. Mark has certainly learned much about Christ from the scriptures. But he would not have been able to learn it had he not believed that Christ was the key to the scriptures. One might argue, therefore, that Christian experience comes first and reflection on the scriptures follows. On the other hand, it is also true that the New Testament writers were largely 'formed' by the scriptures before they ever set eyes on Christ.

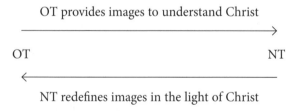

OT provides images to understand Christ

OT   NT

NT redefines images in the light of Christ

Hays argues for a dialogical understanding of the Old Testament in Paul. The Old Testament, he says, is never played off as a foil for the gospel or regarded as sub-standard. Paul's quotations and allusions bring powerful connotations that are not easily silenced. Paul sometimes offers specific interpretations that guide the reader down a particular path. But other times, he places new and old side by side and allows them to mutually interpret one another. Thus Moses is both witness to the old covenant when veiled and witness to God's glory when unveiled. Hays challenges the view that Paul's hermeneutics are Christocentric, arguing that very few of his quotations are actually applied to Christ. However, if one suggests broader themes, such as, 'God's purpose to raise up a worldwide community of people who confess his sovereignty and manifest his justice', then the continuity is more easily discernible.

Another important feature of Hays's work is that while he acknowledges Paul's debt to Jewish exegesis, he does not feel this adequately explains it. To argue that Paul went from text to text by catch-word associations does not explain why he chose these associations rather than others. Even the idea of presuppositional lenses does not adequately explain the choices made or even the process. Scholars expend a great deal of energy trying to trace Paul's steps in such passages as Gal 3.10–14 but it is highly unlikely that Paul went through them one by one in discreet stages. According to Hays, Paul 'seems to have leaped – in moments of metaphorical insight – to intuitive apprehensions of the meanings of texts without the aid or encumbrance of systematic reflection about his own hermeneutics' (1989, p. 161).

Hughes tries to work out a dynamic interpretation for the use of the Old Testament in Hebrews. He notes that some passages emphasize continuity to the extent that the Old Testament heroes are virtually treated as Christians. On the other hand, it is clear that some parts of scripture are treated as obsolete. He thus asks: 'How in one context can the scriptures of the Old Testament function so immediately as a vehicle for the Word of God while in other contexts the covenant which those same scriptures enshrine is unceremoniously dismissed as outmoded?' (1979, p. 71) His answer is not so much exegetical techniques or fixed rules but context and perspective. When the author is thinking of the struggles of the Church, words spoken to Israel in her struggles are an immediate Word of God to the congregation. But when he is thinking of the benefits brought about by Christ, the 'words can only be seen as preparatory, witnessing, some of them at least, to their own futurity and hence infinality' (p. 71).

Finally, we must mention the growing use of the concept of inter-textuality in the study of the Old Testament in the New. Biblical scholars are not the only ones interested in how texts relate to other texts. Students of literature have always been interested in how later writers situate their work with respect to the past. Intertextuality takes this one step further by suggesting that texts are always in a dynamic relationship with other texts. Paul's concentrated use of 'curse' texts in Gal 3 is not only an interpretation of Deut 21.23 and 27.26. It also does something to the word 'curse', so that even historically unrelated writings are affected. This offers a different orientation for the study of the Old Testament in the New. It is not about using the various sources and influences to complete a two-dimensional puzzle, as if that static entity represented the author's use of the Old Testament. Rather, it seeks to describe the complex interactions set in motion when the 'textual matrix' is disturbed by a new text. As Julia Kristeva puts it, we should try and see the interaction of texts as an 'intersection of textual surfaces rather than a point' (1986, p. 36). Scholars in this third category (continuity and discontinuity) agree that we are dealing with a dynamic interaction between new and old. The issue raised by intertextuality is whether this interaction results in a stable resolution (a point) or a range of possibilities (surfaces).

Conclusion

The discovery of the Dead Sea Scrolls and developments in literary criticism has shed new light on the use of the Old Testament in the New. The Dead Sea Scrolls reveal a community that believed the words of the prophets were being fulfilled in their own history and used certain exegetical techniques to prove it. The New Testament authors believed this of their community and used many of the same techniques, indeed some of the same texts, to prove it. As we have seen, much has been published (see Bibliography) but there is still much to do. Questions about hermeneutics (interpretation), the availability of Greek, Hebrew and Aramaic texts in the first century, the role of the Old Testament in the new work and the legitimacy or otherwise of certain techniques will continue to challenge scholars. Furthermore, developments in literary criticism have brought fresh insights into how texts interact with their subtexts. What happens when a text is lifted from its textual moorings and deposited somewhere else? Can the new author control the affects this will have on the reader? Or does it introduce a dynamic that requires the reader's participation? The aim of this book has been to provide an introduction to this fascinating area of study. My hope is that you will now go on to read some of the more detailed works mentioned in the 'Further reading' and begin a 'dialogue with the text and with the texts within the text' (Ruiz, 1989, p. 520). Perhaps in time, you will be writing your own text that interacts 'with the text and the texts within the text'.

Bibliography

Adams, E. (2007), *The Stars will Fall from Heaven: Cosmic Catastrophe in the New Testament and its World* (London & New York: T. & T. Clark).

Ahearne-Kroll, S. (2007), *The Psalms of Lament in Mark's Passion: Jesus' Davidic Suffering* (SNTSMS, 142; Cambridge: Cambridge University Press).

Albl, M. C. (1999), *'And Scripture Cannot be Broken': The Form and Function of the Early Christian Testimonia Collections* (NovTSup, 96; Leiden: Brill).

Allison, D. C. (1993), *The New Moses: A Matthean Typology* (Edinburgh: T. & T. Clark).

—(2010), *Constructing Jesus: Memory, Imagination and History* (Grand Rapids: Baker Academic).

Attridge, H. W. (1989), *The Epistle to the Hebrews* (Hermeneia; Philadelphia: Fortress Press).

Aus, R. (2004), *Matthew 1–2 and the Virginal Conception: In Light of Palestinian and Hellenistic Judaic Traditions on the Birth of Israel's First Redeemer* (Lanham: University Press of America).

Bacon, B. S. (1930), *Studies in Matthew* (London: Constable).

Baker, D. L. (1994), 'Typology and the Christian Use of the Old Testament' in Beale (ed.), *The Right Doctrine from the Wrong Texts?* pp. 13–30.

Barrett, C. K. (1962), *The Epistle to the Romans* (London: A. & C. Black).

—(1978), *The Gospel according to St John: An Introduction with Commentary and Notes on the Greek Text* (London: SPCK).

Bateman, H. W. (1998), *Early Jewish Hermeneutics and Hebrews 1.5–13* (New York: Peter Lang).

Bauckham, R. J. (1999), *James: Wisdom of James, Disciple of Jesus the Sage* (New York: Routledge).

Beale, G. K. (1984), *The Use of Daniel in Jewish Apocalyptic Literature and in the Revelation of St John* (Lanham: University Press of America).

—(1986), 'A Reconsideration of the Text of Daniel in the Apocalypse', *Biblica*, pp. 539–43.

—(ed.) (1994), *The Right Doctrine from the Wrong Texts?* (Grand Rapids: Baker Books).

—(1999), *John's Use of the Old Testament in Revelation* (Sheffield: Sheffield Academic Press).

—(2007), 'Colossians' in G. K. Beale and D. Carson (eds), *Commentary on the New Testament Use of the Old Testament,* pp. 841–70.

—(2011), *A New Testament Biblical Theology: The Unfolding of the Old Testament in the New* (Grand Rapids: Baker Academic).

—(2012), *Handbook on the New Testament Use of the Old Testament* (Grand Rapids: Baker Academic).

Beale, G. K. and Carson, D. A. (eds) (2007), *Commentary on the New Testament Use of the Old Testament* (Grand Rapids: Baker).

Beale, G. K. and McDonough, S. M. (2007), 'Revelation' in G. K. Beale and D. Carson (eds), *Commentary on the New Testament Use of the Old,* pp.1081–161.

Beaton, R. (2002), *Isaiah's Christ in Matthew's Gospel* (SNTSMS, 123; Cambridge: Cambridge University Press).

Belleville, L. L. (1991), *Reflections of Glory* (Sheffield: JSOT Press).

Berkeley, T. W. (2000), *From a Broken Covenant to Circumcision of the Heart: Pauline Intertextual Exegesis in Romans 2.17–29* (SBLDS, 175; Atlanta: SBL).

Bird, M. F. (2009), *Are You the One to Come?: The Historical Jesus and the Messianic Question* (Grand Rapids: Baker Academic).

Birding, K. and Lunde, J. (eds) (2007), *Three Views on the New Testament Use of the Old Testament* (Grand Rapids: Zondervan).

Blomberg, C. L. (2007), 'Matthew' in G. K. Beale and D. Carson (eds), *Commentary on the New Testament Use of the Old,* pp. 1–109.

Bock, D. L. (1987), *Proclamation from Prophecy and Pattern* (Sheffield: JSOT Press).

Bøe, S. (2001), *Gog and Magog. Ezekiel 38-39 as Pre-text for Revelation 19, 17–21 and 20, 7–10* (Tübingen: Mohr Siebeck).

Bonsirven, J. (1939), *Exégèse rabbinique et exégèse paulinienne* (Paris: Beauchesne).

Borg, M. J. (1998), *Conflict, Holiness, and Politics in the Teachings of Jesus* (Rev. edn; Harrisburg: Trinity Press).

Borgen, P. (1966), *Bread from Heaven: An Exegetical Study of the Concept of Manna in the Gospel of John and the Writings of Philo* (Leiden: Brill).

Boring, M. E. (1999), *1 Peter* (Nashville: Abingdon Press).

Brawley, R. L. (1995), *Text to Text Pours Forth Speech: Voices of Scripture in Luke-Acts* (Bloomington: Indiana University Press).

Bredin, M. (2003), *Jesus, Revolutionary of Peace. A Nonviolent Christology in the Book of Revelation* (Carlisle: Paternoster Press).

Brown, R. E. (1982), *The Epistles of John* (AB, 30; Garden City: Doubleday)

—(1993), *The Birth of the Messiah* (Garden City: Doubleday).

Brunson, A. C. (2003), *Psalm 118 in the Gospel of John: An Intertextual Study of the New Exodus Pattern in the Theology of John* (WUNT, 2/158; Tübingen: Mohr Siebeck).

Bryan, S. M. (2002), *Jesus and Israel's Traditions of Judgement and Restoration* (SNTSMS, 117; Cambridge: Cambridge University Press).

Buchanan, G. W. (1972), *To the Hebrews: Translation, Comments and Conclusions* (AB, 36; Garden City: Doubleday).

Caird, G. B. (1984), *The Revelation of St John the Divine* (2nd edn; London: A. & C. Black).

Campbell, D. A. (2009), *The Deliverance of God. An Apocalyptic Rereading of Justification in Paul* (Grand Rapids: Eerdmans).

Carey, H. J. (2009), *Jesus' Cry from the Cross: Towards a First-Century Understanding of the Intertextual Relationship between Psalm 22 and the Narrative of Mark's Gospel* (New York: T. & T. Clark).

Carson, D. A. (1988), 'John and the Johannine Epistles' in D. Carson and H. G. M. Williamson (eds), *It is Written: Scripture Citing Scripture* (Cambridge: Cambridge University Press), pp. 245–61.

Chilton, B. (1984), *A Galilean Rabbi and His Bible: Jesus' Own Interpretation of Isaiah* (London: SPCK).

—(2000), *Rabbi Jesus: An Intimate Biography* (Garden City: Doubleday).

Ciampa, R. E. (1998), *The Presence and Function of Scripture in Galatians 1 and 2* (WUNT 2,102; Tübingen: Mohr Siebeck).

Collins, J. J. (1997), *Apocalypticism in the Dead Sea Scrolls* (London and New York: Routledge).

Conzelmann, H. (1960), *The Theology of Saint Luke* (London: Faber/New York: Harper).

Cranfield, C. E. B. (1977), *The Gospel According to St Mark* (Cambridge: Cambridge University Press).

Crossan, J. D. (1991), *The Historical Jesus. The Life of a Mediterranean Jewish Peasant* (Edinburgh: T. & T. Clark).

Crossley, J. G. (2004), *The Date of Mark's Gospel. Insight from the Law in Earliest Christianity* (JSNTSup, 266; London & New York: T. & T. Clark).

Daly-Denton, M. (2000), *David in the Fourth Gospel. The Johannine Reception of the Psalms* (Lieden: Brill).

Davies, W. D. (1948), *Paul and Rabbinic Judaism* (London: SPCK).

Davies, W. D. and Allison, D. C. (1988), *The Gospel According to Saint Matthew*, Vol 1 (Edinburgh: T. & T. Clark).

Dines, J. M. (2004), *The Septuagint* (London: Continuum).

Doble, P. (1996), *The Paradox of Salvation. Luke's Theology of the Cross* (Cambridge: Cambridge University Press).

Docherty, S. E. (2009), *The Use of the Old Testament in Hebrews* (WUNT 2, 260; Tübingen: Mohr Siebeck),

Dodd, C. H. (1952), *According to the Scriptures, The Substructure of New Testament Theology* (London: Nisbet).

—(1959), *The Epistle of Paul to the Romans* (London: Fontana).

Dunn, J. D. G. (1998), *The Theology of Paul the Apostle* (Edinburgh: T. & T. Clark).

—(2003a), *Jesus Remembered* (Grand Rapids: Eerdmans).

—(2003b), *The Epistle to the Galatians* (BNTC; London: A. & C. Black).

Ellingworth, P. (1993), *The Epistle to the Hebrews* (Carlisle: Paternoster Press).

Elliott, J. H. (2000), *1 Peter* (AB, 38B; Garden City: Doubleday).

Evans, C. A. (1989), *To See and Not to Perceive: Isaiah 6.9–10 in Early Jewish and Christian Interpretation* (JSOTSup, 64; Sheffield: Sheffield Academic Press).

—(2012), *Matthew* (NCBC; Cambridge: Cambridge University Press).

Evans, C. F. (1990), *Saint Luke* (London: SCM Press/Philadelphia: Trinity Press International).

Farrer, A. (1964), *The Revelation of St John the Divine* (Oxford: Clarendon Press).

Fekkes, J. (1994), *Isaiah and Prophetic Traditions in the Book of Revelation* (Sheffield: Sheffield Academic Press).

Fishbane, M. (1985), *Biblical Interpretation in Ancient Israel* (Oxford: Oxford University Press).

France, R. T. (1971), *Jesus and the Old Testament* (London: Tyndale).

—(1994), 'The Formula-Quotations of Matthew 2 and the Problem of Communication' in Beale (ed.), *The Right Doctrine from the Wrong Texts?*, pp. 114–34.

—(2002), *The Gospel of Mark* (NIGTC; Grand Rapids: Eerdmans).

—(2007), *The Gospel of Matthew* (NICNT; Grand Rapids: Eerdmans).

Gheorghita, R. (2003), *The Role of the Septuagint in Hebrews. An Investigation of its Influence with Special Consideration to the Use of Hab 2:3–4 in Heb 10:37–38* (Tübingen: Mohr Siebeck).

Goppelt, L. (1993), *A Commentary on 1 Peter* (Grand Rapids: Eerdmans).

Goulder, M. D. (1989), *Luke: A New Paradigm* (Sheffield: JSOT Press).

Green, G. L. (2008), *Jude and 2 Peter* (BECNT; Grand Rapids, Baker Academic).

Gundry, R. H. (1993), *Mark: A Commentary on His Apology for the Cross* (Grand Rapids: Eerdmans).

—(1994), *Matthew: A Commentary on His Handbook for a Mixed Church under Persecution* (Grand Rapids: Eerdmans).

Guthrie, G. H. (2007), 'Hebrews' in G. K. Beale and D. Carson (eds), *Commentary on the New Testament Use of the Old*, pp. 919–95.

Häfner, G. (2007), 'Deuteronomy in the Pastorals Epistles' in M. J. J. Menken and S. Moyise (eds), *Deuteronomy in the New Testament*, pp. 136–51.

Hanson, A. T. (1974), *Studies in Paul's Technique and Theology* (London: SPCK).

—(1983), *The Living Utterances of God* (London: Darton, Longman & Todd).

—(1991), *The Prophetic Gospel: A Study of John and the Old Testament* (Edinburgh: T. & T. Clark).

Harris, R. J. (1916, 1920) *Testimonies* 2 Vols (Cambridge: Cambridge University Press).

Harstine, S. (2002), *Moses as a Character in the Fourth Gospel. A Study of Ancient Reading Techniques* (Sheffield: Sheffield Academic Press).

Hatina, T. R. (2002), *In Search of Context: The Function of Scripture in Mark's Narrative* (JSNTSup, 232; Sheffield: Sheffield Academic Press).

—(ed.) (2006), *Biblical Interpretation in Early Christian Gospels: Volume 1, The Gospel of Mark* (LNTS, 304; London: T. & T. Clark).

—(ed.) (2008), *Biblical Interpretation in Early Christian Gospels: Volume 2, The Gospel of Matthew* (LNTS, 310 ; London: T. & T. Clark).

—(ed.) (2010), *Biblical Interpretation in Early Christian Gospels: Volume 3, The Gospel of Luke* (LNTS, 376; London: T. & T. Clark).

Hays, R. B. (1989*) Echoes of Scripture in the Letters of Paul* (New Haven: Yale University Press).

—(2002) *The Faith of Jesus Christ. The Narrative Substructure of Galatians 3:1–4:11* (2nd edn; Grand Rapids: Eerdmans).

—(2005), *The Conversion of the Imagination. Paul as Interpreter of Israel's Scripture* (Grand Rapids: Eerdmans).

Heil, J. P. (2005), *The Rhetorical Role of Scripture in 1 Corinthians* (Atlanta: SBL).

Hemer, C. J. (1986), *The Letters to the Seven Churches of Asia in their Local Setting* (Sheffield: JSOT Press).

Holmén, T. (2001), *Jesus & Jewish Covenant Thinking* (Leiden: Brill).

Holmén, T. and Porter, S. (eds) (2011), *Handbook for the Study of the Historical Jesus* 4 Vols (Leiden: Brill).

Holmgren, F. C. (1999), *The Old Testament and the Significance of Jesus* (Grand Rapids: Eerdmans).

Holm-Nielsen, S. (1960), *Hodayot: Psalms from Qumran* (Oslo: Universitetsforlaget).

Hooker, M. D. (1959), *Jesus the Servant* (London: SPCK).

—(1967), *The Son of Man in Mark* (London: SPCK).

—(1988), 'Mark' in D. Carson and H. G. M. Williamson (eds), *It is Written: Scripture Citing Scripture,* (Cambridge: Cambridge University Press), pp. 220–30.

Horrell, D. (2006), *An Introduction to the Study of Paul* (2nd edn; London & New York: Continuum).

Houlden, J. L. (1976), *The Pastoral Epistles* (Oxford: Clarendon).

Hughes, G. R. (1979), *Hebrews and Hermeneutics* (Cambridge: Cambridge University Press).

Human, D. J. and Steyn, G. J. (eds) (2010), *Psalms and Hebrews. Studies in Reception* (LHB, 527; New York and London: T. & T. Clark).

Jeremias, J. (1972), *The Parables of Jesus* (London: SCM Press).

Jobes, K. H. (2005), *1 Peter* (BECNT; Grand Rapids: Baker Academic).

Johnson, L. T. (1995), *The Letter of James: A New Translation with Introduction and Commentary* (AB 37A; Garden City: Doubleday).

Jordaan, G. J. C. and Nel, P. (2010), 'From Priest-King to King-Priest: Psalm 110 and the Basic Structure of Hebrews' in D. J. Human and G. J. Steyn (eds), *Psalms and Hebrews. Studies in Reception,* pp. 229–40.

Kaiser, W. C. (1985), *The Uses of the OT in the NT* (Chicago: Moody Press).

—(1994), 'The Single Intent of Scripture' in G. K. Beale (ed.), *The Right Doctrine from the Wrong Texts?,* pp. 55–69.

Karrer, M. (2010), 'LXX Psalm 39:7–10 in Hebrews 10:5–7' in D. J. Human and G. Steyn, (eds), *Psalms and Hebrews. Studies in Reception,* pp. 126–46.

Keesmaat, S. C. (1999), *Paul and his Story. (Re)Interpreting the Exodus Tradition* (Sheffield: Sheffield Academic Press).

Kim, S. (1981), *The Origin of Paul's Gospel* (Tubingen: Mohr Siebeck).

Kimball, C. A. (1994), *Jesus' Exposition of the Old Testament in Luke's Gospel* (Sheffield: JSOT Press).

Knowles, M. (1993), *Jeremiah in Matthew's Gospel. The Rejected-Prophet Motif in Matthaean Redaction* (Sheffield: JSOT Press).

Koet, B. (2005), 'Isaiah in Luke–Acts' in S. Moyise and M. J. J. Menken (eds), *Isaiah in the New Testament*, pp.79-100.

Köstenberger, A. (2004), *John* (BECNT; Grand Rapids: Baker Academic).

—(2007), in G. K. Beale and D. Carson (eds), *Commentary on the New Testament Use of the Old*, pp. 415–512.

Kristeva, J. (1986), 'Word, Dialogue and Novel' in T. Moi (ed.), *The Kristeva Reader* (Oxford: Columbia University Press), pp. 34–61.

Law, T. M. (2013), *When God Spoke Greek: The Septuagint and the Making of the Christian Bible* (Oxford: Oxford University Press, 2013).

Lee, P. (2001), *The New Jerusalem in the Book of Revelation: A Study of Revelation 21–22 in the Light of its background in Jewish Tradition* (Tübingen: Mohr Siebeck).

Lim, T. H. and Collins, J. J. (eds) (2010), *The Oxford Handbook of The Dead Sea Scrolls* (Oxford: Oxford University Press).

Lindars, B. (1961), *New Testament Apologetic* (London: SCM Press).

—(1994), 'The Place of the Old Testament in the Formation New Testament Theology' in G. K. Beale (ed.), *The Right Doctrine from the Wrong Texts?*, pp. 137–45.

Litwak, K. D. (2005), *Echoes of Scripture in Luke-Acts. Telling the History of God's People Intertextually* (London: T. & T. Clark).

—(2010), 'A Coat of Many Colors: The Role of the Scriptures of Israel in Luke 2' in T. R. Hatina (ed), *Biblical Interpretation in Early Christian Gospels: Volume 3, The Gospel of Luke*, pp. 114–32.

Longenecker, B. W. (1998), *The Triumph of Abraham's God* (Edinburgh: T. & T. Clark).

Mallen, P. (2008), *The Reading and Transformation of Isaiah in Luke-Acts* (LNTS, 367; New York: T. & T. Clark).

Mann, J. (1940), *The Bible as Read and Preached in the Old Synagogue* (New York: KTAV).

Manning, G.T. (2004), *Echoes of a Prophet: The Use of Ezekiel in the Gospel of John and in Literature of the Second Temple Period* (JSNTSup, 270; London: T. & T. Clark).

Marcus, J. (1992), *The Way of the Lord. Christological Exegesis of the Old Testament in the Gospel of Mark* (Edinburgh: T. & T. Clark).

—(2002, 2009), *Mark 1–8, 9–16: A New Translation with Introduction and Commentary* (AB, 27; Garden City: Doubleday).

Marshall, I. H. (1992), *The Acts of the Apostles* (Leicester: Inter-Varsity Press).

Matthewson, D. (2003), *A New Heaven and a New Earth. The Meaning and Function of the Old Testament in Revelation 21.1–22.5* (JSNTSup, 238; Sheffield: Sheffield Academic Press).

McCartney, D. G. (2009), *James* (BECNT; Grand Rapids: Baker Academic).

McKnight, S. (2011), *The Letter of James* (NICNT; Grand Rapids: Eerdmans).

Menken, M. J. J. (1996), *Old Testament Quotations in the Fourth Gospel: Studies in Textual Form* (Kampen: Kok).

—(2000), 'The Quotation from Jeremiah 31 (38).15 in Matthew 2.18: A Study of Matthew's Scriptural Text' in S.Moyise (ed.), *The Old Testament in the New Testament* (Sheffield: Sheffield Academic Press), pp. 106–25.

Menken, M. J. J. and Moyise, S. (eds) (2007), *Deuteronomy in the New Testament* (London: T. & T. Clark).

—(eds) (2009), *The Minor Prophets in the New Testament* (London and New York: T. & T. Clark).

—(eds) (2012), *Genesis in the New Testament* (London and New York: T. & T. Clark).

Montefiore, H. W. (1964), *The Epistle to the Hebrews* (London: A. & C. Black).

Moo, D. J. (1983), *The Old Testament in the Gospel Passion Narratives* (Sheffield: Almond Press).

Moritz, T. (2004), 'The Psalms in Ephesians and Colossians' in S. Moyise and M. J. J. Menken (eds), *The Psalms in the New Testament*, pp. 181–95.

Moyise, S. (1995), *The Old Testament in the Book of Revelation* (Sheffield: Sheffield Academic Press).

—(2000), 'Intertextuality and the Study of the Old Testament in the New Testament' in S. Moyise (ed.), *The Old Testament in the New Testament* (Sheffield: Sheffield Academic Press), pp. 14–41.

—(2008), *Evoking Scripture. Seeing the Old Testament in the New* (London and New York: T. & T. Clark).

—(2010), *Jesus and Scripture* (London: SPCK).

—(2010b), *Paul and Scripture* (London: SPCK).

—(2011), *The Later Writers of the New Testament and Scripture* (London: SPCK).

—(2013), *Was the Birth of Jesus According to Scripture?* (London: SPCK).

Moyise, S. and Menken, M. J. J. (eds) (2004), *The Psalms in the New Testament* (London and New York: T. & T. Clark).

—(eds) (2005), *Isaiah in the New Testament* (London and New York: T. & T. Clark).

Nolland, J. (1989), *Luke 1–9.20* (WBC, 35A; Dallas: Word Books).

—(2005), *The Gospel of Matthew: A Commentary on the Greek Text* (NIGTC; Grand Rapids: Eerdmans).

O'Brien, K. (2010), *The Use of Scripture in the Markan Passion Narrative* (LNTS, 384; New York: T. & T. Clark).

Pao, D. W. (2000), *Acts and the Isaianic New Exodus* (Tübingen: Mohr Siebeck).

Pao, D. W. and Schnabel, E. J. (2007), 'Luke' in G. K. Beale and D. Carson (eds), *Commentary on the New Testament Use of the Old*, pp. 251–414.

Paulien, J. (2001), 'Criteria and the Assessment of Allusions to the Old Testament in the Book of Revelation' in S. Moyise (ed.), *Studies in the Book of Revelation* (Edinburgh: T. & T. Clark, 2001), pp. 113–29.

Perkins, L. (2006), 'Kingdom, Messianic Authority and the Re-Constituting of God's People – Tracing the Function of Exodus Material in Mark's Gospel' in T. R. Hatina (ed.), *Biblical Interpretation in Early Christian Gospels: Volume 1, The Gospel of Mark*, pp. 100–15.

Pietersma, A. and Wright, B. G. (eds) (2007), *New English Translation of the Septuagint* (New York: Oxford University Press).

Piper, J. (2007), *The Future of Justification: A Response to N.T. Wright* (Wheaton: Crossway).

Prior, M. (1994), *Jesus the Liberator* (Sheffield: Sheffield Academic Press).

Resseguie, J. L. (1998), *Revelation Unsealed. A Narrative Critical Approach to John's Apocalypse* (Leiden: Brill).

Rowland, C. (1993), *Revelation* (London: Epworth Press).

Ruiz, J-P. (1989), *Ezekiel in the Apocalypse: The Transformation of Prophetic Language in Revelation 16.17–19.10* (Frankfurt: Peter Lang).

Sailhamer, J. (2001), 'Hosea 11:1 and Matthew 2:15', *Westminster Theological Journal* 63, pp. 87–96.

Sanders, E. P. (1977), *Paul and Palestinian Judaism* (London: SCM Press).

—(1983), *Paul, the Law, and the Jewish People* (London: SCM Press).

Sandt, H. van de. (2009), 'The Minor Prophets in Luke-Acts' in M. J. J. Menken and S. Moyise (eds), *The Minor Prophets in the New Testament*, pp. 57–77.

Schaberg, J. (1995), *The Illegitimacy of Jesus: A Feminist Theological Interpretation of the Infancy Narratives* (Sheffield: Sheffield Academic Press).

Schuchard, S. (1992), *Scripture Within Scripture: The Interrelationship of Form and Function in the Explicit Old Testament Citations in the Gospel of John* (Atlanta: Scholars Press).

Schutter, W. L. (1989), *Hermeneutics and Composition in 1 Peter* (WUNT, 2.30; Tübingen: Mohr Siebeck).

Schweitzer, A. (2000), *The Quest of the Historical Jesus* (Rev. edn; London: SCM).

Seifrid, M. A. (2007), 'Romans' in G. K. Beale and D. Carson (eds), *Commentary on the New Testament Use of the Old*, pp. 607–94.

Selwyn, E. G. (1952), *The First Epistle of St. Peter* (London: Macmillan).

Stanley, C. D. (1992), *Paul and the Language of Scripture* (Cambridge: Cambridge University Press).

—(2004), *Arguing with Scripture: The Rhetoric of Quotations in the Letters of Paul* (New York and London: T. and T. Clark).

Stegemann, H. (1998), *The Library of Qumran* (Grand Rapids: Eerdmans).

Stendahl, K. (1968), *The School of St. Matthew and its Use of the Old Testament* (Rev. edn, Philadelphia: Fortress Press).

Steyn, G. J. (1995), *Septuagint Quotations in the Context of the Petrine and Pauline Speeches of the Acta Apostolorum* (Kampen: Kok).

—(2011), *A Quest for the Assumed LXX Vorlage of the Explicit Quotations in Hebrews* (Göttingen: Vandenhoeck & Ruprecht).

Stockhausen, C. K. (1989), *Moses' Veil and the Story of the New Covenant. The Exegetical Substructure of 2 Cor. 3.1–4.6* (Rome: Pontifical Biblical Institute).

Strauss, M. L. (1995), *The Davidic Messiah in Luke-Acts. The Promise and its Fulfillment in Lukan Theology* (Sheffield: Sheffield Academic Press).

Synge, F. C. (1959), *Hebrews and the Scriptures* (London: SPCK).

Taylor, V. (1966), *The Gospel according to St. Mark. The Greek Text with Introduction, Notes, and Indexes* (London: Macmillan).

Telford, W. R. (1999), *The Theology of Mark* (Cambridge: Cambridge University Press).

Thielman, F. S. (2007), 'Ephesians' in G. K. Beale and D. Carson (eds), *Commentary on the New Testament Use of the Old*, pp. 813–33.

Towner, P. H. (2007), '1–2 Timothy and Titus' in G. K. Beale and D. Carson (eds), *Commentary on the New Testament Use of the Old*, pp. 891–918.

Turner, D. L. (2008), *Matthew* (BECNT; Grand Rapids: Baker Academic).

Vermes, G. (1997), *The Complete Dead Sea Scrolls in English* (London: Penguin Books).

—(2003), *The Authentic Gospel of Jesus* (London: Penguin Books).

Wagner, J. R. (2002), *Heralds of the Good News: Isaiah and Paul 'In Concert' in the Letter to the Romans* (Leiden: Brill).

Watson, F. (2004), *Paul and the Hermeneutics of Faith* (London: T. & T. Clark).

Watts, R. (1997), *Isaiah's New Exodus and Mark* (WUNT 2/88, Tubingen: Mohr Siebeck).

—(2007), 'Mark' in G. K. Beale and D. Carson (eds), *Commentary on the New Testament Use of the Old*, pp. 111–249.

Westerholme, S. (1988), *Israel's Law and the Church's Faith* (Grand Rapids: Eerdmans).

Williams, C. H. (2005), 'Isaiah in John's Gospel' in S. Moyise and M. J. J. Menken (eds), *Isaiah in the New Testament*, pp. 101–16.

Witherington, B. (1998), *Grace in Galatia. A Commentary on St Paul's Letter to the Galatians* (Edinburgh: T. & T. Clark).

Wright, N. T. (1991), *The Climax of the Covenant: Christ and the Law in Pauline Theology* (Edinburgh: T. & T. Clark).

—(1996), *Jesus and the Victory of God* (London: SPCK).

—(2013), *Paul and the Faithfulness of God* (Christian Origins and the Question of God; London: SPCK).

Index of References

19.36 93, 101–2
19.37 93

Acts
1.1–2 65
1.6–8 69
1.8 66, 68, 74
1.16 78
1.17 75
1.20 2, 5, 75, 94
2.17–35 75–6
2.22 54
2.25, 31, 34 78
2.29 76
2.36 69
3.1 111
3.13–25 76–7
3.26 76
4.11–12 77
4.11 68
4.25–6 77–8
4.25 65, 78
4.26 14
4.27 77
4.36 119
6.13 79
7.3–50 78–9
7.42–3 19
7.42 82
7.43 207
7.53 153, 208
8.28, 30 78
8.32–3 74, 79, 82
8.32 42, 58
8.35 80
10.14 36, 111
11.3 111
12.2 75
13.16–52 80
13.47 74
15.13–21 82
15.16–17 207
15.16 82

23.5 82
28.25 78
28.26–7 74, 83

Romans
1.17 125
1.20–5 129
2.13 185
2.24 125
3.4 125
3.10–18 15, 125
3.19–20 125
3.21–6 134, 146
3.23–4 125
3.25–6 126
3.25 134
4.9 25
4.20–1 121
5.12–21 129–130
5.14 129, 206
7.12 185
8.28 136
9.7 208
9.12, 17 124
9.22–4 124
9.25 2, 118
9.32–3 68
9.33 15, 122, 144, 170–1, 207
10.13 145
10.21 122
11.8 83, 123
11.9–10 75, 123
11.24, 26 123
11.27 61, 160
11.32 123
12.14–21 135
12.17 172
13.1 7
13.8–10 35
13.8 135
13.9 52, 185
15.3 94, 127, 165
15.4 2

3.7 181
3.9 181
4.2 182
4.6–10 174
4.6 174
4.11–12 183
5.4 182
5.6 182

1 Peter
1.16 169–170
1.23 170
1.24–5 170
2.3 172–3
2.4–8 68
2.6–8 170–1, 207
2.6 15, 144
2.18 171
2.22–5 171–2
2.22 42
3.10–12 170, 172–3
3.14 173
4.13 170, 173
4.18 170, 173–4
5.5–6 174
5.5 170, 174

2 Peter
1.20–1 2
2.4 176
2.10–11 177
2.22 174–5
3.4, 7 178
3.8 178
3.13 178

1 John
1.7 187
1.8–9 186–7
2.18–28 186
3.12 186
4.7–21 35

2 John
1 186

3 John
1 186

Jude
6–7 176
9 176–7
14 175

Revelation
1.5 198
1.7 102, 194
1.10 203
1.12–16 196–7
1.18 198
1.19 195
2–3 197–8
3.9 2
4.1 195
4.2 203
4.3–8 190–1
5.5–6 198–9
6.16 199
7.3 191
11.3–4 144
12.5–6 200
12.7–9 200
12.13, 17, 200
13.1–7 194
15.3–5 201–2
17.4, 6 192
17.14 199
17.16 192
18.19, 22, 18 192
19.21 193
20.4–5 193
20.8 193
20.12 194
21.10 193
21.15 193
21.22 193
21.23 193
22.2 193
22.6 195

Wisdom of Solomon
5.22 69

4 Maccabees
18.11 186

Sirach
44 163

1 Enoch
1–6 200
1.9 175–6
6–19 176

2 Enoch
29.4–5 200

Philo
Cher 43–4, 47 20

Josephus
Ant 2.205–216

Testament of Dan
5.3 35
7.1–5 186

Apocalypse of Abraham
24.5 186

1QpHab 6.12–7.5 12
1QpHab 7.5 209
1QSb 5.21–29 199
1QH Hymn 4 16–17
4QAmram 177
4QFlor 14, 77, 205
4QpIsa 5.1–14 138
4Q541 73
4Q491 73
CD 5.17–18 177
CD 5.19 146
CD 7.14–21 18–19, 205
11QMelch 18, 73, 166, 205

b.Sanhedrin 106b 99
b.Sotah 35a 95
Deut. Rabbah 11.5 71
Exod. Rabbah 32.9 71
Mek. Exod 16.4 95
Sukkah 3.11 127
Pes. R. 32.3–4 96

Index of Authors and Subjects